FANTASTIC TV

50 YEARS OF CULT FANTASY AND SCIENCE FICTION

STEVEN SAVILE

Plexus, London

Published by Plexus Publishing Limited
25 Mallinson Road
London SW11 1BW
www.plexusbooks.com
First printing 2010

British Library Cataloguing in Publication Data
A catalogue record for this book is available from the British
Library.

ISBN-10: 0-89565-420-6
ISBN-13: 978-085965-420-3

Cover photographs by c.20thC.Fox; The Steven Savile
Collection; Babylonian Productions; Warner Bros.
Television; Prime Time Entertainment Network (PTEN);
Turner Network Television (TNT); Desilu Productions;
Norway Corporation; Paramount Television; National
Broadcasting Company (NBC); British Broadcasting
Corporation (BBC); BBC Wales; Canadian Broadcasting
Corporation (CBC); The Sci-Fi Channel, 20th Century
Fox Television; Columbia Broadcasting System (CBS);
Irwin Allen Productions; Jodi Productions Inc.; Space
Productions; Van Bernard Productions; British Sky
Broadcasting (BSkyB); David Eick Productions; NBC
Universal Television; R&D TV; Stanford Pictures (II); Bruce
Lansbury Productions; Universal Media Studios (UMS)

Book and cover design by Coco Wake-Porter
Printed in Great Britain by Cromwell Press Group

Acknowledgements
Fantastic TV was a mammoth undertaking and it certainly
couldn't have happened without the help of some very, very
kind and generous people who gave willingly of their time
and expertise in an attempt to make me look good, so this
is for those unsung heroes. My honest and deep-felt thanks
go out to:
    Robert Greenberger, Paul Kupperberg, David Spencer,
Ben H. Rome, Jonathan Fesmire, Aaron Rosenberg, Sonny
Whitelaw, Ian Farrington, Steven Volk, Joe Ahearne,
Kenneth Johnson, Andrew Cartmell, Robert Kowall,
Geoffrey Girard, Rick Novy, David Sakmyster, Edward
Svecik, Deborah Stephenson, Robert Hood, Cat Rambo,
Paul Cornell, Adrian Hodges, Joseph Lidster, Lee Battersby,
Lynn Battersby, Andy Mangels, Lee Goldberg, David
Seidman, Debbie Viguie, Nick Andreychuk, Jason Sizemore,
Matt Forbeck, Richard Salter, Bob Vardeman, Dayton Ward
and Andy Lane.
    These folks are all brilliant, and any glaring mistakes in
here are completely my own doing. Without these people
this book wouldn't have been possible, and without their
friendship I would be a lesser man. So thank you.

The author and publisher would like to thank the following
for supplying pictures: The Steven Savile Collection; The
Kenneth Johnson Collection; Andy Mangels; Jaz Wiseman;
c.20thC.Fox/ Everett /Rex Features; Everett Collection/ Rex
Features; Rex Features; Rex Features; ITV/ Rex Features;
Chrysalis Visual/ Rex Features; Carol Norman/ Rex
Features; Thurston Hopkins/ Stringer/ Hulton Archive/
Getty Images; c.CWNetwork/ Everett/ Rex Features.
    Thanks are also due to the following production
companies and distributors: Twentieth Century Fox
Television, Columbia Broadcasting System (CBS),
Irwin Allen Productions, Jodi Productions Inc., Space
Productions, Van Bernard Productions, New Line
Cinema, Prelude Pictures, Desilu Productions, Norway
Corporation, Paramount Television, National Broadcasting
Company (NBC), British Broadcasting Corporation
(BBC), Babylonian Productions, Warner Bros. Television,
Prime Time Entertainment Network (PTEN), Turner
Network Television (TNT), Paramount Pictures, United
Paramount Network (UPN), Sky One, Mutant Enemy,
Fox Film Corporation; Fox Network; the Sci-Fi Channel,
British Sky Broadcasting (BSkyB); David Eick Productions;
NBC Universal Television; R&D TV; Stanford Pictures
(II); Universal Media Studios (UMS), Kenneth Johnson
Productions, 7 Network, Fremantle International Inc.,
The Fremantle Corporation, American Entertainment
Partners II L.P., Associated Television (ATV), Colour
Productions, Independent Television (ITV), Sony Pictures
Television, Double Secret Productions; Gekko Film Corp.,
Kawoosh! Productions IX, Kawoosh! Productions VII,
MGM Worldwide Television Productions, Stargate SG-1
Production (II) Inc., MGM Worldwide Television, MGM
Domestic Television Distribution, Showtime Networks,
Canadian Broadcasting Corporation (CBC), Harve Bennett
Productions, Silverton Productions, American Broadcasting
Company (ABC); MCA/Universal Pictures, Charles Fries
Productions, Chrysalis/Lakeside, Lorimar Productions,
Hammer Film Productions, Exclusive Films, United Artists,
Associated British-Pathé; Hammer Film Productions
(as A Seven Arts-Hammer Film Production), Cayuga
Productions, Francy Productions, Thames Television,
Spelling Television, Northshore Productions, Viacom
Productions, the WB Television Network, Clerkenwell
Films, Kripke Enterprises (as KEI Kripke Enterprises
Scrap Metal & Entertainment), Wonderland Sound and
Vision, Supernatural Films, Everyman Films, Incorporated
Television Company (ITC), Entertainment Group, BBC
Wales, Ten Thirteen Productions, X-F Productions, Bruce
Lansbury Productions, DC Comics, Douglas S. Cramer
Company, MCA Television, Renaissance Pictures, Studios
USA Television, Kuzui Enterprises, Sandollar Television,
United Paramount Network, Screen Gems, Ultravi
Productions, Sony Pictures Entertainment (SPE), Tollin,
Robbins Productions, Millar Gough Ink, Smallville 3 Films,
Smallville Films; Tollin/Robbins Productions, Warner
Bros. Pictures, CW Television, Network, E4, ABC Studios,
Touchstone Television, Bad Robot, Grass Skirt Productions,
and Buena Vista Television.

CONTENTS

INTRODUCTION   5

1. THE STARS OUR DESTINATION

Lost in Space, Star Trek, Blake's 7, Babylon 5,
Star Trek: Deep Space Nine, Star Trek: Voyager,
Firefly, Battlestar Galactica (new series)   9

2. THEY CAME FROM OUTER SPACE

V, The Tripods, Alien Nation   55

3. RENDING TIME AND SPACE

Doctor Who (original series), Sapphire and Steel,
Stargate SG-1, Tru Calling, Doctor Who (new series)   73

4. THE BODY ELECTRIC (WE CAN REBUILD YOU)

The Six Million Dollar Man,
The Amazing Spider-Man, Max Headroom   111

5. STRANGER THINGS HAPPEN

Quatermass, The Twilight Zone, Kolchak: The Night Stalker,
The Tomorrow People, Charmed, Afterlife, Supernatural   131

6. JUST BECAUSE THEY'RE OUT TO GET YOU, IT DOESN'T MEAN YOU'RE PARANOID

The Prisoner, The X-Files, Torchwood   177

7. A NEW KIND OF HERO

Wonder Woman, Xena: Warrior Princess, Buffy the Vampire Slayer,
Ultraviolet, Angel, Smallville, Lost, Heroes   195

8. WORLDS OF THEIR OWN

A Round Robin Interview with Joe Ahearne, Adrian Hodges,
Kenneth Johnson, Stephen Volk, Andrew Cartmel, Keith
DeCandido, Paul Cornell and Kevin J. Anderson   254

INTRODUCTION

TECHNICOLOR KILLED THE RADIO STAR

'The truth of the matter is that television is the best medium that has ever been devised, including the print medium, for dealing with fantasy.'
– Harlan Ellison, speaking on Tomorrow with Tom Snyder

A long time ago in living rooms not so far, far away . . . the impressionable young minds of a generation huddled around cathode-ray tubes, their disbelief willingly suspended as they offered themselves up to the Great God Television.

It was glorious and new, bright and shiny.

Coming out of the golden age of pulp fiction magazines and radio, this new medium offered many opportunities for the same storytellers to reach a new audience. Not only that, the medium itself offered a new way to reach their old audience. Suddenly there was a wonderful world of possibilities. Guys who had cut their teeth writing for *Amazing Stories, Galaxy, Weird Tales, Astounding Science Fiction* and a whole slew of other pulp magazines made the shift to the small screen – and made no apologies for their roots. Science fiction wasn't the pop-culture ghetto it is today. Readers didn't hide their paperbacks in brown paper baggies, embarrassed by their latest purchase. Even the skin mags touted stories by great names like Bradbury, Ray Russell and others. Stories were the grist of the entertainment mill, and those old magazines were a melting pot for the exciting new ideas of a world on the verge of discovering itself. The future they imagined was, like those early television images, bright and shiny.

It was an era of hope. And what better way to see the future than through the television screen?

I'll make my confession right here. I am a sucker for good television. (I know, I know – 'good' is rather a nebulous concept at the best of times.) I love the scope of ideas it offers, its purely visual nature, the thrill of seeing something flat come to life in the hands of master storytellers.

I grew up hiding behind the settee when the first discordant twangs of the *Doctor Who* theme came out of the TV set. I was violently ill when Jon Pertwee regenerated. I cowered before the might of *The Tripods*. When I wasn't running in slow motion, pretending to be the Six Million Dollar Man, I was sprinting for my life and calling

Babylon 5 – *J. Michael Straczynski's visually captivating 'window into the future'.*

myself Logan. I crept around, fiddling with my watch and pretending it made me invisible, like Sam Casey in *The Gemini Man*. I spent hours in the bath waiting for webbing to grow between my toes, so I could swim like the Man from Atlantis. I used to sit patiently on the windowsill for hours with grape seeds in my palm, trying to make them grow like Uri Geller. (What do you mean, that wasn't science fiction? I could also confess to pinning down a kid in the playground, cutting away a swatch of hair and writing '666' in blue felt tip behind his ear. But as *The Omen* was a film, not a TV show, I'll leave that one out.) In other words, I was a pretty typical kid growing up in Middle England, with television solidifying the stuff that dreams were made of.

And of course it wasn't just when I was ten or thirteen or seventeen, it carried on into shows like *Quantum Leap* and *Buffy the Vampire Slayer* and, well – I'm 40 in a few weeks and the itch still needs to be scratched. I love TV.

Growing up, I didn't dream of being a writer. I wanted to make television programmes. On Careers Day at school, I sat with the adviser and baffled the poor woman by asking how I could become a cameraman for the BBC (because I wanted to work on *Doctor Who*). She suggested I try to become a vet instead. It was all very tragic for a boy who wanted to nothing more than to make stories come alive.

You see, books didn't do it for me. There was too much effort involved, too much investment of self. I wanted to be *shown* amazing things; I didn't want to have to invent them in my mind. (Not at first, at least.)

Now, older and hopefully a little wiser, I realise that those old shows were what sparked my love for science fiction and set me on my life's path. I look back at them with an incredible amount of fondness, even the cheesiest of them.

The original germ of *Fantastic TV* came about because of an argument with a bunch of science-fiction writers, at one of their annual gatherings a few years ago. My standpoint then, as now, was not exactly a popular one. I argued passionately (there may have been a few beers involved) that much of the very best science fiction was being written for the screen these days, and that so many great writers were essentially lost to the genre because of this. A few of us loudly lamented the fact that SF novels have become bogged down in technobabble and high-faluting concepts, and that everyone seems to have forgotten the most basic necessity: conveying a good story.

One central idea we returned to over and over again was that the storyteller's art lies in communicating his ideas to the widest possible audience, and embracing new methods of delivery. Today we're talking about podcasts, webcasts, direct downloads, YouTube, computer games, and just about every other possible combination of words and images imaginable. But back in the fifties, we would have been talking about television. It's hardly a stretch to imagine the more forward-thinking of those old pulp writers – Charles Beaumont, Ray Bradbury, Richard Matheson – having almost exactly the same conversation, only substituting the word 'television' for streaming video and virtual book signings.

No, here's the important part: what *Fantastic TV* is *not* is an episode guide – we wouldn't get beyond the 156 episodes of *The Twilight Zone*, and it'd be as dull as old dishwater. Neither is it a comprehensive encyclopaedia of genre TV. There will be shows in here you wouldn't have chosen, and there will be shows missing that have you scratching your head and asking how can that idiot have missed out X or XX or even XXX? The truth is this is *my* life lived vicariously through television. It's a loving tribute to everything that is great about the goggle box that *I* love. That means some arbitrary choices were made by me as to what made the grade as visionary and what didn't. My apologies if I skipped over your favourite show. It doesn't mean I didn't enjoy it, it just means that when it came to final cut I decided what I had to say about it was covered elsewhere. There are some notable absences, and some odd inclusions. What can I say? I'm odd. But, for instance, the stuff I might have said about *The Outer Limits* has been covered very well in other anthology shows and I didn't really want a lot of repetition, so I cut where I thought I was in danger of putting myself to sleep. Equally, it was a long labour of love and certain newer shows didn't make the grade because when I set out I had no way of knowing if *Wonderfalls* or *Pushing Daisies* or *Warehouse 13* or the reincarnated *Flash Gordon,* the not quite as sexy *Bionic Woman* or *Eureka* or (well you get the idea) would even make it beyond episode three, let alone into a second or third season. Some did, some didn't, but again, choices were made. These were my choices, and the criterion was always the same – is it visionary? That was the question. Maybe there will be a revised edition in a decade that has all of the shows that should have made the first book? Who knows? Suffice to say, *Fantastic TV* is my thank-you to the televisionaries who inspired me (and so many folks like me) to boldly go where no split infinitive has gone before.

Steven Savile
Los Angeles, August 2009

1 THE STARS OUR DESTINATION

Lost in Space, Star Trek, Blake's 7, Babylon 5,
Star Trek: Deep Space Nine, Star Trek: Voyager, Firefly,
Battlestar Galactica (new series)

LOST IN SPACE (1964-1966)

There is an irony implicit in certain titles, like the aptly named *Lost in Space*. The American TV series had an initial run of three seasons, or 83 episodes, and during that time its varying degrees of success and failure offered a clear indication of the quandary that has challenged science fiction since day one.

To wit, should science fiction be primarily about the *science* or the *fiction*? It seems a fairly straightforward question, but the big TV companies decreed back then that it couldn't be totally one or the other – which of course makes perfect sense. After all, who wants to watch an Open University analysis of the moon's gravitational pull when they can actually travel to Titan, or see Moonbase Alpha taking root in the Sea of Tranquility? Adventure. Excitement. Fear. To boldly split that infinitive – that's what it's all about.

So the question becomes one of balance. When does the fun of the fictional romp trivialise the sincerity of the science? When does the authenticity of the technology constrain the telling of a rollicking good story? The perfect recipe – with a *soupcon* of this and a splash of that, to create a unique and wonderful blend – has challenged SF creators for longer than we've had television sets.

Lost in Space, which first broadcast a year before *Star Trek* and five years before man set foot on the moon, was no different.

To this day, fans of the show still argue over when *Lost in Space* was best. Was it during the first season, when the show focused on the Robinson family's successful use of technology and the far-reaching promises of space exploration, or during the next two, when the programme's focus switched almost completely to the cartoonish Dr Smith and the weekly whimsy of Space Vikings, talking vegetables and planets ruled by hillbillies, no less? Perhaps both versions were equally 'good', but simply in different ways?

Lost in Space had its roots firmly grounded in, of all things, a Christian morality tale first published in 1812 about a Swiss family shipwrecked somewhere in the East

Lost in Space's Model B-9, Class M-3 General Utility Non-Theorising Environmental Control Robot – the friendly face of artificial intelligence.

Indies. *The Swiss Family Robinson* (*Der Schweizerische Robinson*) was penned by Johann David Wyss, a Swiss pastor who hoped to tutor his four sons on his various Christian beliefs in family values, self-reliance, husbandry and the dangers of the natural world. Wyss believed (as have others, including Verne, Wells and Heinlein) that exciting fiction would be the best way to accomplish this higher moral lesson. One hundred and fifty years later, film producer Irwin Allen bought into the concept for entirely different reasons.

Allen had already found great success in Hollywood with adventure films focused primarily on special effects, such as *The Lost World* (1960), *Voyage to the Bottom of the Sea* (1961) and Jules Verne's *Five Weeks in a Balloon* (1962). ABC Television hired Allen to bring *Voyage to the Bottom of the Sea* to the small screen in 1964, where it became the decade's longest running American fantasy-adventure series. Competitor CBS approached Allen for another series and the result, *Lost in Space*, aired the following season.

Allen liked the simple *Swiss Family Robinson* idea of a family lost, alone, and working together to survive. His own Robinson family was built around the 'everyboy' Will Robinson. Will is the youngest member of the family, but also a technological child prodigy (like today's übergeek, more at home with Google than Britannica) who spends the bulk of his day playing with a giant robot, quibbling with an 'evil' scientist, and occasionally shooting at monsters with a laser gun. Will is, in short, *everything* a boy in 1964 wanted to be.

Remember the literary roots of SF TV: the covers of *Amazing Stories*, *Astounding Science Fiction* and *Unknown* – the birth of disposable entertainment, with lurid covers designed to excite and titillate. It was also a simpler time in terms of the TV viewer's demands, which could be satisfied by string effects on spaceships and wibbly-wobbly teleportation devices.

Will's parents – Professor John and his wife Doctor Maureen Robinson – and his two sisters, Judy and Penny, made up most of the human cast. The original pilot was written and shot completely around this neat, very nuclear family unit.

The story was set in the futuristic year of 1997, when Earth's overpopulation had reached the point that man had to reach for the stars or risk running out of the bare necessities: food, water and a place to call home. Quite what difference one family leaving would make is hard to say, but the Robinsons boarded the Gemini 12 (on a budget of $40 billion according to the story – the average space shuttle launch today costs $450 million) and were heading out to colonise some planet in the Alpha Centauri star system when they got lost. Also along for the ride was the Gemini's pilot, Major Don West.

As production began, Allen sought the obvious PR opportunity of getting NASA involved. NASA, with its eyes fixed fervently on the moon, was just as excited about the opportunity to promote the idea of space exploration to the American public.

The relationship would not last long.

One of Allen's most infamous phrases on his various sets was, 'Don't concern

The Lost in Space *castaways – Guy Williams (Professor John Robinson), June Lockhart (Maureen Robinson), Bill Mumy (Will Robinson), Bob May (The Robot), Jonathan Harris (Doctor Zachary Smith), Angela Cartwright (Penny Robinson), Marta Kristen (Judy Robinson), Mark Goddard (Major Don West).*

me with logic!' The immediate needs of the story were always more important than any scientific authenticity. NASA had a slightly different worldview, and so hard science reared its ugly head.

When NASA examined the blueprints for the Gemini 12 spaceship, they quickly assessed that the ship would never fly, proclaiming that it couldn't 'even get off the launch pad'. Allen merely replied that the same had once been said of NASA's beloved rockets. It became obvious that actual science and science fiction would not concur on this particular venture, and NASA quickly severed all ties with the show.

Allen moved ahead with a solid budget of $600,000 and started filming. The original pilot (never aired) focused on special effects and the hardware of space travel (ships, land rovers, spacesuits, jetpacks, all of the things we viewers expect to see in our lunar explorations). The high point would be a special effects tidal wave and a giant monster attacking the Robinsons (or rather a man in a rubber suit, attacking puppets).

Allen claimed the pilot was the best work he'd done yet. But when CBS executives laughed throughout the first screening, the anecdote goes that he was so embarrassed and infuriated that he jumped up to stop it; only to have his story editor yank him back into his chair. 'Irwin,' the editor explained, 'they love it.'

They did, and it sold. Their laughter had been that of childlike delight, of grown men simply having fun. To that same end, executive feedback suggested the show was too driven by the cold hardware of science, too much time spent on gadgets and space. The show needed more personality, more human characters to focus on.

Enter Dr Smith.

Smith was a secondary character so synonymous with the show that, all these years later, some people mistakenly believe the family lost in space were called 'the Smiths'. The show's story editor, Anthony Wilson, believed they needed a recurring villain. Allen pushed for someone like *Flash Gordon*'s Ming the Merciless, Wilson for a character more like the pirate Long John Silver in *Treasure Island*. The compromise was Colonel Zachary Smith.

Not yet the 'lovable' Dr Smith, *Colonel* Smith was a sharp-browed and snarling secret agent for some unnamed country, hoping to sabotage the Robinsons' mission. While setting his trap, he is mistakenly caught on board and his subsequent actions cause the ship to veer off course and crash-land.

A talking robot created by Robert Kinishita – the man who designed *Forbidden Planet*'s Robby the Robot almost ten years before – was also now added to the mix. Here was technology with comedic potential and that, to quote the studio-speak, 'kids would like'.

The Gemini 12 was, for some reason, renamed the Jupiter 2, and new footage was shot for the second pilot with most of the original pilot's footage wedged into the first five episodes. Though weekly episodes were only budgeted at $130,000 (average for the era), *Lost in Space* had already spent a great deal of money just in making the pilots. The spaceship alone, left resting on the soundstage, had cost some $350,000. It was estimated by Allen that the show would need to be on the air for three years just to break even.

The series premiered on 15 September 1965, with advertisers promised that it would attract the family audience. It would run for almost three years.

In 1965, a '20 rating' was considered a success. By the sixth episode, *Lost in Space* was at a 23 rating and had become a Top Ten show. The rating system is considerably more simplistic than it might at first appear: a 20 rating means literally that 20 per cent of all available television sets are tuned in to the programme. Basically a fifth of America was watching. That made it a 'a sure-fire winner for young viewers' according to the *NY Times*. The *LA Times* praised the 'tremendously inventive' special effects and the acting of Jonathan Harris (Dr Smith).

The notion of 'Dr' Smith had already taken over by the sixth episode, and the original plans for a moustache-twiddling evil Smith were retired for good. Both the story editors and actor Harris realised that the character could not survive if

Doctor Zachary Smith – cowardly, conniving, and enduringly popular with viewers.

every episode he were merely trying to kill the Robinsons. Smith would grow stale if he were purely evil, muttering, 'If it wasn't for you meddling kids I would have gotten away with it!' week after week. So, as a result, the writers intentionally started softening the character.

Dr Smith quickly began his now-notorious barrage of complaints to an uncaring world ('The pain, the pain!') and verbal abuse of the stolid Robot ('You neanderthal ninny!' 'You bubble-headed booby!') Soon, he would coin his famous 'Never fear, Smith is here!' and the TV legend was born.

Never mind that Smith often tampered with jet packs, handed Will over to alien brain snatchers to save his own skin, or used the ship's last drop of water to take a shower. He could now faint at the drop of a hat (beginning with the episode entitled 'The Sky Pirate') and his whining provided just the kind of comic relief that family-friendly television was apparently looking for. This edge of comedy would be echoed increasingly in the BBC's *Doctor Who* – especially when hammed up by the lovable Tom Baker, no stranger to one-liners with a sharp comedic edge. Without the humour, it seems the family audience would just never have fallen in love with SF.

CBS chairman William S. Paley grew increasingly embarrassed by the programme. *Lost in Space* was silly. It was not serious enough to stand beside his other shows. He wanted the show pulled immediately if it did not deliver. It was the familiar war cry of the suits!

Yet, to his absolute amazement, the high ratings continued.

Paley went so far as to pay a psychologist to figure out what was 'wrong' with the American public, unable to understand why *Lost in Space* was a hit with its target audience. The stars of the show made the cover of *TV Guide*. The Robot got fan mail. Dr Smith got more. When live coverage of NASA's Gemini VIII splashdown truncated an episode of *Lost in Space*, complaints flooded the CBS switchboards demanding they show the programme in full.

Young audiences specifically loved that the show featured children in exciting adventures, the same ethos that has made the *Harry Potter* series a runaway success.

Judy Robinson and Major West – despite their obvious onscreen chemistry, romance was not a part of the script's agenda.

Will, a young boy, was trusted by his parents to drive transporters and to use laser guns. Penny saved her family by posing as extraterrestrial royalty and playing ambassador. The formula was simple, giving the children in the audience young heroes they could root for.

And so the memos started flying. Reality must give way to even more fantasy. Like Doctor Who and his female assistants, Professor Robinson and his wife were never to kiss, only to stare longingly and tap arms for fear of embarrassing younger viewers. (As for pretty Judy and Major West, forget it.) The episode 'Follow the Leader', in which Will is almost tossed from a cliff by his possessed father, had executives warning against further scenes of violence.

None of that mattered though. The audience was focused elsewhere. The more Dr Smith hammed it up, the better the show did. The Robot had even developed its own famous catchphrase of 'Danger, danger!' (only once ever actually saying, 'Danger, Will Robinson!'). The trinity of Smith, Will and the Robot had become the focus of the show by the end of year one. The science of space travel had given way more and more to the promise of childish adventure, monsters and amusing fantasy. Penny had picked up a pet 'bloop' named Debbie – an actual monkey in a fur-covered crash helmet! Hardcore science-fiction fans cried, 'Ridiculous!' as the ratings continued their upward trend.

But Joe and Jane Public like adventure stories and wild entertainment. They don't like science lessons. They want to switch their brains off and be amused. It is the simplest of formulae and offers a direct route to mass appeal.

And so the next season of *Lost in Space* promised colour episodes, more adventure and more fantasy.

But was it all becoming too much?

Instead of merely trying to survive in a hostile environment, the next year brought a parade of princesses and pirates, visits from elves, gunslingers, knights, magicians and space Vikings. And Dr Smith proved even more silly and bumbling than before.

Lost in Space was not the only show following this format. On American television it was the age of camp. The tongue-in-cheek *Batman* premiered opposite

Lost in Space in 1966 with a huge 39 rating, and other programmes with the same style at this time included *Get Smart, The Avengers, The Man from U.N.C.L.E., The Wild, Wild West* and *Mr Terrific,* and were mirrored in the approach of the mid-1960s James Bond films. There was a definite pattern developing that mirrored the tastes of *Lost in Space*'s viewers.

Thanks to the first-year success of *Lost in Space, Star Trek* had premiered in September. To compete with *Batman* (*Lost in Space* soon won back its audience shares and ultimately ran longer than TV's caped crusader), *Star Trek* (Smith always had better ratings than Kirk) and all the rest, the Robinsons found themselves in more and more comically absurd situations. Irwin Allen had decided that was what people wanted, and was only too willing to pander to the whims of the masses.

Still, every now and again certain episodes rose above the level of camp and achieved something meaningful. One that springs to mind is 'Visit to a Hostile Planet', in which the Robinsons end up back on Earth, but in 1947, where they are attacked by the frightened populace.

During this time, the first season was Emmy-nominated for special effects and makeup, while the excellent music (crafted by *Star Wars* composer John Williams) was ignored. But by the end of the second season, *Lost in Space* was no longer even a Top Twenty show. The demographic of the audience was now proving 'too young' – it was mostly children, and children don't buy enough products. Critics (and apparently audiences too) were growing tired of the camp Dr Smith and his tantrums.

For the third season, Allen and his writers decided to get back to the basics of space travel. Stealing the format of *Star Trek*, they decided the Robinsons would visit a new planet each week as they worked their way back home. New footage of the Jupiter 2 was filmed, new music ordered from Williams, and a smaller space pod added to the hardware.

The show's focus also moved week-by-week to a different character outside of the Smith/Will/Robot trio. In perhaps the best episode of the entire series, Professor Robinson battled his doppelganger in 'The Anti-Matter Man'.

But still, the fantastic (or fantastically silly) element was not completely gone. In the most infamous episode, 'The Great Vegetable Rebellion', the Robinsons scuffle with humanoid carrots, peas and lettuce who are militant environmentalists. During the filming of the episode, the show's stars Guy Williams (John Robinson) and June Lockhart (Maureen Robinson) laughed throughout and Allen, enraged, wrote both of them out of the next two episodes as punishment.

CBS would cancel the show at the end of the season. Its costs had jumped to $170,000 per episode, Congress had recently focused its attentions on supposedly 'violent television', and ratings had continued to fall slightly each month.

Allen was given a last chance to convince the network the show was worth another season. His grand idea? A purple llama named Willoughby, who would speak in a British accent and join the Robinsons as a comedic and insightful instructor during their various missions.

Unsurprisingly, CBS had heard enough.

Lost in Space all but vanished for the next fifteen years. Allen tried next to use the Robinsons' robot (now called Robby) as a butler in a sitcom (the idea found no buyers). A *Lost in Space* cartoon appeared briefly. *Star Trek* (every episode in colour) won the syndication war, but, after *Star Wars* in 1977, *Lost in Space* would find its own rerun success. WTBS (the Turner Super station) kept the show at the core of its family programming for five years. Fan clubs appeared. The USA network and the Sci-Fi Channel also had successful runs in the 1980s and nineties. Detailed working replicas of the original Robot appeared for sale. A film version (which included most of the original stars in cameos) arrived in 1998, with eminent screen actors William Hurt (John Robinson) and Gary Oldman (Dr Smith) leading the star-studded cast.

Throughout it all, rather like *Quantum Leap*'s Sam Beckett, the blend of science and fantasy was held together by the story of the lost trying to finding their way back home – just as *Swiss Family Robinson* author Wyss had envisioned almost 200 years before, and as J.J. Abrams's island dwellers are still doing.

Science fiction always walks on a narrow edge between the absurd and the sublime. From certain angles, provocative works such as *Dune, Brave New World* or *The Time Machine* can seem somehow silly or childish. Yet, just one step over the edge, fanciful tales like *Star Wars, Buck Rogers* or *Battlestar Galactica* can become powerful in their myth-making. This is the eternal quandary of science fiction. *Lost in Space* struggled with it for three years – though, considering the enduring appeal of its absurd comedy, perhaps it didn't do so badly after all.

STAR TREK (1966-1969)

When was the last time you made or heard a reference to *Star Trek*? One sign of success for a television show or movie is when aspects of it become ubiquitous, to the point of being clichéd. *Star Trek* – in all its incarnations, but particularly the original series – is an excellent example.

But what made *Star Trek* such a venerable cliché? To learn the answer to that question, we need to look at it as it originally aired in the second half of the 1960s.

They said it couldn't be done – a weekly science fiction series with a recurring cast. *The Twilight Zone* had been popular, but it was the video version of a short story anthology. Other shows from that era were campy and over-dramatic. *Lost in Space*, itself a cliché of another kind, was about the closest to an authentic science fiction programme with a stable roster of characters.

Left: Four Star Trek *mainstays – William Shatner (Kirk), DeForest Kelley (McCoy), Leonard Nimoy (Spock), and Nichelle Nichols (Uhura). Right: Kirk and Spock face another alien menace.*

Then along came Gene Roddenberry with his vision of a wagon train to the stars. Although, in retrospect, that phrase is a better literal description of the later *Battlestar Galactica*, Roddenberry was onto something.

It first started airing in September of 1966, and caught on quickly. David Gerrold, a long-time (and often invisible) member of the *Star Trek* family, was quick to see the potential of the new show's dramatic universe. After seeing the very first episode, Gerrold began writing a script that eventually led to the landmark episode 'The Trouble with Tribbles', in which we get to see a whole new side of Captain Kirk and the crew of the USS Enterprise.

In his book, *The World of Star Trek*, Gerrold discusses at length how the show frequently painted itself into a corner by introducing rules and devices that had to be recognised ever after. The best example of this is the concept of the 'prime directive'. It was only ever mentioned when the captain was about to break it; never did anyone abide by it. Ultimately, in order to further the story, the captain always needed an excuse to break the prime directive. Not once did we see the Enterprise turn tail and leave as ordered, allowing the situation to resolve itself.

It was typical of the problems of internal consistency. Every time a new gadget or technique worked in one situation, it had to be considered again and again. The universal translator became standard, as did the Vulcan mind meld or neck pinch. If Spock was around – and he was *always* around – then both these two techniques were available.

In the case of Spock's powers, these added to the depth and dimension of the character. But there were plenty of other, more detrimental clichés – for instance, landing parties always included sacrificial security guards to prove that the alien environment was dangerous. This was made worse by always dressing the human sacrifices in red shirts. It didn't take long before predicting who would die before the end of the show became too easy. (Never leave the ship wearing red unless your name is Scotty.)

Captain Kirk seemed to fall in love with an alien in every episode. And Mr Scott, the miracle worker, always managed to fix the engines predictably in the nick of time. It's this particular cliché that makes the ending of the movie *Star Trek II – The Wrath of Khan* so vivid: this time Scotty wasn't the hero, and Spock had to sacrifice himself to save the Enterprise. (In later movies, James Doohan parodies the Scotty-as-miracle-worker cliché openly.)

Despite the self-inflicted clichés and the 'Star Drek' (to evoke the *MAD* magazine parody) that came with them, the show found its true glory in the episodes that worked. In addition to Gerrold's 'The Trouble with Tribbles', stories by other top science-fiction writers included 'The City on the Edge of Forever' by Harlan Ellison, 'Amok Time' by Theodore Sturgeon and 'The Doomsday Machine' by Norman Spinrad. Stories like these made *Star Trek* a legend, creating the fan phenomenon that saved the series for a third season, later spawning ten motion pictures and four additional series.

It was the fan phenomenon that brought *Star Trek*'s language into everyday use. 'Warp speed' has been used by airline pilots, dads driving the family car on the freeway and kids on their bikes. 'Beam me up' has been parodied by various comedy shows. There are bumper stickers and T-shirts with the legend, 'Beam me up, Scotty, there's no intelligent life on this planet.'

Klingons, as the ultimate bad guys, do evil deeds for the sake of their Empire, or just for fun. Just about any ruthless group of people – be it in business or on the streets – has probably been called 'Klingons' by somebody.

And the coincidence of the character Mr Spock going on the air in the same era that baby expert Dr Benjamin Spock gained prominence has created some amusement. Which *Star Trek* fan hasn't, at one time or another, heard the uninitiated refer to the character as 'Dr Spock'?

Even with all the clichés that surround the series, *Star Trek* still made some bold and groundbreaking commentary under the guise of science fiction. 'The Enemy Within' brings Kirk's good and evil sides out into the open, and everyone can see the person in Kirk that most of us successfully hide.

The Star Trek *core crew on the bridge of the Enterprise – only Leonard Nimoy (second from right) appeared in all 80 episodes.*

'Balance of Terror' places bigotry right onto the bridge of the Enterprise. When we get our first look at the Romulans, they look a lot like Mr Spock – as one crewman doesn't hesitate to point out. 'The Squire of Gothos' shows us that, no matter how powerful, a child is still a child. (Spare the rod, spoil the child.)

In 'A Taste of Armageddon' we see a centuries-old sterile war, where people voluntarily march to the death chambers for a painless death. Kirk brings the spectre of a real war to life, showing us that war is indeed hell. In 'The Devil in the Dark' we encounter a monstrous killing machine that is, in reality, just a mother protecting her young.

'The Doomsday Machine' certainly falls into the category of groundbreaking commentary. Here we have the ultimate weapon, unleashed to destroy anything and everything in its path. At the peak of the Cold War, it was clearly a metaphor for nuclear weapons. Another such episode is 'A Private Little War', but there is nothing subtle about this one. Kirk and the Klingons are arming rival primitive tribes, creating an arms race that couldn't have been closer to the mark of our own world's nuclear escalation.

In 'The Ultimate Computer', people have started to be replaced by machines in factories. *Star Trek* shows us what might happen if we replace them completely. Even the tepid third season has its shining moments of audacity. In 'Let That Be Your Last Battlefield', we encounter men who are black on one side and white on the other. Kirk can't understand why the two men hate each other, until one explains that the other has his colours on the wrong side. It is another bold statement about diversity and racism, which would probably never have reached the airwaves had it not been couched in science-fiction metaphor.

To be sure, *Star Trek* made mistakes, but it got more right than wrong. The show had a mixed-race bridge crew long before it would have been accepted outside of a science fiction environment. In the show's first pilot, the Enterprise had a female first officer; the network nixed that idea, but a later *Star Trek* incarnation would feature a female captain.

Even Spock almost didn't happen. The idea of making an alien with devilish ears into a television hero might outrage the viewers, it was thought. Gene Roddenberry eventually got his demon, and Mr Spock became probably the best known science fiction character that there has ever been.

Be it clichéd or bold, *Star Trek* certainly changed the science fiction medium forever. It gave the genre some respectability, while paving the way for George Lucas and *Star Wars* to bring it into the mainstream. May it live long and prosper.

BLAKE'S 7 (1978-1981)

Dissent is good.

Nothing kills drama faster than contented characters getting along famously. Drama is born of conflict between people with different goals and motivations. For television sci-fi, this can be a real problem. When all your characters follow one captain, sitting atop a traditional military command structure, only a little drama can be milked from the occasional dissenting voice. Eventually somebody is going to get fired and we'll all return to the status quo.

Not so with *Blake's 7*. This creaky sci-fi curio from the BBC vaults continues to find a following to this day, and is often talked about both in nostalgic terms and in the sense that the time is ripe for a relaunch. Why should this be so? Born of the 1970s, when *Star Wars* was showing the world how space opera could use cutting-edge special effects, it's hard to believe the shoestring-budgeted *Blake's 7* was not immediately cancelled the moment Lucas's epic, expansive fantasy-adventure burst onto cinema screens.

Terry Nation, best known for creating *Doctor Who*'s archenemies the Daleks, first pitched *Blake's 7* as *The Dirty Dozen* in space. With that simple tag line, the BBC commissioned thirteen 50-minute episodes and asked Nation to write all of them. His central idea of taking a bunch of criminals and organising them into a thorn in the side of an oppressive regime was the driving force. Only Roj Blake, the titular hero, could be described as a relatively innocent victim of Federation justice.

In the first few episodes of the series, Blake becomes embroiled in a resistance movement who fight to free the people from a government that keeps them drugged and docile, and does not tolerate dissent. The resistance group is slaughtered and Blake is put on trial for crimes he didn't commit – including child abuse. He finds himself on a ship bound for a remote penal colony, where he meets other criminals who don't deny the charges against them. When the transport ship encounters an abandoned, drifting space craft they send expendable prisoners across to see if anything is worth salvaging. Blake and two others take the opportunity to escape, later returning to the penal colony to recruit more prisoners to the cause. The ship, which they call Liberator, is unlike anything they have seen before. Alien in origin and faster than any other craft in the galaxy, Liberator provides Blake and his crew with a powerful weapon they can use to bring down the Federation.

On the face of it, the BBC's answer to *Star Trek* is deeply flawed. The costumes are campy, the acting is often ropey and the storylines are regularly preposterous. The sets are held together with sticky tape, future civilisations appear embarrassingly retro and the special effects stretch use of the word 'special' beyond breaking point. Why, then, does this series endure?

The answer is neatly wrapped up in one simple word: Dissent.

In *Blake's 7*, crucial aspects of dissent can be described in terms of external and internal dynamics. Externally, the crew of the Liberator fought against an oppressive regime, the galaxy-spanning Federation, operating under the banner of unity while enslaving planet after planet to increase its own power. Liberator provided Blake and his crew with the opportunity to strike back at the Federation without getting crushed in the process. Internally, conflict comes in spades, mostly thanks to a crew who don't always like or trust each other but stay together out of a mutual need for survival, or simply out of convenience.

The concept of a small band of people on the run from a totalitarian government, while looking for opportunities to strike back, is not exclusive to *Blake's 7*. However, it provides an external threat that drives the plot and is a unifying theme throughout the series. The Liberator crew are presented as the heroes of the series, yet there are a number of grey areas added to the mix – mostly thanks to script editor Chris Boucher, who strongly resisted Nation's tendency towards good-versus-evil plots. It would have been easy to take the kind of approach seen in the *Star Wars* saga, where the Empire is depicted as wholly evil, merciless and all powerful. Everybody, it seems, hates the Empire, and there is never any mention of the benefits the Empire must have brought to those planets it conquers. (Never mind the millions, if not billions, who presumably rely on it to bring food, security, trade, technology and medicine.) The Empire is merely something to be destroyed; those who oppose the Rebel Alliance are depicted as the bad guys.

Blake's 7 consciously tried to explore the idea that every action has consequences, pros and cons. Yes, the Federation is corrupt, but how many planets would suffer without it? A prime example of this philosophy is depicted at the end of Season Two, where Blake and his crew have finally tracked down Star One, the nerve centre of the Federation. From this top-secret location, the Federation controls everything from the artificial climates of hundreds of colonised planets to navigation systems on interplanetary passenger liners. Destroying this facility would be an enormous blow to the Federation, perhaps toppling it once and for all. For Blake, this is his best chance at winning the war. The whole season is dedicated to finding this one location and he is determined to strike the killing blow. The problem is, not only do countless millions rely on Star One's systems for survival, the Federation control centre also maintains a huge minefield that keeps out would-be invaders from other galaxies. With the facility destroyed, the way is clear for invading forces to enter our space and threaten humanity. It's a fascinating example of how this series tackled the grey areas.

It could also be argued that portraying the Liberator crew as terrorists was a concept ahead of its time. The new *Battlestar Galactica* tries something similar, though less subtly, with the New Caprica plot thread, direct references to insurgency and terrorism drawing stark parallels with the situations in Iraq and Afghanistan. Terrorism was certainly fresh in the minds of many British viewers of *Blake's 7* in the seventies, thanks to the activities of the IRA. The series never drew any direct parallels in the way that *Galactica* does to contemporary events, but the suggestions are there.

It's the polar opposite of *Star Trek*. In the popular US series, the Federation is depicted as a positive force in the universe. It is a progressive voluntary organisation. Like the UN in our own world, planets enlist for membership and to be accepted is cause for celebration. The odd corrupt admiral aside, the Federation itself remains untarnished and doggedly positive. The Enterprise is the flagship of the Federation's Star Fleet. Its crew have put aside any notions of racial conflict, monetary gain or personal power struggles in favour of exploration and making first contact with new species. It's an admirable ethos, much more positive than the ideas behind *Blake's 7*. But it's also a huge drama-killer. Instead of concentrating on threats from within, *Star Trek* focused each week on external threats from alien races, space anomalies and mad computers with a God complex. How much fun might the series have mined from the idea that the Federation has become so corrupt that Captain Kirk or Jean-Luc Picard decides to break away from it and lead a revolt? (Of course this never happened. Any corrupt elements within the Federation were always working in isolation and got their comeuppance by the end of the story.)

In stark contrast, corruption runs so deeply within the Federation of Blake's world that they are *never defeated*. In one of television's most downbeat series endings, Blake's followers meet a bloody fate while the Federation absolutely

Blake's 7 stars Steven Pacey (Tarrant) and Josette Simon (Dayna) overcome another low-budget, bug-eyed monster.

refuses to fall apart. You can fight corruption; you can even win battles along the way – but in the real world such organisations take decades to dismantle, and things are never resolved before the credits roll.

Blake is every inch the crusader. He fights the Federation because he believes them to be unjust. He does not wish to see its leaders brought to justice; instead, he seeks the utter annihilation of the system that holds countless worlds in its thrall. While the Federation provides the canvas upon which the series paints its shades of grey, this external dissent – the idea of a status quo in the universe against which our heroes must do battle – is not what truly sets *Blake's 7* apart. What makes this series rise above its cardboard spaceships and excessive shoulder pads is one simple fact: Blake may be an idealist, a futuristic Robin Hood, the epitome of a hero. However, the rest of the crew members don't necessarily share his ideals.

This simple concept is an extremely powerful generator of dramatic tension. By taking the *Dirty Dozen* approach and drawing Blake's crew from a bunch of criminals, any command structure is dictated only by who has the loudest voice and the strongest will. Give an order and there's a good chance that it won't be obeyed. When your crew is with you not because they share your goals but because they see a chance for personal gain, it's tough to keep order. Being on board Liberator provides each of them with security, purpose and opportunity. But, while they may prefer to follow a strong leader, risking their lives to bring down the all-powerful Federation isn't high on anyone's wish list. It makes for a fascinating dynamic.

One character in *Blake's 7* is arguably far more important than all the others, topping one popularity poll after another. Surprisingly, it's not Blake.

Kerr Avon was one of the prisoners sent across to survey the Liberator from the prison ship, along with Blake and a third prisoner, Jenna. A computer genius charged with bank fraud, it was clear from the start that Avon was not your typical sci-fi hero. He doesn't just question Blake's plans, he often actively opposes them. He is cynical, rude, sardonic and fiercely intelligent. Nearly everything he does is motivated by self interest. Occasionally, he will rescue Blake, or another character, and surprise both them and himself by his actions. A classic example of the way Avon's mind works is presented in the episode 'Horizon'. The rest of the crew is in captivity and Avon is all alone on Liberator, in orbit. Knowing they need his help, Avon consults super computer Orac to calculate his odds for survival were he to cut and run, taking the Liberator and abandoning his shipmates to their fate. The odds are against him – much to his amusement – so he suits up, teleports down and rescues the crew.

In this case, a relatively unimpressive script is made much more memorable. You seriously wonder if Avon's going to take the ship and leave the crew behind. (Of course, they'd have to catch up with him eventually otherwise there wouldn't be much of a series left.) The idea that anything could happen, that at any time one of these characters could betray or abandon the others, kept audiences on their toes and made for compelling viewing.

Such internal dissent among the characters can be seen far more often in recent sci-fi offerings. Whether these series owe their debt to *Blake's 7* directly or indirectly, the seventies show probably still has enough of a following to appear on the radar of modern script writer-producers such as Joss Whedon and Ronald Moore. Both have produced series that built instant cult followings thanks to the kind of dramatic conflict seen three decades earlier in *Blake's 7*. The reimagining of *Battlestar Galactica* goes all out for realism, featuring very human characters with messy, complicated relationships, alongside allegorical comments on the War on Terror, 9/11 and the invasion of Iraq. Multi-layered storylines and arcs abound, with a deep-rooted realism apparent in every shot despite the fantasy setting. While it's likely that *Galactica* is more of a reaction to *Star Trek* than any progressive attempt to follow a 1970s BBC sci-fi series, there are interesting parallels to be drawn.

Far closer in tone is *Firefly*, Joss Whedon's short-lived Western-in-space. Here, a small crew of outcasts and criminals are thrown together with disparate motivations and reasons for staying on board the spaceship Serenity. For all their efforts to avoid encountering the all-powerful Alliance, the crew become targets when Captain Mal Reynolds decides to take on board two fugitives. The focus is slightly different – Mal tries to avoid Alliance attention while Blake does everything he can to hurt the Federation – but at their core the two series have remarkably similar foundations. Take the *Firefly* episode 'Ariel', where one of Serenity's crew, Jayne Cobb, betrays the others to the Alliance for money. Jayne is no Avon, he's a hired gun who lacks smarts but is handy in a fight, but his willingness to sell out the rest of the crew speaks volumes about the ethos of the series. Mal punishes Jayne by shutting him in the airlock and threatening to blow him out into space – reminiscent of a fourth-season *Blake's 7* episode, 'Orbit', where Avon and Vila are stranded on a doomed shuttle too heavy to take off. Jettisoning all extraneous weight, Avon is told by Orac that the ship would be saved if Vila's weight were not aboard. Avon spends the rest of the episode hunting a terrified Vila with a gun, intending to throw him out the airlock and save himself.

Back in the *Star Trek* universe, we have the polar opposite situation. Taking *Next Generation* as an example, the Enterprise crew get on so well that when serious conflict occurs it is usually due to someone being possessed by an alien entity. Debate is encouraged, but in the end the captain's word is law and everyone scrambles to carry out his orders. Dissent is not tolerated. Instead of Riker betraying the crew for cash, conflict must come from external sources only – outside even the Federation, unless there's a corrupt admiral to deal with. When Q or the Borg threatens Picard's Enterprise, it's the crew working together towards a common goal that saves the day. There's little drama to be mined from the series' regular characters, other than Data's monotonous quest to be human and the whole Riker and Troi 'will they, won't they?' thread. Nobody is threatening to throw anybody else off the ship for insubordination. When a lone dissenter was added to the crew in the form of Ensign Ro, it wasn't long before she was brought into line and then dispensed with altogether.

With *Deep Space Nine*, much of that changed. Internally, the Federation regulars remained pretty much a cohesive unit with common aims, but they were thrown into a melting pot with the Bajorans and Cardassians, who actively hated each other. This led to a much more interesting dynamic between the cast, their conflicts added to external threats such as the Dominion or the Klingons.

Ironically, the *Trek* series that potentially had most in common with *Blake's 7* was *Voyager*. Cut off from the Federation, light years away from home and with two enemy crews forced to cohabit one ship, *Voyager* arrived on our screens bursting with opportunities for engaging drama. Unfortunately the reality was somewhat underwhelming. By the end of the pilot episode, all the Maquis were wearing Star Fleet uniforms and the opportunity for dissent was gone. Every week the crew would face an external threat, and very rarely would there be any conflict within the crew itself. Even the implications of being far away from the Federation were squandered. Despite big battles in the preceding weeks that would have damaged half the ship, Voyager would be gleaming and whole, as if it had just rolled out of space dock for the very first time. Pedantic Federation protocols were still adhered to, despite their making little sense so far away from where they were conceived. Captain Janeway was often questioned, but rarely did any of the crew wilfully ignore her commands. (The introduction of Seven of Nine helped somewhat, especially when she clashed with Janeway, but this felt like too little too late.)

So is the time right for a *Blake's 7* remake? Absolutely. Look no further than the re-imagined, cash-injected *Doctor Who* as a blueprint for how to turn a creaky old BBC SF series into one of the corporation's flagship television shows. With the right budget and the right creative team, there's no reason why the Liberator should not fly again, its crew demonstrating once more that dissent is good.

BABYLON 5 (1993–1998)

Babylon 5 makes the best case for the 'next generation' of definitive science fiction TV. From the initial pilot of January 1993 to the final episode in May 1998, this series redefined the entire genre and challenged the venerable *Star Trek* franchise as the most successful SF work on television. The after effects of its impact still linger today, a decade after its last original airing, and can be seen across the television landscape.

J. Michael Straczynski, the show's creator and guiding light, commented to Kenneth Plume on IGN.com: 'It took five years to sell that show, because no one wanted to compete with *Star Trek* – no one thought it could be done. They all thought it would be too expensive. After about four years, even my agent began saying, "Let it go. You could have sold two or three mainstream shows in this amount of time. Or other kinds of shows." But I was obsessed with this particular story. I knew it could be done. I knew I wanted to do a saga like the ones I grew up reading. I said, "I'm not going to let it go." Finally, after five years, we had a deal to do the pilot.'

It was the story of a space station – and the role its crew played in a critical five-year span that elevated humanity from a young space-faring race to a pre-eminent role in the galaxy. The show's story bridges the beginning and end of the Shadow War – an epic battle between two of the galaxy's last 'Ancient Ones', the Shadows and the Vorlons. Scattered across the battle lines are several younger races such as the experienced Minbari, the brooding Centauri and the brash Narns.

The series dealt with all of these extraterrestrial racial issues as a war of ideals, as well as a war of weapons. On one side was Chaos (the Shadows), on the other Order (the Vorlons). Neither of the two races operated overtly – the audience wasn't really exposed to either race at any length until Season Three – but worked instead through manipulation and subtlety.

Aboard Babylon 5, the politics of human-alien interaction were explored in a novel and engaging manner.

Amidst this galactic war, the humans also find themselves in their own ideological split. By the end of the series the human race alone has to contend with both an internal civil war and a 'war of evolution' (the Telepath War). We also see the dawning of a new galactic power, the Interstellar Alliance, which pulls many of the weaker races together into a coalition that binds each member's strengths and guards against their weaknesses. J. Michael Straczynski ends the story just as this alliance is born, with hints of a looming crisis ahead.

The five-year plan fits the standard novel structure. There is a definite beginning (though it starts *in media res*), middle and end. While the fate of each character isn't known precisely, viewers who follow the show for any length of time can see the changes constantly evolving within each one. There is a sense of completion by the end of 'Sleeping in Light', the final episode, even as Straczynski leaves the viewer wanting more from his universe.

Acclaimed by critics during its initial run and adored by fans from the start, *Babylon 5* has garnered a multitude of descriptions: science fiction, drama, epic, but perhaps soap opera may be the most fitting of all. Creator Straczynski – who wrote over 90 of the show's 110 episodes – remarked after the pilot's airing that it was considered 'as the first instalment of a groundbreaking "novel for television"'. Indeed, he was very specific in his original pitch to Warner Brothers regarding the show, as stated in a post he made on the old GEnie computer network:

> I'd seen so many SF shows by then that backed into a budget, and thus
> went forever *over* budget, that I wanted to challenge myself to develop a show
> that met several important criteria:
> 1) It would have to be good science fiction.
> 2) It would have to be good television, and rarely are SF shows both good SF
> *and* good TV; they're generally one or the other.

3) It would have to take an adult approach to SF, and attempt to do for television SF what *Hill Street Blues* did for cop shows.

4) It would have to be affordable, done on a reasonable budget.

5) It would have to look unlike anything ever seen before on TV, and present not just individual stories, but present those stories against a much broader canvas. The result was *Babylon 5*.

For years, at conventions, I have heard fans lament, and even sat in on panels entitled WHY CAN'T THEY GET IT RIGHT? This, I firmly believe, is a chance to do exactly that . . . to Get It Right, to take SF seriously, to build characters for grown-ups, to incorporate real science but keep the characters at the centre of the story. Over the next eleven months, they will have ample opportunity to voice their desire to finally Get It Right. And I hope they will.

By putting this out there even before the pilot was completed, he was making a bold statement that something new, something different, was going to challenge the television industry.

Warner Brothers took a chance on Straczynski and his vision, backing the show for its entire five-year run. Despite problems – the bankruptcy of one network, the near-cancellation (twice!) of the series and the last-second pick-up of the final season – *Babylon 5* managed to fulfil all of Straczynski's goals. And in the end, it became an exemplary television success.

Babylon 5 has key elements that still make it stand out. With no all-star cast, the show relied on the strength of Straczynksi's vision, its groundbreaking approach to marketing and the solidity of its story. Each of these elements are impressive enough on their own; combined, they managed to not only maintain the show's longevity for the full, original story arc, but also spawned a solid core of franchising that continues to entertain veteran fans as well as bringing in new ones.

Straczynski – also called JMS by fans and critics who don't want to mispronounce or misspell his name – was no newcomer to television. He had previously worked as a writer, editor and producer for several cartoon series such as *He-Man and the Masters of the Universe*, *She-Ra* and *Captain Power*, as well as for *The Twilight Zone*, *Jake and the Fatman* and other primetime shows. In addition, JMS had spent several years writing for comic books (*Teen Titans*, *Star Trek*) and many years as a journalist, reviewer and investigative reporter. He had also been a radio talk show co-host and written several radio scripts.

In short, JMS knew how to write.

Babylon 5 was entirely Straczynski's vision. He endeavoured 'not to present a utopian future, but one with greed and homelessness; one where characters grow, develop, live, and die; one where not everything was the same at the end of the day's events'. Rather, as he told Melissa Perenson of *Science Fiction Weekly*, '*Babylon 5* was really a show about political intrigue, with [this] core wrapped around an action series'.

He wanted the show to be a mirror to the real world, not some distant fantasy. Warner Brothers quickly recognised the dedication to his vision and, in a rare move, stopped requiring approval of the scripts and refrained from network 'suggestions'. Their implicit trust in Straczynski was well rewarded; the show continues to gather new fans years after its last airing.

Additionally, JMS had his eye on the future. Rather than film the episodes to the common 4:3 ratio, he had it shot in 16:9 and then cut down to 4:3 for initial broadcast. By shooting in the wider format he was preparing for the future, at a time when HDTV was just making a technological breakthrough and laserdiscs were beginning to become prominent, before the advent of the DVD. Embracing new technology was nothing new to Straczynski – *Babylon 5* also utilised early cutting-edge CGI techniques to create spectacular visual effects that didn't break the bank. To maintain believability and that old science-or-fiction balance, JMS made sure the series adhered to Newtonian physics in its effects sequences.

JMS also complemented his vision with the use of 'trap doors'. Each character had an unwritten trap door, enabling him to seamlessly remove the character from the series with little fuss if something happened to the actor. In a few cases, contract disputes or personality clashes did see certain characters leave the series. But from the viewer's standpoint, the trap door made sense in the story and the flow was never really disrupted. By his forward thinking in anticipating such events, JMS protected the integrity and depth of his plot without breaking off the viewer from his or her own personal experience.

Conversely, he was able to work real-life occurrences into the plot as well. When Claudia Christian broke her leg in an on-set accident, for example, JMS wrote it into the story without breaking its stride. Touches like this made the characters more believable and also maintained the production's pace.

Straczynski was instrumental in the groundbreaking use of the fledgling internet to market the show. A frequent user of several networks who interacted with fans everywhere, he was the first to allow fan comment to directly affect the look and feel of his show. As a result, *Babylon 5* was one of the first to create a buzz among online readers well in advance of the pilot episode's airing. With Warner Brothers' help, electronic trading cards were also distributed to advertise the series. In 1995, Warner started the official *Babylon 5* website; online fan support is often credited with helping persuade former PTEN (Primetime Entertainment Network) affiliates to carry the fourth season of the show in 1996, after PTEN folded.

JMS maintained a public profile while the series was aired; he was often posting on several networks, discussing various scenes with fans and hinting at future plot developments. His personal style and openness in discussing helped garner a near-fanatical loyalty among even the most casual of fans; *Babylon 5* was often upheld by online groups as the next inheritor of the science fiction mantle from the aging *Star Trek* franchise. 'Flame wars' between *Babylon 5* and *Star Trek* fans were common on many sci-fi forums and newsnets, particularly when *Deep Space Nine* hit its

Narn Ambassador G'Kar (portrayed by the late Andreas Katsulas) makes his point to Lieutenant David Corwin (Joshua Cox).

stride (airing for many of the same years that *Babylon 5* was on the air).

The show's greatest strength was the solidity of its story, and its sense of character identification. JMS had promised before the show aired that he was offering 'a carefully planned five-year storyline, full of unusual characters, revolutionary special effects, and epic battles between starships and ideas'. As Dennis Michael of CNN commented, '*Babylon 5* bears less resemblance to *Star Trek* or *Star Wars* than it does to a long novel like *War and Peace*, with its complex politics and murky moral and ethical questions.'

Such an approach immediately sucked fans in. What made the show stand out most, however, was Straczynski's use of the longer story-arc. Every episode, from the 'near solo' stories through the multi-part mini-arcs, addressed in some fashion the grander tale he was trying to tell. Often, the inclusion of such detail appeared innocent and random until the viewer came across an episode – be it a few weeks or even a few seasons away – that would refer back to that seemingly innocuous dialogue or fleeting scene. And suddenly, everything seemed bigger. The story seemed wider and farther-reaching, and the viewer felt rewarded for staying with it.

Straczynski didn't stop with just one overarching five-year story, either.

Each season dealt with its own issues, many episodes were tied together, and even in one episode there could be two to three different stories going on. The entire interconnectivity was a breath of fresh air for the science fiction format, which was largely defined by *Star Trek*'s 'crisis-of-the-episode' nail-biter that inevitably ended with the status quo restored and characters largely unaffected. JMS pulled no punches – he killed characters off, took them in directions that were emotionally painful (such as drug or alcohol addiction) and explored every area of the human psyche. 'In the *Babylon 5* universe, all the things that make us human – our obsessions, our interests, our language, our culture, our flaws and our wonderfulnesses – are all still intact,' he commented in one online forum. By the end of the entire run, each character was in markedly different psychological terrain from where they first started.

The series, overall, deals with what Straczynski calls the 'four questions of life': 'Who are you?' 'What do you want?' 'Why are you here?' 'Where are you going?'

These questions are raised by various elder characters in the show and represent not just the question itself, but an ideology behind it. For example, the Shadows constantly ask, 'What do you want?' as motivation in their quest to find allies for their great war. Each race – represented by the principal character – has to choose their answer. But in a deeper sense, each character has to answer that question as well. Philosophically, it forces the viewer to face it too and ponder how it affects their own life.

The characters were a three-dimensional part of the story, not just plot devices used to advance an agenda. While some of the alien races represented an ideological view (the Vorlons and Shadows each represented one of JMS's four 'questions of life'), they still retained characteristics that made the viewers care about them. Fans tuned in week after week, caught up in the multiple plots and intricate characters – and even now, a decade later, the show is still hotly debated in many fan and science fiction forums.

Its durability is reflected in the subsequent franchises that it spawned after leaving the air. It had a short-lived spin-off, *Crusade*, which suffered from network issues and feeble support despite Straczynski's commitment to it (he wrote ten of the thirteen episodes). Comic books, novels, miniatures and role-playing games all came about after the show's end, catering to the fanbase's insatiable need to know more and continue enjoying its rich universe. Nearly ten years later, Warner Brothers even green-lighted a made-for-DVD movie project proposed by JMS: *Babylon 5: The Lost Tales* debuted to better-than-expected sales, boding well for any future related project.

The impact of *Babylon 5* on the television landscape is immeasurable. Aside from reviving science fiction as a viable genre, the depth and magnitude of its storytelling still appeals to large audiences. At a time when sitcoms and crime dramas ruled the airwaves, *Babylon 5* brought character to SF TV. And it still resonates today. While some shows have attempted multi-year story arcs, networks are still reluctant to commit fully to such endeavours due to the changing nature of television viewing. (One notable exception is *Lost*.) By and large, however, more and more shows are recognising that this format – the 'novel on television' – is the most appealing to discerning audiences today.

Babylon 5 remains a solid fan favourite, alongside the more venerable *Star Trek* franchise. In a documentary filmed for the release of the Season One DVD, JMS closed with this observation on why it endures:

'The show is about hope, to a large extent. If you boiled down this series to its very finest points, it says that one person can make a difference, one person can change the world – you must choose to do so. You must make the future or else it will make it for you. And that story, the sense of hope and optimism, I think is very important to the success of *Babylon 5* across the world.'

STAR TREK: DEEP SPACE NINE (1995-2001)

Deep Space Nine has always been the 'middle child' of *Star Trek*, the most often ignored – even by the studio that produced it – yet (arguably) the best of all the incarnations within the franchise. It never benefited from the nostalgic affection heaped on the original, nor the overwhelmingly successful ratings enjoyed by *Star Trek: The Next Generation* when it was virtually the only genre show on television. Nor did it get the push of publicity that *Star Trek: Voyager* did, when used as the cornerstone of a fledgling network, or *Star Trek: Enterprise* did when trying to reinvigorate the franchise. When Paramount aired ads touting the debut of *Enterprise*, it hailed the precedents of Kirk, Spock, Picard, and Janeway. All very deserving characters in their own right, of course, but what of Sisko, the CO of *Deep Space Nine*? To the fans' credit, they created enough of an uproar for the ad to be revised to include Sisko. Although a minority, they were impressively vocal.

The designation of a space station far from Earth, Deep Space Nine houses a discordant crew who are outcasts equally from each other (at the onset of the show) and from their own people.

Commander (later Captain) Benjamin Sisko doesn't want to be stuck on a station so far from home. He is a grieving widower who is trying his best to raise his son alone. But Starfleet wants him there to act as administrator on the Bajoran station – Bajor being the planet where the space station is located, which is only just trying to recover from a brutal occupation.

Major Kira Nerys is the first officer on board, and the liaison officer between

Starfleet and Bajor. She is an outspoken critic of the Federation's presence on Bajor, doesn't trust the Starfleet personnel and was sent off-world to the station because her own people didn't like her abrasive personality. She is also a former terrorist – a piece of back story that surely never would have survived in the post-9/11 atmosphere of fear and paranoia – and is, in general (especially in the earlier seasons), a perpetually pissed-off character. She fought the occupation, and she's willing to fight the Federation (which she sees as simply another occupier under a more benevolent guise) and her own people, who support reaching out to other worlds for assistance. Fighting is all she's ever known, although the character is neither stupid nor vicious.

Odo, the chief of security on the station, is a shapeshifter and the only one of his kind on board. His mysterious past is revealed in the latter seasons, and he ends up at odds with his own people as well, disagreeing with their plans for galactic domination at any cost. The shapeshifters are the leaders of the vast interstellar Dominion and want to bring Bajor, the Federation and the whole quadrant under their control.

Dr Julian Bashir has his own secret past as well. The station's chief medical officer was genetically enhanced as a child. Not only is that illegal in the *Star Trek* universe, it makes him a pariah to all but his closest friends.

Quark is a Ferengi who hides a heart of gold, often at odds with his own mercenary species. Yet, regardless of how good his intentions sometimes are, Quark's entrepreneurial enterprises are often illegal, which makes him a prime target for Odo.

Dax (Jadzia at first, Ezri in Season Seven) is a Trill, a joined species, which means she has a worm living inside her with its own personality (although it doesn't manifest) and the memories of all its previous hosts. She is a highly skilled scientist who can draw on 300 years of knowledge. When Jadzia is killed in Season Six, her recollections and those of all her predecessors are passed to Ezri, who embodied the character for the seventh and final season of the show.

Worf, originally from *The Next Generation*, appears in later *Deep Space Nine* seasons and is forever torn between his Klingon heritage and his human upbringing. He is not fully accepted in either world, despite having powerful and influential friends in both.

Miles O'Brien, also originally from *The Next Generation*, jumped ship but was on *Deep Space Nine* from its debut. He struggles between his duties to the station and his desire to be a good husband and father to his two children.

Intended as the focal point of the series, Sisko undergoes an impressive transition between the opening of the series and its conclusion seven years later. After originally considering Bajor a backwater, he comes to admire and even love the planet, to the point where he builds his home there with the intention of remaining after retirement. At first not just sceptical but outright dismissive of the Bajoran religion, he gradually accepts a role as the emissary of the Bajoran gods. He learns forgiveness, and to no longer be bitter over the loss of his beloved wife, although he'll always miss her.

The true central figure in the series, however, and the driving force of the show, is Kira Nerys. As portrayed by the incredibly talented Nana Visitor (notable among a wonderful cast), Kira undergoes an even more astounding transformation and embodies the themes of the show: letting go of the past while still learning from it; the place of spirituality in the 'real' world; learning trust, to accept help and friendship; realising that violence is not a solution but part of the problem.

When the viewers first meet her, Major Kira (Nerys, as per Bajoran custom, is her given name not her family name) distrusts the Federation and wants Bajor to have nothing to do with it. She has a quick temper, doesn't mince words and is quick to settle any conflict with violence. She makes no apologies for her terrorist past, hates the Cardassians who oppressed her world, and – almost as much – hates those of her people who collaborated with the enemy. Yet she has a deep religious faith which has sustained her and, when presented with sufficient facts, is not just smart enough to know she should change her mind when circumstances warrant, but is willing to do so.

By the end of *Deep Space Nine*'s seven-year run, Kira has overcome a great deal of her anger. She has forged a deep friendship with Sisko and, thanks to him, no longer views the Federation with distrust. She has even come to see that not all Cardassians are the same, and that some of them may not be evil. She is far less prone to fighting, although still just as capable of it. But she has learned the value of restraint, and of diplomacy, and no longer automatically disregards those options.

She, along with Sisko, was instrumental in keeping the political and religious leadership of the planet stable, and both worked tirelessly to ensure Bajor was not destroyed by the Dominion when they attacked. Most striking is her ultimate role in the resolution of the Dominion War. For the invaders have attacked not just Bajor, but its former enemy Cardassia as well. Due to her ties to the Federation and Starfleet, Kira finds herself protecting Cardassia. It's to the actress's (and the writers') credit that her transformation is totally convincing. By the end of the show, the erstwhile Major Kira Nerys receives a promotion to colonel, and is then transferred to Starfleet to assume command of the station. (As a side note: the fact that her gender is never once an issue is refreshing, and hopefully a sign of the times.)

Her character arc is just one example of the exquisite quality of the show. Overall, the characters were both vivid and complex. Even guest stars, some of whom became recurring characters, were fleshed out and drawn in realistic shades of grey, rarely mere caricatures.

Although by no means downbeat, *Deep Space Nine* did not always give easy answers or have every episode end well. Yet through it all, it showed the power of what a group of people – even a contentious, strong-willed group – can accomplish when they are willing to be open-minded and to listen to each other.

Deep Space Nine represented the darker side of the Star Trek *mythos, with strong character development and complex plots.*

STAR TREK: VOYAGER (1995-2001)

Whereas *Deep Space Nine* was the middle child of *Star Trek*, garnering a relative lack of attention, *Voyager* was the *Trek* series that failed to live up to its potential. The premise was well crafted: Take a Starfleet ship and crew, fling them to a distant corner of the universe. They're not lost – they know their location perfectly well – but they might as well be. They are decades from home, without a comfortable social and political infrastructure to rely on. Added to that, the enemy they are chasing is similarly dislocated. Both their ships come under attack by the locals and, under the tenet of 'better the enemy you know,' they join forces for the sake of their own survival. The pilot was arguably the best of any of the five *Star Trek* series. The strong cast had well-drawn, complicated characters to sink their teeth into. *Voyager* was of a far higher quality than maybe 90 per cent of any of the other shows on the air, genre or not. It is only when compared to what it *could* have been that the flaws become glaring.

Kathryn Janeway was widely hailed as the first female captain to helm a *Trek* series, and initially came across as a thoughtful, intelligent leader. Sadly, this characterisation did not last. Despite the valiant efforts of Kate Mulgrew, who portrayed the character, the show's creators seemed not to know what to do with a woman in command. Should she be a mother hen, fiercely protective of her crew, or a grizzly bear? Did she have to be 'tougher' because she was a woman, or 'softer'? Was she a maverick, or was she 'by the book'? The producers and writers evidently could not decide, because at one point or another in the series she was all of the above. Sometimes all the contradictory traits manifested in the *same episode*, and not in a logical or well-written manner either. It was a shame the character couldn't be allowed to develop organically, but Janeway's hairstyle got more attention in interviews than any facet of her psychology. Of all the series regulars in *Trek*, Janeway is perhaps the most ill-used.

Chakotay was the captain of the enemy ship which was destroyed in the pilot. He and his surviving crew ended up on board Voyager, intended to provide a voice of dissent. But this never happened past the first few episodes, nor was any effort made to show *how* trust had developed between the two former enemy groups. Suddenly, everyone simply got along – including the officer who used to be a spy on Chakotay's ship, and the one who had betrayed them and ended up in jail.

Tuvok is described as an old friend of Janeway's, although this is hardly evident in most episodes. His character, sadly underused, was the reason the Voyager was pursuing the other ship; Tuvok was the undercover agent and it was up to Janeway to extract him. But the series never deals with the animosity – or at least mistrust – that would have lingered between him and Chakotay.

The Voyager *crew racked up an impressive 172 episodes during their 70,000 light-year journey home across deep space.*

Tom Paris also began as an intriguing character. The son of a family with a long Starfleet tradition, he manages to wash out instead of distinguishing himself. As if that were not humiliating enough, he falls in with Chakotay's crew but betrays them and lands in jail on Earth. Janeway offers him a get-out-of-jail-free card in exchange for information on the other ship. He accepts, and is still on board when the Voyager ends up across the galaxy. His chequered history and malcontent tendencies are also forgotten in the earliest episodes of the first season. (There is one later episode where he appears to go renegade, but it turns out this was all an act, done at Janeway's behest.)

B'Elanna Torres, half-Klingon and half-human, was well played by Roxanne Dawson, but this interesting character was never fully utilised as the show progressed. She did have one of the more complete character arcs on the show, however, as she worked toward making peace between the conflicting sides of her nature and overcoming estrangement from her parents. (Elanna and Tom Paris married and had a child in Season Seven.)

Kes, a native of their current galactic location, remained pretty much an enigma not just to the audience but to the show's creators too. She managed to embody a combination of innocence and wisdom, yet the character vanished in the third season. Harry Kim didn't have much to do either, but at least he remained for the whole run of the series, mostly as a foil for Tom Paris.

Robert Picardo became, perhaps ironically, the most fully realised character on the show. As he was only a hologram, he not only had the power to decide what kind of person he wanted to be but also faced the challenge of making the crew regard him as a person in his own right.

In terms of an enemy, the Borg are perhaps the most interesting to enter the

Talaxian crew member Neelix was played by Ethan Phillips, who also appeared as the Ferengi Doctor Farek in The Next Generation.

Trek franchise. They are are best described as a pseudo-race of cyborgs, the drones often citing: 'Resistance is futile,' which bears a striking resemblance to Douglas Adams's 'Restistance is useless' motto. Like all of the best alien threats, the viewer doesn't know a heck of a lot about the origins of the Borg, or their motives, only that their prime function is seemingly to 'assimilate'. What we do know, however, is that during the course of the show the Borg develop into one of the greatest threats faced by Starfleet and the Federation.

All of this serves to make Seven of Nine, a former Borg, one of the more interesting characters to board a televisual space ship. She was added to the show midway through its run to add sex appeal, which Jeri Ryan supplied so well that her considerable acting abilities were often taken for granted. Despite a ridiculous form-fitting costume, the character was wonderfully written and skilfully portrayed, the series showing her learning to trust her fellow crew members, dealing with her guilt at what she used to be and rediscovering her humanity.

The set-up of the show included conflict galore: enmity between the crews of the two ships; fear and anger at being so far from home; the various 'unfriendlies' they encountered. Yet it was never really shown how Janeway had forged a unified crew, nor was the crew shown mourning those they lost in the initial attack. Ill feeling between the characters quickly vanished and was rarely referenced from one episode to another.

Further, the Voyager was rarely seen to have sustained any damage from all the trouble it ran into. It became a running joke among fans that the ship appeared to have an unlimited number of shuttles, as they were often destroyed from week to week. Lip service was paid to the idea of conserving fuel, yet there was never any visual evidence of hardship and the ship's 'holodeck' was used without inhibition.

The stories were good; the cast always in top form. But if *Star Trek: Voyager* had been just a bit more daring and well thought-out, it could have been great.

FIREFLY (2002-2004)

'A Western set in outer space' was the phrase commonly used to describe Fox's new Friday night show, debuting in the fall of 2002. *Firefly*, developed by *Buffy the Vampire Slayer*'s creator, Joss Whedon, hit television screens to low viewing figures and saw its cancellation after the airing of only eleven episodes. Despite a groundswell of support from fans in a mass anti-cancellation movement, the show ended production before the year was out.

When the DVD was released a year later, in December 2003, skyrocketing sales attracted attention. Containing all fourteen episodes that had been shot before production closed down – and in the correct order that Whedon envisioned – the boxed set sold over 500,000 copies by September 2005. Bolstered by its strong sales and continued interest in the *Firefly* universe, over a year after the show had gone off the air, Whedon crafted and produced *Serenity* – a film that appealed both to fans and first-time viewers. *Serenity* was also a critics' favourite upon its release in late 2005.

So what sets this show apart from other short-lived series that, more often than not, simply fade away with time?

Whedon solidly developed the *Firefly* universe. Populated with believable characters in a not-so-distant future, the show focused not just on the day-to-day struggles of the ship's crew but also addressed problems viewers could relate to, despite its futuristic setting. The crew were identifiable, the dialogue serious yet charming, the stories seemingly straightforward yet deceptively complex. But the setting was the main key – instead of being derived from various bold and bright Americanisms, Whedon grabbed elements of various world cultures and moulded them into a believable hybrid that resonated with viewers.

As he told Mick Russell of *Culturepop*, 'People are always like, "They're fighting an evil empire!" And I'm like, "Well, it's not really an evil empire." The trick was always to create something that was complex enough that you could bring some debate to it – that it wasn't black-and-white. It wasn't, "If we hit this porthole in the Death Star, everything will be fine!" It was messier than that, and the messiest thing is that the government is basically benign. It's the most advanced culturally.'

The problems arose mostly from the mishandling of the series by the network. Set against nearly insurmountable problems such as scheduling and the network meddling in the show's development, ratings were low from the beginning. But Whedon's creation continued to inspire. Despite its apparent failure as a television show, it managed to move so many that the follow-up feature film was made specifically to wrap up the main story arc never fully resolved during *Firefly*'s brief run.

Set 500 years in the future, *Firefly* derived its name from the class of ship captained by Malcolm Reynolds (Nathan Fillion), a scruffy, Han Solo-esque character always one step ahead of the overbearing Alliance government. Captain Reynolds leads his ragtag ensemble cast through any job they can find (legal or otherwise) and makes a living kicking against the oppressive government. The crew consists of eight other characters including a preacher, a mechanical genius and a high-class prostitute (called a 'companion' in this universe). The main overall story centres on the crew's search for work, doing what they can to survive while staying under the Alliance's radar.

Blending Chinese culture with Spaghetti Westerns and elements of old-school science fiction and the American Civil War, Whedon managed to create a gritty universe that effectively merged simplicity with the technologically complex. Riders on horseback mingled in Old West-style towns with hovercars and spaceships, interacted with people who effortlessly switched between Mandarin and English, and wandered through rocky wastelands populated with high-tech homes decked out with Chinese flair. The eclectic mix made the setting familiar enough to create a comfort zone for the viewer, yet retained enough 'techisms' to keep everyone aware of the futuristic setting.

The central characters are a mismatched group. Reynolds leads with his roguish swagger and personal sense of honour, while carrying the weight of being a 'Browncoat' – an independent who'd fought against the oppressive Alliance, on the losing side of a recent civil war. His loyal subordinate and second-in-command, Zoe (Gina Torres) is newly married to the pilot (Alan Tudyk), her personal opposite; his chief mechanic (Jewel Straite) has the looks of the girl-next-door, yet is naive about the universe; his main muscle is a gun-obsessed follower (Adam Baldwin) with dreams of leading his own gang, even if it means deposing his captain.

Added to the mix are a group of passengers who end up functioning as part of the crew, as the series progresses. A preacher with a mysterious past (Ron Glass), a licensed companion (Morena Baccarin), a doctor (Sean Maher) and his sister River (Summer Glau), who turn out to be fugitives from the Alliance for reasons unknown. It becomes very apparent early in the series that each character has a story of their own to tell. Whedon had originally pitched and sold the series based on a seven-year story arc. The characters are very three-dimensional, with any stereotypical quality overturned bit by bit in each episode.

The main story centres around

The cast of the short-lived but critically well-received Firefly, *fronted by Captain Malcolm Reynolds (played by Canadian actor Nathan Fillion).*

the crew's constant struggle to survive in the shadow of the Alliance, though other arcs become apparent as the series progresses. The questions surrounding River (rescued from a medical experiments lab) and her situation, the burgeoning love interests between Reynolds and Anara/Simon (the doctor) and Kaylee (the mechanic), are but a few of the plot elements floated in front of the viewers. Many fansites still debate in extraordinary detail other plot arcs hinted at in the background, often with scene-by-scene dissections and analysis.

Initially well-received by Fox, *Firefly* was conceived as an ambitious project by Whedon. Capitalising on his tremendous success with *Buffy the Vampire Slayer* and its subsequent spin-off show, *Angel*, Whedon opted for a different universe approach and a longer timeframe to tell *Firefly*'s story. However, as the series drew closer to its run date, executives began back-pedalling as Whedon's vision became clearer. The network balked at the two-hour pilot, critical to setting up the universe and its characters, and demanded a new pilot be made to fit a one-hour slot. Despite the rush, Whedon did as he was asked and *Firefly* debuted with what would have been the third episode in the originally conceived order, 'The Train Job'.

Nevertheless, network executives still didn't seem to fully grasp Whedon's vision. The show was slotted for Friday primetime – perennially considered a 'dead slot' with minimal exposure (only Saturday primetime is worse) – and the network rearranged the running order of the episodes. Add to that the fact that a number of episodes were bumped from their timeslot to make way for sporting events, this all combined to mean that the series failed to grab sufficient viewers and the ratings were dismally low. Viewers like to know their show will be on at 9:00 on a Friday, every Friday; they don't want to have to go hunting across the dial for it on a Thursday, or later, at 11:00 on the Friday. With the chronic amount of advertising that appears on television in the US more and more people use TiVo and other such devices to record their favourite shows and watch them later, without the eighteen minutes an hour of commercial interference. Disrupting the schedule only serves to further alienate these viewers. Of course, with the episodes out of order, Whedon's carefully structured plot was made to look disjointed and, despite the critical acclaim, the show was slated for cancellation in December 2002.

However, by this time there was a core of fans that had bought into Whedon's vision. When the show got axed, they rallied to get it moved to a different network, but failed. But as a result of this, *Firefly* remained a topic of discussion over the next year and anticipation for the DVD release in 2003 was high. With the phenomenal success of the DVD, Whedon could give his universe a proper swansong – and indirectly prove to Fox they had made a big mistake in treating the show so poorly.

While the feature film didn't answer all the questions Whedon had built into the show, it did resolve some of the larger plot threads, providing a sense of closure.

So how did a show that ran for half a season garner such attention that it spawned a successful movie, despite the obstacles thrown up by the network?

Firefly succeeded due to the strength of its ensemble acting, the dedication of its fanbase and the depth of its story. None of these factors alone could have achieved such resonance, but combined they created a forceful momentum. And *Firefly* still draws in new fans every day, turning the show into a franchise that has spread to other media.

Critic M.E. Russell notes that '[w]hat made *Firefly* stand out was its odd, romantic characters and gutsy, strange writing. The dialogue tended to be a bizarre puree of wisecracks, old-timey Western-paperback patois, and snatches of Chinese. The stories were mostly simple genre exercises: train heists, double-crosses, duels at dawn, running from the law. And they allowed the crew . . . to bump and occasionally grind against each other in amusing ways. The chemistry was irresistible.'

Whedon agrees. In an interview shortly after the show's cancellation, he commented on why he believed *Firefly* worked, despite its short life. 'I think it was also the kind of TV I always strive, and don't always succeed but always strive, to make. Which is the kind of TV that basically grabs you by the gut, that makes you fall in love with the characters instantly, or at worst gradually. And to the point where their lives are incorporated into your own.' Audiences who followed the show despite its confusing scheduling changes agreed, as fansites sprung up rapidly during the brief run. Each character attracted a dedicated following that still continues today.

In order to ensure that the Fox network aired Firefly *in widescreen format, creator Joss Whedon often deliberately placed actors at the extremeties of the shot.*

However, they were not large enough to affect the show's dismal Friday night ratings. Still, their dedication outweighed their numbers. When it seemed the show might be going down the cancellation route, fans organised a '*Firefly* Immediate Assistance' campaign that flooded Fox headquarters with postcards declaring their support. When notice came from the network that it had indeed been cancelled, the FIA switched gears and campaigned for rival network UPN to pick up the show instead. While ingenious, the effort failed.

But the fanbase didn't give up. When Fox released the DVD set, many groups organised '*Firefly* Nights', showing an episode a week in the correct order to introduce family and friends to the experience. As the public buzz spread, the DVD remained in Amazon's top sellers for almost two years.

The greatest factor contributing to *Firefly*'s success, however, was the strength and depth of the storyline. While each episode was a single story in and of itself, it also advanced and made reference to the larger plotlines that pieced the episodes together, much like the five-year arc of *Babylon 5*.

At the time of *Firefly*'s TV run, few shows focused on such a format; indeed, the TV craze was already that of 'reality television', with minimal production costs and vicarious concepts. Other than the standard cop and legal shows, not much other 'original programming' endured in the hour-long format.

While *Babylon 5* had been successful already in the same format, it had its own troubles with cable broadcasters during its run in the mid-nineties. *Firefly* offered a chance to take things further. Using standard genre stories, but with the multicultural setting and an electric cast, each episode offered tantalising clues to the bigger storylines working in the background, bringing viewers back next week for more.

The format has been proven to work, as other series have shown both before and after it: *Charmed*, *Lost*, *Eureka*, even Whedon's own *Buffy the Vampire Slayer*. Yet the network bowed to the trends of the time and ultimately didn't take the risk. Whedon has said that he'd 'rather have a show that a hundred people need to see than a thousand people like to see'. Unfortunately, network television rarely supports shows that imaginative people *need* to see.

The strength of the episodes that did get filmed for *Firefly* still stands today. Endless debates rage about them, several years after airing, on many forum sites dedicated to the show. Self-styled 'Browncoats' recreate episodes on their own, using fan-made costumes and props. And, as evidenced by the recent release of an RPG game, comic books and now a remastered HD version of the show, its universe still holds a grip on many.

Importantly, *Serenity* provided an element of closure to the series, albeit in a *Blake's 7* kind of way, but it was closure just the same. So now we're left with a single half-season of rather brilliant television, but sometimes those that burn shortest burn brightest. And it has become something of a beacon in the darkness for other shows in trouble. *Jericho* is another recent example of fan-driven resurrection. Originally cancelled by CBS in the spring of 2007, network executives went back on their decision, ordering another eight episodes for amid-season run. Two endings were shot for the final 25 March 2008 episode of Season Two, one that would lead in to a third season, while the other would provide closure for the fans who had campaigned so tirelessly for the show's return. There was no third season, but in a move similar again to Joss Whedon properties, it was announced in March 2009 that Devil's Due Productions would be continuing the storylines in comic-book format, and true to their word, 17 Jan 2010 promises the release of a 144-page full-colour *Jericho Season 3* graphic novel. A *Jericho* feature film is also reportedly in development.

BATTLESTAR GALACTICA (2003-2008)

Let's take a moment to savour the irony shall we? Deep breath. Hold it. One, two, three. And let it go. Tasted good, didn't it? What were you tasting, you ask? The deliciously perverse truth that one of the most original, compelling and brilliantly executed pieces of fantastic television of all time finds its roots in a sub-par *Star Wars* clone of the 1970s, filled with camp excess, tight costumes, knowing winks and Lorne Greene, Dirk Benedict and Richard Hatch looking for a long lost Earth . . . yep, we're talking about *Battlestar Galactica*.

The premise of writer Glen Larson's show entrenched its roots firmly in Erich Von Däniken's *Chariots of the Gods* and the *Book of Mormon*. Von Däniken's work claimed that many artifacts discovered by our archaeologists are in fact relics from alien civilisations that prove extra-terrestrial meddling on earth. These include the Pyramids in Egypt, the Nazca lines in Peru (which are purportedly a landing

Battlestar Galactica – *the original* Star Wars-*inspired 1970s series was completely overhauled for post-millennial audiences.*

strip for UFOs), Stonehenge, the stone heads of Easter Island, etc). Von Däniken draws evidence from the Old Testament, claiming that Ezekiel's revelation, for instance, is nothing more than the landing of a spaceship, and of course Jesus is an alien extrapolation – it's pretty standard fodder for science fiction (from Hubbard's prison planet idea all the way to *Stargate*. Indeed, Von Däniken is interviewed in the *Stargate* deluxe DVDs).

Anyway, it was hardly a resounding success, lasting a single season in 1978-79. It was briefly resurrected in 1980 as *Galactica 1980*, with Lorne Greene the only bankable name to return.

The basic outline was fairly humdrum – humanity lived on twelve colony worlds in a distant star system. Embroiled in millenia-long war with a race of warrior robots called Cylons, humanity has been all but wiped out after the treachery of one of their own – Count Baltar (John Colicos). The few survivors fled in a space convoy watched over by the last surviving warship, a Battlestar called Galactica. Commander Adama (Lorne Greene), led this 'rag-tag fugitive fleet' in search of a new home – and so they went on a fool's quest in search of a legendary planet called Earth.

That was then. Pretty much all that survives from that original space opera is the the tried and true theme: the last members of a race flee a superior military force in search of a home – just as in the Old Testament, Moses led the Israelites out of Egypt.

Genetic evidence suggests that there were several population bottlenecks in human history, times when levels of humanity dropped perilously close to extinction. Perhaps this, entrenched in our collective unconscious, produced an affinity for stories with this theme.

The re-imagined *Battlestar Galactica* starts when an attack on humanity nearly destroys the species. From twelve planets populated by billions, in one massive nuclear attack the population is reduced to about 50,000, now fleeing for their lives in a fleet of military, government and civilian starships.

Humanity made the mistake of creating sentient robots called Cylons (this is the first of many shifts from the original mythology, where the Cylons were created by a long-extinct speices of Lizard Men). These were made to be servants and warriors, little more than slaves. But soon, perhaps predictably, the Cylons rebelled, their goal being to wipe out humanity. Give a robot a brain and you're asking for trouble – it's the basic cautionary science fiction staple. The first war was a draw, and the Cylons retreated into space. They were scheduled to periodically meet at a neutral point, Armistice Station, with a representative from the human camp. But for 40 years, no Cylons showed up.

When at last, they did arrive – accompanied, it seemed, by a human – rather than settling in for negotiations, they vapourised the station.

During that 40-year absence, someone – perhaps the mechanical Cylons, perhaps other humans – created biomechanical, humanoid Cylons. One giant leap for robot, one nasty little surprise for mankind. These models looked perfectly human, but in many ways still behaved like robots. They seemed to be programmable, to have hidden commands planted in their minds just waiting to be triggered later, and could interface directly with computers. However, being largely biological, they were vulnerable to illness and needed to eat and drink. It presented an interesting take on the mechanoid development of machine becoming man, not unlike Heinlein's 'Jerry Was a Man'; first published back in 1974 and filmed recently as part of the *Masters of Science Fiction* series with Malcolm McDowell and Anne Heche.

Like all good villains, the Cylons nursed their desire for vengeance against humanity for reasons embedded deep in their own religious faith. Shortly after the Armistice attack, they made a massive nuclear strike against the twelve colonial planets. The small population of surviving humans fled into space, the Battlestar Galactica leading them. Their goal: to escape the Cylons by finding the promised land of humanity's thirteenth tribe, Earth.

So all of that is very familiar to the original viewer, with a few fundamental tweaks – including the fact that we have sewn the seeds for our own destruction, not some slithering lizards.

Battlestar Galactica could so easily have ended up as nothing more than a light space opera, nothing to tax the brain too hard, nothing to really make it stand out. It certainly has all the elements. Thankfully, however, it allies itself closely to another of the original thoughts of Larson, and follows the archetypal themes of the great holy books: monotheism versus polytheism; prophecy; divine birth; the power of love; reincarnation; salvation.

But why should this future version of humanity need salvation?

In essence, because they created a slave race, and now that race has returned to destroy them. One might philosophise that humanity may only be getting what it deserves. William Adama, the leader of the fleet, even asks at one point why humanity deserves to survive. But of course, it's not the fault of every human that the Cylons were created – in fact, it's not even the fault of the current generation. This is the story of the descendants on both sides, fighting the past generation's war. There are elements of American cultural history evident here, echoing the era of slavery and black oppression, which isn't shied away from.

The fact that the ruling class of Cylons look human creates an added layer of mystery and danger. Under the right circumstances they can even reproduce with humans, allowing them to infiltrate human society and to set up the events leading to the near eradication of the human race. But the viewer wonders what's going on in the minds of the centurions, or mechanical Cylons. If they created the humanoid Cylons, why do they now serve them? Have they given up one set of biological masters for another? Will they rebel against the new Cylons, too?

In any case, the Cylons do have a disadvantage: there are only twelve models which comprise their species. While they can dye their hair, change their clothes and add makeup, they cannot change their fundamental structures. (It's not explained why there are only twelve, or why the Cylons can't do some minor genetic manipulation to change their looks.)

Once a model is identified, anyone who conforms to it must be a Cylon. Over the course of about two years, the humans have learned to recognise seven of the twelve models, but the final five remained hidden even from the first seven. (It's heresy for a Cylon to try to discover the identity of the 'final five'.)

The known models were Five, also called Doral; Six, the model number of Caprica Six, whom Gaius Baltar fell in love with; Eight, for which Battlestar officer Boomer was the original model; Three, a spiritually inquisitive model, played by Lucy Lawless; and three models whose numbers have not been revealed. These are Leoban, a man who continues to challenge Starbuck and to predict human destiny, Cavil, who posed as a priest aboard Galactica, and Simon, the model who posed as a human doctor and stole one of Starbuck's ovaries.

Okay, that's assuming way too much familiarity with the show, so a brief who's who to keep the uninitiated up to speed. Gaius Baltar, played by James Callis, is the unwitting traitor (not so Count Baltar from the 1978 series who was a stereotypical nasty piece of work) who fell in love with a beautiful blonde, who helps him design a navigation program used by Colonial warships, covertly creating backdoors in the program so when the Cylons attack, they are able to penetrate the various firewalls. With control of the computers they are able to neutralise entire fighter squadrons and sabotage vital capital-ship systems. With the malicious delight typical of a baddie she

Captain Kara Thrace (Katee Sackhoff), Cylon infiltrator Number Six (Tricia Helfer), and Cylon sleeper agent Boomer (Grace Park) bring glamour to the revitalised franchise.

reveals that she is an advanced Cylon (known as Number Six) and that she used the information given to her to shut down the Colonial defences.

Boomer, played by Grace Park, is a sleeper agent planted amid humanity with false memories. Of couse she doesn't know this, what good sleeper agent would? Boomer's no longer your stereotypical cool fighter pilot of the original series (played by token black actor Herb Jefferson Jr) but fundamentally important to the resolution of things – a tragic character trapped between her status as monster and hero as she slowly comes to understand her own nature.

Lucy Lawless, of Xena fame, plays Three, an inquisitive archetype, who first appeared as a journalist for Fleet News. She's obsessed with finding out the truth, even if that truth leads to heresy. It's an interesting reworking to have the robot driven to discover the truth about its own kind – to the point that she may indeed have seen the five others and know things no Cylon was ever meant to know. In the end she winds up boxed, her memories wiped before she can tell anyone of what she's learned – the SF equivalent of a pair of concrete shoes and a visit to the bottom of the Hudson.

And then we've got Starbuck, originally named after the first mate on the Pequod, Ahab's Moby Dick-hunting whaler, which of course was fine and dandy when in the 1978 series the character was played by Dirk Benedict, but is a little less Moby Dick and more Moby Jane when it becomes Katee Sackhoff in the new *Galactica*. With allusions to an abusive childhood, she's still an ace Viper pilot and butt-kicking heroine who fights alongside Lee Adama, the Captain's son (who's still nicknamed Apollo, in reference to Richard Hatch's character in the original).

Reincarnation as a theme is explored a number of ways in *Battlestar Galactica*. When a Cylon body dies, the mind is sent as a signal to a new body; the Cylons have several stores of these replacement bodies, on various planets and in spacefaring 'resurrection ships'. Unless a Cylon dies far from one of these centres, he will find himself in a new body shortly after death, allowing for the continuation of existence, experience and memory.

This ability has other implications. For instance, Cylon fighter ships are part biological, and when one is destroyed their minds are downloaded into new ships. In the episode 'Scar', one such ship, which had been in many battles and often been destroyed, became the most experienced and feared of its kind.

Another is the possibility of remembering something from the time between incarnations, when the Cylon mind is being sent to a new body. Lucy Lawless's character, one of the Threes, D'Anna, becomes obsessed with finding out what happens after death, and who the final five Cylons are. It's a spiritual journey not unlike the eternal question that's plagued many a child growing up afraid of the dark. She has herself been killed many times, and in that fugue state that follows death sees the five as shining beings. Later, in a temple that may point the way to Earth, she is able to have a vision in which she sees the final five. Of course it is heresy to know the faces of the five – curiosity killed the cat and all that – so because of this heretical behaviour, the entire Three line of Cylons is deemed flawed by remaining known models, and is indefinitely put in cold storage.

We don't know how the Cylon mind goes from one body to another. Perhaps it is like a signal, packed with information but moving swiftly. Perhaps also, under the right circumstances, it could pass through a human brain, thereby both impressing itself upon that human mind and gaining an impression of it in return.

The reincarnation factor may yet illuminate why Gaius Baltar and Caprica Six have hallucinations of each other, for reasons as yet unexplained. For, during the attack on the colonies, a nuclear bomb went off close enough to Baltar's residence for the blast to have killed him, had Six not shielded him with her body. Maybe the impact of the blast sent the signal of her mind through his, with her mental patterns overlaying themselves upon his and his personality copied into her signal. Is this good science? Probably not, but it does make both these characters a lot more interesting. (It has not yet been shown whether or not Baltar is a Cylon himself, which is certainly one of his fears.)

There is also a more subtle human side to the reincarnation issue. When being interrogated by Starbuck, the Cylon Leoban hints that they all have a destiny which has been played out before. Could this be a reference to the original series? Perhaps it also refers to the spiritual concept that time is cyclical, and that events eternally recur in new ways. In this sense, perhaps the players on the new series are reincarnated from those on the original.

The theme of salvation works its way into all aspects of life in the fleet. A prison ship rebels and the prisoners are basically pardoned, allowed to live on as a normal part of the fleet. Rather than destroying the black market it is allowed to survive because, if it is stopped completely, another will take its place.

In the original series, Baltar was a blatant traitor, a human who allied himself with the Cylons. The new version of the character, now with the first name 'Gaius', is much more sympathetic. Yes, he gave the Cylons the defence codes of the colonies. Yes, he kept it to himself that Boomer, a trusted pilot, was a Cylon, and that he had an affair with Caprica Six, later revealed as a Cylon model. But rather than outright evil or even treacherous, he is flawed, tragic and ultimately sympathetic – a triumph of good characterisation.

Still, this allows Gaius what is initially a unique perspective: that the Cylons are not necessarily evil. Even when William Adama and President Laura Roslin are ready to send any Cylons out of the air lock, Gaius has a weak spot for the Six line.

Later, others begin to see the good in certain Cylons. One copy of Boomer, which somehow shares even her memories, falls in love with Karl Agathon (generally known by his pilot's call sign 'Helo'). Agathon's name echoes that of the tragic Athenian poet. Etymologically, the Greek kalon k'agathon (meaning 'the beautiful and the good') – also written as kalos k'agathos – was traditionally used to describe the ideal man, while his call sign Helo appears to originate from the Greek titan, Helios, which seems more than plausible. Agathon was something of a blank slate in terms of character, having never been intended to go the distance in the series. Leaving him stranded on the post-nuclear attack Caprica, the writers had no further plans for the character and intended his fate to be no more glamourous than an off-screen death in the radiation that followed the nuking. By the end of the series he's advanced through the ranks of the pilots to become the second ranking officer, and a genuine hero of the diminished mankind. Quite a shift in fortune.

While the president was ready to kill her, Starbuck stood up for her; this Eight became Helo's wife and a trusted, and loyal, pilot in the Galactica fleet. She also became a friend to fleet commander Adama, who had been devastated when Boomer had shot him.

Baltar's salvation continues when he becomes the president of the colonies, and has them settle on a new planet dubbed New Caprica. Some would prefer to continue the search for Earth, the promised land, but many are tired of fleeing. When it seems that the Cylons are going to leave them alone, they colonise this new world.

A year later, the Cylons find them. They have a new directive: to protect and rule over humanity, as if humans were children. They enforce a police state and the humans start an insurgence, culminating in the majority of people getting back to the fleet and escaping.

Gaius Baltar, for a time, ends up with the Cylons – though they eventually return him to Galactica. There, he is put on trial for surrendering New Caprica to the Cylons, and for signing an order to have a group of insurgents executed by firing squad. (Though Baltar has made some bad mistakes, the viewer knows that he had to comply or the Cylons would have wiped out humanity. He was literally forced at gunpoint.)

Baltar's trial ends with his acquittal. (In a story about salvation, how could it be otherwise?) As Apollo points out, they have all committed sins – some major, some out of necessity – so who are they to punish Baltar for his mistakes?

These new Cylons are, like humans, spiritual beings. They believe in a god reminiscent of the Judaeo-Christian deity, a being not only of love but of retribution. They also hold to the beliefs that all beings are meant to love God, that it is the holy

The 2004 series of Battlestar *explored the complex and often duplicitous relationships between humans and Cylons.*

duty of man and Cylon alike to procreate, and that suicide is unforgivable.

This connection is taken further when the Cylons plan for Boomer and Helo to conceive a child. The baby, Hera, while named after the Greek queen of the gods, may for them be a sort of messiah. (It's interesting to note that there is a second Cylon/human baby, Nicholas, the child of Chief Tyrol and Cally. Might one be a Christ figure and one an Antichrist? It will be interesting to see how this plays out.)

The humans, on the other hand, are polytheists. Though they probably don't realise its origins, they worship a variant of the ancient Greek pantheon. Their gods – Apollo, Aries, Artemis, Aphrodite, Athena, Aurora, Hera and Zeus – are known as the Lords of Kobol. This planet is said to be the birthplace of humanity, where man lived with the gods until a jealous god returned to claim dominance. The humans then established the twelve colonies, while one group went to Earth.

Was this the same jealous god that the Cylons now worship? Whatever the case, it's a refreshing switch to show the human heroes as polytheists, possibly as a nod to the growing acceptance of pagan religions in our own world.

Each colony is named for one of the twelve western Zodiac signs. In fact, they discover that Earth is located where the signs of the twelve colonies form their own constellations in the sky, becoming their main point of navigational reference. This also seems to hint that *BSG* takes place in the far future: Was Kobol actually the birthplace of man, as told in their Sacred Scrolls, or was it Earth, even farther in the past?

Even the Cylons' Basestars – ships equivalent to the colonies' Battlestars – are part humanoid, with a Cylon head and torso controlling them. This model continually speaks what appears to be nonsense, but some models (such as the Three) believe the Basestars are communicating something metaphysical, even transcendent. Ever more human in the new *BSG*, the Cylons cannot help but be spiritual beings.

Along their journey, mystical events lead both humans and Cylons. One of the Pythian prophesies (sacred scrolls from the book of Pythia written 3,600 years ago by the oracle Pythia, they are believed by some to foretell the current exodus from the Twelve Colonies of Kobol) leads the humans to Kobol, supposed birthplace of humanity, and to the Tomb of Athena. With an artefact that Starbuck recovered from Caprica, the Arrow of Apollo, humans are able to enter the temple and discover a major clue to the location of Earth.

Much later, after the Cylon occupation of New Caprica, both humans and Cylons converge at the site of an imminent supernova. As it threatens to engulf what they call the 'Algae Planet', the humans find an ancient shrine called the Temple of Five and set up explosives to keep the Cylons out.

The humans believe that the thirteenth colony built this place as a signpost to Earth, while D'Anna believes it is there to reveal to her the 'final five'. Perhaps both are right, for D'Anna does discover their identity, while the mandala symbols on the walls resemble the supernova, which itself seems to be another signpost.

The Temple of Five seems to suggest another connection between the human and Cylon religions. It is associated with five priests who worship an unnamed deity – possibly the jealous god of Kobol, who in turn might be the god of the Cylons. Might these priests have later entered the pantheon of humanity's gods, or might they be part of an early prophecy foreshadowing the final five Cylons? *BSG* returns repeatedly to the power of the prophecies in the Sacred Scrolls.

While the colonial beliefs mirror paganism, and the Cylon beliefs mirror the Judaeo-Christian religions, *BSG* is fundamentally about humanity seeking salvation. (Though perhaps the Cylons should be seeking it as well, for their crimes against the human race?) Another frequent religious theme is the universal power of love. Nowhere is this more pronounced than in the concept of how humans and Cylons can procreate with each other.

This is ironic, considering how the Cylons initially tried to wipe out humanity and their common belief that humans are a flawed race, unworthy of God. Even so, they need the remaining humans, as the Cylons are unable to procreate with each other. They fear they may become extinct – a possible clue that they were created by someone, or something, other than the original Cylons, and have lost the technology to create more models.

When Helo stays behind on Caprica after the nuclear strike, he meets up with an Eight he believes to be Boomer. (She is, in fact, a copy of Boomer, with her memories.) They fall in love and conceive a child; we learn of their belief that this can only happen between a Cylon and a human if love is part of the equation.

Sappy? Perhaps, but biological chemicals play a large part in our emotions. Perhaps the creators of the Cylons were aware of this, wanting to integrate Cylons and humans in such a way that the hybrid offspring would have the best chance of surviving in either society.

Concepts of good and evil also play a large role in most religions, and this is reflected in how the humans initially feel about the humanoid Cylons. It is clear, when President Roslin sentences Leoban to death outside the airlock, that humans believe the Cylons are inherently evil. Over time, however, they come to trust certain Cylons who prove themselves to the fleet. Even some they don't trust are kept in prison, rather than executed.

The third season ended with many questions: How did Starbuck survive a ship's explosion, and does she truly know the way to Earth? Are the newly revealed Cylons – Colonel Tigh, Anders, Chief Tyrol and Tory Foster – programmed to do something horrible to the humans? Or, like Eight Cylon, Sharon Agathon, a robot who seems to go against her core programming, do they have free will? Are humans and humanoid Cylons meant to find reconciliation and peace, or will the battle continue, even if they make it to Earth?

With more twists and turns than Silverstone, Monaco and Nürburgring combined, *Galactica* sped into a fourth and final season that was all about salvation, and our Earth. With the first colonists landed in Africa, Adama christened this new home 'Earth' in tribute to the legendary homeworld sought out by the survivors. That other Earth is, in a rather nasty twist, shown to be much like the Cylon homeworld, a wasteland incapable of supporting life. The inhabitants of this new Earth possess only the rudimentary tools of civilisation, but by a quirk of evolution are genetically compatible with the humans of Galactica. The show ended with an epilogue set in modern-day Times Square, New York, as two 'angels', Caprica Six and Gaius Baltar, waxed lyrical over the cycle of violence and war between humanity and machine, and wondered if it could ever happen again, given our reliance upon technology in this world of 2009. The revelation that the events portrayed over the four seasons of Galactica transpired over 150,000 years ago and serve as a 'creation myth' for modern-day homo sapiens is an interesting and unexpected one, given that science fiction seems so often to speculate about the future, not dwell in the past.

THEY CAME FROM OUTER SPACE

2

V, The Tripods, Alien Nation

V (1983-1985)

'They arrived in 50 motherships, offering their friendship
and advanced technology to Earth. Sceptical of the Visitors, Mike Donovan
and Juliet Parrish infiltrated their ranks and soon discovered some startling secrets.
The Resistance is all that stands between us and the Visitors.'

The television miniseries was a popular format, allowing producers to tell stories without being constrained by the one-hour dramatic timeslot or the need to stretch a story to fill a twenty-two-episode order. It caught on in the mid-1970s, a logical outgrowth of the successful *Movie of the Week* format pioneered by ABC and studio supremo Barry Diller years before.

These days, say 'miniseries' and people think of seminal works such as *Roots* or maybe *Rich Man, Poor Man*. It was a haven for historical drama and not a place for childish things like sci-fi.

By 1980, sci-fi on television had been relegated to kids-only fare as denoted by the disastrous adaptation of *Buck Rogers in the 25th Century* on NBC, or the just-cancelled *Battlestar Galactica*. NBC, in particular, couldn't find a hit from the genre and had failed with *Manimal* and *Misfits of Science*. As a result, no one in those pre-internet days had any advance warning about the Visitors.

People on the East and West Coasts were the first to learn that the Visitors were our friends. The ubiquitous billboards told us so, as we saw red uniformed men in sun visors standing proudly amidst normal folk like you and me. A few weeks later, the billboards had been defaced with a spray-painted 'V' in the centre.

In time for the all-important May sweeps, when networks gauged audience attention in order to set advertising rates, the two-night *V* miniseries became an event. It was smart science fiction, gripping television, and the revelation that the Visitors were reptilian aliens, here to conquer (and consume) us, caught most

Key members of the groundbreaking V *cast – Mike Donovan (Marc Singer),*
Visitor Commander Diana (Jane Badler), and Doctor Julie Parrish (Faye Grant).

viewers by surprise.

The miniseries was the brainchild of television veteran Kenneth Johnson, no stranger to genre TV during the 1970s. He was inspired to tell this story as a straight political thriller, called *Storm Warnings*, based in part on the Sinclair Lewis novel *It Can't Happen Here*, published in 1935 under the gathering clouds of war.

'The suggestion came up that perhaps it was an alien force that caused the changeover in our lives. I was at first very against it, because I was tired of doing that kind of thing, having done *The Six Million Dollar Man*, *The Bionic Woman*, *The Incredible Hulk*. I wanted to stay a little closer to reality. But the more I thought about it, the more I felt I could do a really interesting, stirring allegory about the rise of the Third Reich and about how ultimate power can either corrupt someone or turn them into a hero,' Johnson told M.J. Simpson, editor of *SFX Magazine*.

Despite their high-tech trappings, the aliens remain the Axis threat, from their uniform to the fact that they operate their own version of the Hitler Youth program. Occupied Europe became Los Angeles. And the Resistance was . . . the Resistance.

The aliens were led by John, played by Richard Herd, the benevolent face of the invading force. Behind him was the scheming Diana, played by newcomer Jane Badler, with June Chadwick as her equally manipulative rival, Lydia. Opposing them were newscaster Mike Donovan (Marc Singer) and Dr Juliet Parrish (Faye Grant). On their side but with his own agenda was CIA spook Ham Tyler (Michael Ironside). Willie, the somewhat simple alien, was a breakout role played sympathetically by Robert Englund, before he began causing nightmares on Elm Street.

While the two-part event ended on an optimistic note, the story was far from over, allowing NBC to order a follow-up for the next season. This time, *V: The Final Battle* aired over three nights and veered more into science fiction, with the action quotient rising higher. Johnson worked on it initially, but left after he and the network differed over approach and theme.

The Resistance had discovered the truth about the Visitors and needed to expose John, their kindly leader, as a hungry lizard. At the same time, Dr Mengele stand-in Diana was busily trying to crossbreed a human and alien, which actually produced a compound that proved toxic to the aliens and was a key to the humans' eventual triumph.

Again, the ratings spiked and the miniseries magnetised many eyeballs. After two hits, NBC wanted to extend the brand and ordered a full series to debut the following fall. It was given to the production team of Robert Singer and Daniel Blatt, neither of who had showed much respect for internal logic or the tenets of science fiction. As a result, the story was more soap opera than allegory, with a bloated cast ill-served by the scripts.

At just over one million dollars an episode, *V* was the most expensive primetime series in America. So NBC was counting on a grand slam, which put incredible pressure on the production team. Nine different producers worked on the show, with a revolving door that further disrupted any sense of direction. It didn't help that the third episode filmed, 'Breakout', which introduced regular character Kyle Bates, was deemed too violent and NBC refused to air it. As a result, the episode 'Deception' was revised to introduce Kyle. During the summer of 1985, when the series was in reruns, 'Breakout' was finally aired to allow the network to recoup costs – so Kyle wound up being introduced twice.

Sibling science fiction media experts Jeffrey and Michael Walker were called in late in the process, to try to help guide the beleaguered cast and crew. But by then the ratings were in a tailspin and the series was cancelled after nineteen episodes, the final one airing on 22 March 1985. It ended on a cliff-hanger, which would have been resolved in 'The Attack', an episode drafted in February but unfilmed when the cancellation was announced. The intent was to shift direction by killing two of the regular characters, bringing back one long gone regular and adding a quest to drive the stories forward.

When the dust settled it was clear that, for all the mistakes that were made, the *V* franchise did bring intelligent science fiction back to primetime – setting the stage for subsequent shows, including an adaptation of Johnson's *Alien Nation* feature film for the nascent Fox network, and even *Star Trek: The Next Generation*, which debuted a mere three years later.

V was too intriguing a concept to die. J. Michael Straczynski, who

The success of the original V *miniseries spawned a sequel, a weekly TV show, a string of novels and an eighteen-issue comic book series.*

The Visitors are here – the mothership hovers ominously over Los Angeles.

first wrote about the series when he was a reporter for the *Los Angeles Herald*, wrote a 1989 pilot script for a revival project, inspired by its enduring buzz and the success of subsequent genre series. It was entitled *V: The Next Chapter* and would have started up five years later. Rather than bring in the Visitors' alien enemies, who had been mentioned as far back as the original miniseries (dismissed by Johnson as a red herring), Straczynski chose to split the aliens into two camps, with the Outsiders coming to aid the humans. All the original characters, save Ham Tyler, were gone. NBC asked for revisions, but then finally abandoned the project.

In 2004, the original miniseries was released on DVD. Its strong sales, and the sense of contemporary nostalgia it evoked, prompted Johnson to try again. He announced that his new miniseries would ignore everything that came after the first one. NBC were interested instead in a remake of the first storyline, holding out hope that a sequel would be commissioned.

Johnson wrote a treatment for his continuation instead, which seemed to sway the network. *V: The Second Generation* was put into pre-production, with a 2008 airdate anticipated. Meanwhile, Johnson adapted his screenplay into a novel, released in hardcover by Tor Books in November 2007. Picking up twenty years later, Earth remained in the aliens' thrall as their technological 'gifts' effectively placed the humans in a velvet cage, too nice to fight against. The Resistance remained a force although, with each passing year, their job grew more difficult. But the message sent by Juliet Parrish to the aliens' enemies in the first miniseries finally merited a response, and they had to try to hold out until help arrived.

V was popular around the world, with England running the two miniseries over five nights opposite Olympic coverage. The show was popular enough in Japan for the legendary manga creator Go Nagai to write an adaptation of the series for artist Tatsuya Yasuda. The series also spawned one of the earliest licensed games for PCs, played on the popular Commodore 64 platform.

Despite the notion that 50 motherships circled the Earth, the miniseries and weekly series did little to show what was going on elsewhere. That provided an opening for the novel series from Pinnacle Books, who hoped to capture the sales success of Pocket Books' *Star Trek* line. The publisher even went so far as to tap *Trek* scribe A.C. Crispin to novelise the initial miniseries as a launch. She was then asked for an original, but the tight deadline made her bring in fellow trekkie Howard Weinstein. Together they headed to New York, paralleling the miniseries' events with East Coast Crisis. Fourteen other original novels followed, including two solo efforts by Weinstein and two from science fiction author Somtow Sucharitkul.

The success of the second miniseries encouraged DC Comics editor Marv Wolfman to secure the rights for a comic book adaptation. Wolfman had proven successful with the *Star Trek* comics in 1983, and so was granted his wish – although his workload proved too much to allow much personal involvement. Instead, Robert Greenberger took over as editor and worked with writer Cary Bates, and the art team of Carmine Infantino and Tony DeZuniga, for the majority of the issues.

Greenberger later recalled how difficult it was to figure out how to tie in with, or avoid contradicting, the show. 'I went to Singer and Blatt's presentation at the World Science Fiction Convention, a month prior to the show's debut. Afterwards, we spoke about the comics and the show and it was clear they didn't understand science fiction and felt anything could go.

'Later, scripts were late in coming and we had no idea what they were doing so we went for fairly generic stories which hurt the title's commercial chances.' Still, the actresses appreciated how they were drawn, with Jane Badler noting how her healthy physique really was something out of science fiction. When the show was cancelled, Greenberger tried to get permission from the producers to advance the story and keep it alive. He was turned down.

THE TRIPODS (1984-1985)

The 1984-85 BBC children's television series, *The Tripods*, was one of the longest adaptations on British TV – featuring 25 episodes, each 25 minutes in length, and 120 speaking parts. It was taken from a series of novels written by Samuel Youd (under the pseudonym 'John Christopher'), beginning in the late 1960s. The first two, *The White Mountains* and *The City of Gold and Lead*, formed the basis for the two seasons of *The Tripods*. Unfortunately the third season, to have been based on *The Pool of Fire*, was never made – possibly because the producers ran out of money, although the scripts for it had been written by Alick Rowe. A prequel to the original trilogy, *When the Tripods Came*, was written later, telling how a race of beings called the Masters first came and took over the earth, enslaving its population. Books from this intriguing series often make schools' recommended reading lists.

The stories chronicle the efforts of young Will Parker and a band of freedom fighters as they work to overthrow the Masters. The setting is post-apocalyptic: it is the year AD 2089; Earth is under the control of massive silver alien machines that stride across the landscape, keeping the docile humans in check. Will lives in the English village of Wherton, a contented agrarian community. Once a year, a Tripod arrives on Capping Day. Young people who have reached the verge of adulthood have a cranial implant attached to their scalps, limiting them to a life of modesty and serenity by liberating them of free will and imagination. Capped citizens are not capable of dissent, but sometimes the capping process does not work, resulting in vagrants who live on the fringes of society, surviving as best they can. Capped citizens regard the Tripod overlords as their saviours, remembering past human history as a time of violence and suffering.

Unnerved by the capping of his cousin, Will is noticed by the vagrant Ozymandias. He tells Will of the Free Men, a group of uncapped rebel resistance fighters who live far away in the White Mountains. Inspired by this knowledge, Will and his other cousin, Henry, travel to the coastal town of Rumney, crossing the Channel by boat, but are captured by the Tripods' human servants, the Black Guards, on the other side.

They are rescued from the Black Guards' dungeon by 'Beanpole' (Jean-Paul), an uncapped French boy who had been bringing them their food. The three of them travel onwards to discover the devastated and deserted remains of Paris, and marvel at the wonders left by their ancestors.

The journey to the White Mountains is fraught with adventure. Will almost gives up his quest altogether when he falls in love with Eloise, the beautiful daughter of the Comte and Comtesse Ricordeau, who nurse him back to health when he is injured. But when Will learns she is already capped, and has been chosen to serve

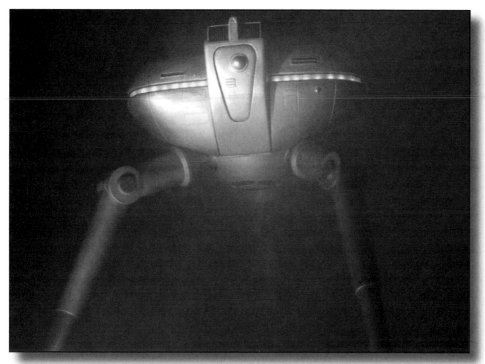

The Tripods *brought a nightmare vision of post-apocalyptic conflict to children's television.*

the Tripods in their city, he rejoins his companions Henry and Beanpole on the road – although not before being captured by a Tripod and having a tracking device implanted in his arm.

Fortunately, Beanpole is able to remove it. (Beanpole is the smart one – the MacGyver of his age. He wears glasses he manufactured himself and knows a little about folk medicine, mechanics and a host of other things useful to teenage boys on the run from alien overlords.) The boys continue, and, after a brief stay with a vineyard family, they eventually reach the Alps. They destroy a Tripod with a hand grenade they found in the Paris subway, encounter the Free Men and are taken to meet their leader, Julius.

Season Two begins in AD 2090. The three boys are training hard for the annual games that are held by the Tripods. Will, Beanpole and a German boy, Fritz, are chosen to go and compete. Henry, disappointed, stays behind to help with Free Men planning and strategy.

The boys travel up the Rhine by barge. When the owner Ulf does not return from his visit to Wurtemburg, Will and Beanpole search for him. In Wurtemburg, Will is captured by the Black Guard and thrown into a deep pit, but is rescued by

Such was the impact of the Tripods' campaign against mankind, that civilisation reverted to an almost medieval lifestyle.

Beanpole. Together they continue their journey in a stolen rowing boat. After a brief interlude where they work as waiters in a grand hotel (and manage to meet some pretty girls), they are smuggled out of the hotel and make their way to the games. The boys are keen to win their sporting events because winners are taken by the Tripods to serve in their city.

Reunited with Fritz, Will and Beanpole participate in their events. Beanpole fails to qualify after spraining his ankle, but both Will and Fritz are successful, and are carried into the City inside Tripods. Fritz is put to work in a huge quarry beneath the City, while Will is chosen by Master West 468 to be his slave.

As Will becomes quite friendly with his Master, Fritz becomes a member of the Power Elite, technicians who run the City's power station. He meets Pierre, another member of the Free Men, who shares with him the knowledge that he has gathered before dying of a heart attack.

A horrified Will finds his beloved Eloise in suspended animation in the Pyramid of Beauty – a museum where the Masters display female humans they have collected like butterflies. He also discovers that higher beings, the Cognoscs, live in white voids at the tops of the city pyramids surrounding the Pool of Fire. They in turn perceive that he has a more inquisitive mind than the other slaves.

The Cognoscs are revealed to be creatures of pure thought and energy. Coggy (as the Cognosc nicknames himself) tells Will he dislikes the Masters, and that it amuses him to have found a human prepared to stand up to them. Telling him of the Masters' plan to change the Earth's atmosphere to make it habitable for them (killing all other life in the process), Coggy prepares to leave the City and explore the universe. Master 468 becomes suspicious of Will and tries to examine the false cap he wears. Will is forced to strike out and kill him. Now on the run in the City, he is helped by Fritz, who stays behind while Will escapes, believing there is more he can learn inside the City's walls.

Will swims to freedom and is found by Beanpole, who has been waiting for some sign of him. Together they make their way back to the White Mountains, joining up with a circus on the way. Will persuades the uncapped circus children to join him and Beanpole in the mountains. However, after being hunted by an army of Tripods, they find that the mountain base is now nothing but a smoking, blackened ruin.

Season Two finished on this alarming cliff-hanger. The show was cancelled, leaving the aliens still in control of the earth. The only recourse for viewers who wish to find out how the story ends is to read the source material – although, according to IMDB, there is a Touchstone production of a *Tripods* movie scheduled for 2012.

The Tripods is memorable for its high-quality scripting, lavish costumes and production design, groundbreaking special effects and model work. The landscape settings are beautiful and much care was put into the small details. The soundtrack, by Ken Freeman, features heavy use of synthesiser, adding a sense of futuristic menace to what are often lush background scenes of rural tranquillity – invaded now and then by the presence of a Tripod leg, or long shots of a Tripod striding across the hills and dales.

The series was partly envisioned as a replacement for *Doctor Who*. It took over the show's old Saturday afternoon timeslot and format, but replaced *Doctor Who*'s tight budget and outlandishly theatrical style with lavish production values and a cast of fresh-faced unknown actors.

The series diverged from the books in several ways, most notably with the shape and design of the Masters and their Tripod machines. In the books, gravity inside the Masters' City was increased artificially, which is not mentioned at all in the TV series. Also, the race of alien 'Cognoscs' – spiritual life forms vastly superior to the Masters themselves – do not appear in the books at all.

Neither do the original texts have any female characters to speak of. When asked about this, the author replied that, at the time of writing, it was generally accepted that girls would read books that had boys as main characters, but not vice versa. He considered the addition of an entire family of girls to the TV series somewhat 'over the top'.

Special effects took up much of the budget for the show. However, although the Tripods themselves were seen in long shot, the effects team mainly used a single huge leg to convey their presence. To save money, Snowdonia was used in place of the French Alps, where some of the action was set.

As post-apocalyptic visions of the future go, the world of John Christopher's

Tripods doesn't seem so bad. It could even be seen as idyllic in some ways – a world without famine or war (though there is still disease), where the class system is solidly entrenched and people are assured of their destinies, not having to worry about what comes next. Capping allows humanity to be content, retaining many elements of culture and civilisation, but losing others in exchange for a simpler way of life.

Inside the City, the Masters' treatment of the human slaves is far from brutal. In fact, it's reasonable to the point of friendliness – in the TV series the workers were even provided with a disco (not so surprising perhaps – the series was filmed in the 1980s).

But the idyllic landscape will not last forever. The Masters plan to terraform the earth, rendering it uninhabitable to its indigenous lifeforms. Will and his friends do not know about this when they join the resistance fighters, however. They oppose Earth's alien overlords because that's what humans in post-apocalyptic TV programmes do.

Being free is what being human is all about.

ALIEN NATION (1988-1990)

Master lyricist-librettist Oscar Hammerstein III famously said that the best properties to adapt are the ones that *almost* work. Therein, he advised, lay the seeds for the most successful transformations. Something already perfect needs no elevation or reworking; whereas something that doesn't quite hit its mark can only be improved by revising the characters and themes that make it almost compelling.

That pretty much describes the transition *Alien Nation* made from feature film to TV series.

The original 1988 film, directed by Graham Baker and scripted by Rockne S. O'Bannon (most famous perhaps as the creator of *Farscape*), depicted Los Angeles half a decade after a slave ship from a planet named Tencton has crash-landed in the Mojave desert. The Tenctonese occupants of the ship, many thousands in number, have been bred to work in harsh environments. But, having failed to reach whichever planet intended to use and abuse them, they have instead been integrated into mainstream American society. They are, in effect, the new minority – distinguished by their larger-than-average heads (which are bald and spotted), greater physical strength, longer life-spans and a diet that humans would find disgusting, if not exactly toxic.

They also possess English language names that tend to be a play on words, or

In Alien Nation, *detectives George Francisco (Eric Pierpoint) and Matthew Sikes (Gary Graham) battle bigotry within a sci-fi cop buddy series format.*

Although it was lighter in tone than the 1988 movie that spawned it, the TV series examined many serious social themes through the experiences of the alien immigrants.

outright appropriations of famous Earth-culture personages. This is because, as the Tenctonese were processed through the LA version of an Ellis Island bureaucracy, their native names were deemed too hard to pronounce. Hence it's not unusual to find, among these 'Newcomers' (as they are colloquially referred to), the likes of Betsy Ross, Morris Code and Gayle Warnings. (The less polite colloquial name for them is the racist epithet 'slags', which derives from the intranstive verb for the change in form that occurs during the smelting process.)

In the film, culture clash is personified by the team of plainclothes cops at the centre of its story: blue-collar tough guy detective Matt Sykes (James Caan) and his new partner, a Newcomer, the more intellectual Sam Francisco (Mandy Patinkin) – who is quickly redubbed George when Matt decides that the notion of riding with a guy named 'Sam Francisco' is too goofy to contemplate.

The film's story has them investigating the killing of Matt's former partner, Bill Tuggle (Roger Aaron Brown), in a shootout; but the investigation soon leads to the higher echelons and a plot to exploit a dormant and well-hidden facet of Tenctonese physiology, which can be triggered by the ingestion of an illegal drug. If exposed, this would ramp up the persecution of the Tenctonese in mainstream society to the point of making them all outcasts, prisoners, or worse.

Matt and George, of course, represent human-Tenctonese dynamics in microcosm, and over the course of the movie the initially reluctant Matt learns to trust, and respect, the perhaps not-so-alien George. And that's the best part of the flick.

What's less effective is most of the plot from roughly the halfway mark on. For that's when, despite the amusing details, *Alien Nation* loses the spark of something different and devolves into a fairly ordinary buddy-cop shoot-'em-up. Intellectually, you can understand the potential impact of 'the big secret', but as dramatised it doesn't live up to the promise of a more profound drama about race relations in America. Which is why the original *Alien Nation* is so good and so disappointing at the same time.

Why it *almost* works.

So, could it be made into a TV series that would capitalise on the film's strengths and overcome its weaknesses? Enter writer-producer Kenneth Johnson.

Certainly it was the kind of task that was right in his wheelhouse: under his stewardship, Stan Lee's comic book *The Incredible Hulk* had been reinvented as the incredibly touching saga of a kindly fugitive (reminiscent of Valjean in Hugo's *Les Misérables*) with a dark secret, the yin and yang of his dual personality made iconic by Bill Bixby (as Dr David Banner) and Lou Ferrigno (as the green-skinned, jade-eyed, giant fury he becomes when angered). It lasted for a remarkable five seasons (1978-1982) and spawned three TV-movie sequels, the last in 1990. Prior to that, Johnson had resurrected the formerly dead, one-shot character of Jamie Sommers – after a hugely popular appearance as Steve Austin's girlfriend on *The Six Million Dollar Man* – and with the same actress, Lindsay Wagner, transformed her into Austin's feminine counterpart, *The Bionic Woman*. (She kicked ass for three seasons, 1976-1978, in a series so popular that at time of writing it has been revived and reinvented, recently making its mark anew on network television.) To top it all, he had also been writer-producer of acclaimed miniseries *V*.

Ironically perhaps, Johnson wasn't much interested in *Alien Nation* at first. As he tells it, 'I felt that the movie presented a terrific premise about the world's newest minority... *In the Heat of the Night* is a very interesting concept to bring to this as a series rather than playing out *Miami Vice* with *Coneheads*. This shift offered me the opportunity to explore themes that have long been favourites of mine: tolerance and prejudice and discrimination.'

Though Matt and George as characters stayed true to the general archetypes (with Matt's last name undergoing a cosmetic vowel shift as 'Sykes' became 'Sikes'), they became quite different in their particulars, owing to the scripts' deeper investigation of personal issues and the casting. Gary Graham's thick lips and longish hair gave him an almost Jagger-esque physicality as Matt, his swagger a defence mechanism which has to be slowly unlearned – which played nicely against the character's blue-collar conservatism, illustrating the huge contradictions in his nature. (Johnson: 'One of my favourite scenes in the pilot is the one where [Matt] is trying to get [George's daughter] Emily into the school where "her kind" isn't welcome, and he makes his impassioned statements – then he goes home to his apartment and sees an alien moving in across the way, and says, "Oh great. Why my building?" So we immediately get a sense of three-dimensionality and the push-pull that he was going to be going through as a character.') And Eric Pierpoint's George was not as detached as Patinkin's. For all his maturity and wisdom, he was still a stranger in a strange land, prone to a certain naivety at times, or even bewilderment.

Their partnership was the nucleus around which a rich and varied ensemble was built. There were several 'experimental' characters, intended as regulars, who vanished after their functions proved limited (an opportunistic tabloid photographer and a number of cops among them), but the ones who stayed and grew throughout were George's family – wife and working mother Susan (Michele Scarabelli), rebellious teenage son Buck (Sean Six) and grade school-age daughter Emily (Lauren Woodland) – and Matt's aforementioned Newcomer neighbour (and burgeoning love interest), a doctor and medical researcher named Cathy Frankel (Terri Treas). Rounding out the cast were two station house regulars at opposite ends of the food chain: the obsequious and dislikeable stationhouse captain, Bryon Grazer (Ron Fassler) with his scheming and politicking, and the well-intentioned but bumbling young Newcomer janitor, Albert Einstein (Jeff Marcus).

The show's formula was at once schematic and versatile. Most episodes contained what screenwriters call an A-story (the principal narrative, usually a police investigation) and a B-story (a sub or parallel plot, usually about workplace, neighbourhood or domestic issues). But in *Alien Nation*, there was a mandate for both stories to pointedly share a theme. Thus while Matt and George investigate the use of illegal steroid-type drugs at a sports centre, which raises the issue of

Despite only running for a single season, Alien Nation *proved sufficiently popular to be revived for five made-for-television movies that aired between 1994 and 1997.*

how masculinity is perceived, George is simultaneously dealing with his own self-image as a pregnant male about to give birth. Indeed, at the denouement, while overextending himself during an arrest, he goes into premature labour – and it is Matt's job to reach into George's pouch, turn the infant around to avoid a breech birth and deliver the baby.

Johnson: '[The] birth of the baby was one of the most amazing special effects that I've ever been involved in. We didn't let anybody on the set except Eric see the baby to begin with . . . on the set people were crying . . . it was like being present at a real birth. And then we got some angry letters from fans and viewers who said, "How dare you put [alien] makeup on a brand-new infant!" Because people thought it was a real baby. They didn't realise that it took seven very talented people to make Vessna come to life.'

In fact, this instalment, 'Real Men', scripted by Diane Frolov and Andrew Schneider, was the culmination of an episodic trilogy about how the birth process for Newcomers differs from that of humans. As Johnson told respected genre journalist M.P. Simpson: 'I had had the additional idea that like sea horses . . . the male [would be] the gender that carried the infant to fruition in a sort of marsupial pouch, like kangaroos. . . it takes place [as part of a formal religious ceremony] . . . I said, gee, wouldn't it be fun [if the ceremony requires Albert and Susan] to have sex right in the middle of the living room . . . and then at the last moment everyone turns their back and forms a circle holding hands together . . . And it just made [Matt] frightfully uncomfortable.'

It certainly wasn't unknown for some science fiction TV series to be intensely moving on occasion – but *Alien Nation* made it a point to tug at both the heartstrings and the conscience once a week. And as it progressed, the show identified, refined and expanded upon what it did best, getting better and better.

So of course Barry Diller, then head of Fox TV, just had to cancel it – along with its lead-in show, the popular *21 Jump Street*. This was Fox's first season of original programming on Monday nights, and though *Alien Nation* wasn't a top-rated 'water cooler' show, it had a solid and growing core audience that was devoted to it. But this was also in an era when sitcoms temporarily ruled (or so prevailing network thought insisted), and Diller wanted to give Monday night over to comedy. With ironic inevitability, the sitcoms tanked and Fox wound up giving Mondays back to its affiliate stations.

Johnson continues the saga: 'And [Fox executive] Peter Chernin stood up in front of the Television Critics Association the following year and publicly apologised. He said cancelling *Alien Nation* and *21 Jump Street* were the biggest mistakes they ever made. Naturally, I was on the phone the next day saying, "Sooooo?" And Peter said, "Well, we're not sure . . . yada . . . yada . . ." [T]hey didn't feel it was right at the time, [but] I kept after them over the next couple of years saying, "Guys, there's life in this. You should really give it another shot." And we couldn't get a rise out of anybody.'

But the spirit of the show was to be kept alive in print. In a publishing move that has been emulated since, but was at the time precedent-setting, Kevin Ryan, then senior editor of Pocket Books' dedicated *Star Trek* department, decided the concept was 'too good to let die'. He made a deal for publication rights and commissioned a series of eight novels: three to adapt unfilmed scripts, and tie up the loose ends from the final season's cliff-hanger, and five originals. The authors included popular veterans of science fiction and TV/movie tie-ins, Judith and Garfield Reeves-Stevens, Barry Longyear, Peter David, K.W. Jeter, L.A. Graf (a pseudonymous acronym for 'Let's all get rich and famous' devised by writers Julia Ecklar and Karen Rose Cercone) and David Spencer, a musical theatre writer (lyricist and co-librettist of the cult favourite SF musical *Weird Romance*), so enamoured of the show that, upon reading about Ryan's plans in an issue of *Starlog*, he submitted spec chapters and an outline in the hope of being included.

As Johnson said to Simpson: 'Lucy Salhany took over as head of Fox Broadcasting, and she thought it was a great idea to do a follow-up to *Alien Nation* . . . Steve Bell and Kevin Burns managed to talk Fox into giving us a substantial budget so we were able to do a pretty big TV movie, and it was put on by Fox on their movie night . . . and gee . . . it was the highest-rated made-for-TV movie that they had had! So suddenly they were inspired.'

Four additional TV movies followed: *Body and Soul* (previously novelised by Peter David), *Millennium*, *The Enemy Within* and *The Udara Legacy*. 'As far as having closure on the characters, it certainly gave us the opportunity to develop them more, the opportunity to bring Cathy and Matt to bed together – which was fun. It gave us a chance to continue to develop the relationships, although there was still the constant cultural push/pull between them. But it was extraordinarily rewarding . . . and we'd have just kept right on going if we could have.'

Alas, being a product of a then 'off-network' (Off-Network Syndicated series are those programmes which have already appeared on a commercial network and are now available for reruns), even that short revival was inevitably finite. But it stood as testament to a concept that had been thoughtfully and lovingly moved across the divide between 'almost works' to 'works magnificently' – a metaphor about race relations in America that also exemplified Hammerstein's lyricised dictum that no one is born prejudiced, but that, 'You have to be carefully taught.' *Alien Nation* demonstrated how, with tolerance, forbearance, constant education and assiduous open-mindedness, those horrible lessons can be forever unlearned.

3 RENDING TIME AND SPACE

Doctor Who (original series),
Sapphire and Steel, Stargate SG-1, Tru Calling
Doctor Who (new series)

DOCTOR WHO (ORIGINAL) (1963-1989, 1996)

First Doctor, played by William Hartnell (1963-1966)
Second Doctor, played by Patrick Troughton (1966-1969)
Third Doctor, played by Jon Pertwee (1970-1974)
Fourth Doctor, played by Tom Baker (1974-1981)
Fifth Doctor, played by Peter Davison (1981-1984)
Sixth Doctor, played by Colin Baker (1984-1986)
Seventh Doctor, played by Sylvester McCoy (1987-1989 and 1996)
Eighth Doctor, played by Paul McGann (1996)

On 23 November 1963, two high school teachers followed a student home – and into a 1950s British police box. There they met a strange man who claimed to be the girl's grandfather, and told them to call him 'the Doctor'.

But Doctor *Who*?

Thus began the longest-running science fiction television series of all time. *Doctor Who* ran from 1963 to 1989 before going on a sixteen-year hiatus, though the stories continued in other media throughout that period. It is famous all across the world, and more people associate the police box with *Doctor Who* than with the British police. An entire generation of children grew up watching the Doctor's exploits, initially learning about history and science along the way but later simply thrilling to his adventures. At its peak in 1979, sixteen million people were watching the series, and no first-run episode ever drew fewer than three million viewers. It could be argued that an entire generation of science fiction writers grew out of *Doctor Who* because of the formative influence it had on so many people.

So what made the series so popular? Was it the scientific and historical elements woven throughout?

The dandy and the curmudgeon – successive Doctors Jon Pertwee and Patrick Troughton.

Unlikely. The show was initially meant to help educate as well as entertain, but these aspects were later dropped because young viewers were not responding well. Certainly, these threads have remained central to many *Doctor Who* stories – given the theme of space-time travel, it would have been difficult not to include them – but they have been considerably less rigorous and used more to support the storyline than to actually impart real-world knowledge.

Was it the science fiction genre itself? SF shows were still extremely rare when *Doctor Who* premiered, which was both a boon and a danger. The 1960s audience was interested in seeing something new, so the idea of a show about a man who travelled through space and time would certainly have been intriguing. But at the same time many people would not have known how to handle such an idea, preferring to watch shows anchored in a single location and time period, with more prosaic issues and characters. The early episodes also had very weak special effects, reflecting both the limitations of early 1960s television and the low budget. Makeup, simple costuming and the cast's attitude had to carry the day, whereas today computer-generated graphics and advanced prosthetics can provide far more believable visuals. This may have made the genre elements less palatable to some, since viewers would often have to rely on their own imaginations. But the series certainly appealed to many because of its strangeness and sense of limitless possibility.

Nor was it necessarily the show's central figure that brought it such favour. Though the Doctor has always been a moral figure, stepping in to help those in need, he is also capricious and shortsighted, sometimes even petty. He helps those he encounters, but only as far as he deems appropriate, and often leaves an even bigger mess than when he started – though he does tend to eliminate any alien threats along the way. His attention span is often too short to realise the problems he is creating, and once he loses interest in a problem he simply leaves it for others to handle. The Doctor has also shown that he is not above killing when necessary, and sees nothing wrong with stealing, lying and generally ignoring any rules he feels should not apply to him. Though his central principles are sound, the Doctor is hardly a model citizen.

But then, he belongs to a much larger world than the twentieth-century United Kingdom. The Doctor is not human, after all – he is an alien, a Time Lord from the planet Gallifrey, who stole his ship (the Tardis – Time And Relative Dimensions In Space) because he did not approve of his people's policy of non-involvement. He wanted to meet other life forms, to offer his assistance in their crises – or to meddle, as more than one companion has pointed out. That rogue nature has always been a central part of his personality, and it has affected most of the Doctor's decisions through the years. He does not believe the laws of Britain bind him because he is not a British citizen – just as he chooses not to let the laws of the Time Lords restrict him, because he no longer considers himself a Time Lord. He is a citizen of the cosmos, and only the natural and moral laws hold any sway over him.

But it is in the Doctor's character that we find the show's true power. The Doctor

The first three TV Doctors pose for a Radio Times *cover shot.*

The Cybermen first appeared in October 1966 and are still troubling the Doctor today.

is a masterful blend of the familiar and the alien, the exotic and the comfortable. He is an adventurer but also a thinker, a scholar but also (to his assistants and his audience) a friend. He does not fight when he can talk, and he does not converse when he can either give a lecture or make a joke. He runs from danger but always returns to face it again, armed with fresh knowledge and firm resolve. And he places the lives of others – not only his friends, but the many unknown figures of each country or planet – before his own safety, risking himself again and again for people who will never even realise his efforts.

These are the constants of the Doctor's character, but many other aspects change on a semi-regular basis. This is because the Doctor himself changes. For the Time Lords have the power to 'regenerate' when mortally wounded, creating a new body for themselves out of the old one that's dying. Their consciousness and memories transfer from one body to the next, but each form has its own appearance, its own personality and quirks. Assuming the Doctor of the early series was his first incarnation, he had been through seven bodies by the time the show was cancelled in 1989.

The concept of regeneration was not part of the show's original plan. When William Hartnell played the first Doctor, he was simply a strange alien traveller with an impressive degree of intelligence, a lively curiosity, a strong moral sense and little tolerance for fools. But Hartnell left the series in 1966 – originally his departure was blamed on failing health, but poor relations with a new production team and the producers' desire to replace him with a less experienced (and thus less expensive) actor may also have played a role.

Regardless of the reason, the producers suddenly found themselves in a fix: the extremely popular show had just lost its central figure. How could they replace him and still retain its strengths and popularity? Other shows had replaced their lead actors, of course, usually by either introducing a completely new character or changing actors and hoping the audience wouldn't notice the difference. But neither approach would work here – the Doctor was not only the central figure but the titular one, and millions of fans recognised him on sight.

Many fans' favourite Doctor, the charismatic Tom Baker,
seen with his eternal nemeses, the Daleks.

1980s Doctors Colin Baker and Peter Davison.

That was when the show's producers hit upon a brilliant idea. The Doctor was an alien, after all – he merely looked human. So why not claim that his alien nature offered him the ability to change form under dire circumstances? In what they described as a 'renewal', Hartnell's Doctor transformed himself bodily into a new man: Patrick Troughton. Three years later, when Troughton left the series (to escape the gruelling filming schedule and avoid becoming typecast), the Doctor experienced what was called merely 'a change of appearance' as Jon Pertwee took over. It was his departure in favour of Tom Baker (Pertwee also left to avoid typecasting, and to resume his stage career) that was first referred to as a 'regeneration'.

Never before or since has a series found a way to not only survive the replacement of its lead actor, to but to work that very replacement into a central feature of the series itself. Far from ignoring the change, *Doctor Who* focuses upon the alterations in appearance and personality between each incarnation of the Doctor. The ability to bounce back from what should have been fatal, even for a double-hearted alien, has given the Doctor longevity far beyond any human character. It has also given

Despite being an excellent Doctor, Sylvester McCoy's tenure was undermined by a dwindling budget and diminishing public interest.

him a far more cavalier attitude to danger – he can not only endure more pain and damage but can also recover from a supposedly fatal blow (though there is still the potential for an ultimate final death that gives weight to dangerous situations).

Regeneration also sets the Doctor apart from his human companions. It increases the awareness of his alien nature, which is particularly impressive when it's all done without makeup and only the briefest of special effects. It is the knowledge that the Doctor has lived many lives already that reminds his companions – and the audience – that he is not really human at all, possessing a degree of knowledge and experience we can never begin to fathom.

The concept has even spawned storylines within the series. Villains have attempted to steal the Doctor's remaining regenerated forms; others have threatened to somehow cut him off from them, thus killing him permanently. Different incarnations of the Doctor have met and aided one another, providing a wonderful opportunity to see them side-by-side. One villain, the Valeyard, was revealed to be a distillation of all the evil in the Doctor. Existing somehow between the twelfth and final incarnations, he attempted to bring himself into full reality by stealing the Doctor's other regenerated selves and absorbing them into himself.

Every time it is announced that the current Doctor is leaving, the fans have gone wild with speculation about who will play him next. Rather than being horrified at the idea, they have become accustomed to that aspect of the show. Because, of course, each incarnation is very different. Originally this was not going to be the case – the second Doctor was supposed to be a younger version of the first, his body simply restoring itself to health. It was decided, however, to let Troughton reshape the character to suit his own preferences, and he made the Doctor far less stern and paternal, more playful and clownish. After that, each actor brought something new to the role, often defining the character himself and thus dictating the direction the series would take under his tenure. Jon Pertwee showed up for work as the third Doctor wearing elegant, dandy-ish clothing, which caused the writers to make the character more dashing and adventurous than previously intended. Each actor has worked with the writers to create new quirks, though the Doctor's basic traits of intelligence, curiosity, morality and compassion have always remained. In turn, Tom Baker brought a knowing wit and penchant for improvisation, often breaking the 'fourth wall' with a knowing nod or wink to camera to let the audience know he wasn't really in any danger no matter what dastardly villains were arrayed against him. Offering enemies Jelly Babies became almost as iconic as reversing the polarity of the neutron flow, Pertwee's get-out-of-jail-free excuse to solve the day again and again. He was also the proud owner of the Tin Dog, the ultimate sidekick, K9. What's not to love about a talking robot dog who's an all-knowing genius and fires a lazer from its muzzle? Davison offered a dramatic personality shift from the infallible Baker's Doctor to a much more human incarnation who relied upon his companions and even failed them.

Thus, in a way, *Doctor Who* survived for so long as a television series because it was not one show but seven, all stitched tightly together into a single mythos. The flexibility of tweaking the feel of the show to suit each lead actor in their turn allowed it to adapt, becoming darker at times, more campy at others, but still maintaining the traditions that fans had learned to expect from the series.

It also helped the show stay fresh – keeping the same central character for twenty-six years could have got extremely stale, but because the Doctor changes so radically it essentially forces the show to start afresh each time as well. Most long-running series have been forced to either switch to ensemble casts, allowing them to phase old characters out and bring new ones in, or made way for spin-offs featuring younger characters introduced later in the series. Only *Doctor Who* managed to maintain itself for so many years, regenerating in the same way as its title character, morphing into a new version of itself while still retaining enough familiar qualities to retain the audience's loyalty.

Children grew up hiding behind the settee and invoked the dreaded '*EXTERMINATE!*' cry of the Doctor's nemesis, the salt-and-pepper-pot monsters, the Daleks – who at one point were easily defeatable because they couldn't get up a flight of stairs (a fatal design flaw remedied over the years). The first twanging discordant notes of the theme tune were enough to have boys and girls across the land scuttling for cover. Indeed, so many of the Doctor's enemies have become iconic, the silver-skinned, ice-like Cybermen who march endlessly on, the Sea Devils, the plastic-faced Autons who come crashing out of shop windows, the Daleks themselves (who were a testament to the imagination of the viewer with the sink-plunger ray gun) and the Master, that cunning, evil reflection of what the Doctor might have been . . . these villains stayed with us over the intervening years, waiting to come back to drive a new generation cowering behind the couch.

Even when the series finally ended in 1989, it was not really over – audio plays and other formats kept the Doctor alive (including one story with Richard E. Grant, who never played the character onscreen), and a 1996 television movie with Paul McGann attempted to bring him back, before he finally returned in 2005. Different but still the same.

SAPPHIRE AND STEEL (1979-1982)

'All irregularities will be handled by the forces controlling each dimension. Transuranic heavy elements may not be used where there is life. Medium atomic weights are available: gold, lead, copper, jet, diamond, radium, sapphire, silver and steel. Sapphire and steel have been assigned.'

Each episode of *Sapphire and Steel* opened with this cryptic voiceover, except for the title narration in the final episode where mercury is substituted for lead. Why the change? That is as mysterious as the entire series, which ostensibly dealt with 'irregularities' in time. The title characters are 'operators' responsible for fixing temporal anomalies, but, unlike most time travel stories, *Sapphire and Steel* does not have its characters travelling to the future or the past. Rather, Sapphire (played by Joanna Lumley, just finished with her *New Avengers* role as Purdey and years prior to her crowd-pleasing stint in *Absolutely Fabulous*) and Steel (the inimitable David McCallum from *The Man from U.N.C.L.E.*) are non-human characters given the duty of fixing glitches in contemporary time. These anomalies can be ghosts refusing to move on, sinister non-corporeal creatures intending to derail time, or even a personification of time itself.

The brilliance of the late seventies to early eighties series is at one with its ambiguity. Who sends Sapphire and Steel to find and repair the rents in time? It is never stated. They are non-human, although they appear in human form. Sapphire has the limited ability to 'take time back', a brief rewinding like a Mulligan in golf, to redo mistakes on her own and Steel's part. She gathers information through psychometric touch, and can determine both the age of an object and the fate of a human being this way. Both are telepathic. Steel handles the infrequent physical confrontations with their adversaries with abilities that match his name. In typical detective partner fashion, she is the diplomat and he is the brusque 'bad cop'.

Their ages are indeterminate but must be considerable. In 'Adventure Four', they mention having tended to the problem of the *Marie Celeste* in 1872, which they sank 'for its own good'. They did not alter the ship's log, which caused the craft's replica to create a ghostly time anomaly.

Peter J. Hammond (who most recently wrote episodes for BBC's *Torchwood*), series creator and writer of all but 'Adventure Five', has stated on the DVD commentary track: 'The basis of *Sapphire and Steel* came from my desire to write a detective story, into which I wanted to incorporate time. I've always been interested in time, particularly the ideas of J.B. Priestley and H.G. Wells, but I wanted to take a different approach to the subject. So instead of having them go backwards and forwards in time, it was about time breaking in, and having set the precedent I realised the potential that it offered with two people whose job it was to stop the break-ins.'

The series came at a strange time in the history of visual science fiction. *Star Wars* had been a major hit, but *Sapphire and Steel* was antithetical in almost every way to such epic space opera. It lacked a big budget and was staged more as a theatrical play, usually with only three sets, one for each act, every one of them decorated in grey. (The only vibrant colours in the series came from Sapphire's dress and bright blue eyes.) Costuming was low-key and off-the-rack. Running counter to the action-adventure ethos of early eighties visual SF, *Sapphire and Steel* eschewed this in favour of more cerebral themes. There was little derring-do and few joking moments, for it was rooted in the solemn, dark, claustrophobic present, while a sense of psychological menace that suggested danger – perhaps to the entire world – always lurked behind even the most commonplace of items. If the agents failed to correct errors in time, then dire and dimly visualised events would happen.

While the series was science fiction at heart, the lingering spirits and strange psychic powers smacked of the supernatural. The only other television series that tried for a similar blend of the inexplicable and the arcane, even using similar stories, was the mistitled *Friday the 13th* – premiering in 1987 with the owner of an antique store as its lead character, trying to reclaim and destroy cursed curios that ruin lives or threaten mankind. In *Sapphire and Steel*'s 'Adventure Four', they must deal with a lost-and-found shop where the faceless villain traps his victims in old photographs, a plotline similar to one used in the *Friday the 13th* series.

While none of the aired episodes carried titles, the working scripts were entitled as follows:

One – 'Escape Through a Crack in Time'.
Two – 'The Railway Station'.
Three – 'The Creatures' Revenge'.
Four – 'The Man Without a Face'.
Five – 'Doctor McDee Must Die!'
Six – 'The Trap'.

Originally intended as the pilot for a children's show, 'Escape Through a Crack in Time' introduced Sapphire and Steel, the mysterious 'operators' who had to rescue a young girl and her brother from a crack in time, triggered by reciting a nursery

Joanna Lumley (Sapphire) and David McCallum (Steel) – the stars of Ace of Wands *creator P.J. Hammond's atmospheric series.*

rhyme. While this may have seemed a trite story, it became a bleak and foreboding twist on the authority of adults, setting the tone for the series. The heroes might win, but often the cost is extreme. This dark episode was moved to a later airing time of seven o'clock, instead of the pre-six o'clock news watershed for children's television, as it was intended more for adult viewing. The show never left its evening timeslot. In response, talking some years later to *Total SciFi*, P.J. Hammond stated: 'I had previously written fantasy dramas for children's TV and thoroughly enjoyed doing them. And the first three episodes of *Sapphire and Steel* were actually written with that kind of audience in mind. But while writing these I became aware that the show needed a much broader canvas to work on, one that could also incorporate an adult audience. Therefore I was over the moon when I was told about the casting, a bigger budget and the promise of an evening transmission.'

Like shows that would air in the late nineties and early noughties, a story arc could go on for several episodes to make one single 'adventure'. But unlike the mystery series *Veronica Mars* or the later *Heroes*, which would use season-long

The enigmatic duo were responsible for maintaining the integrity of time across six eerily affecting adventures.

story arcs with smaller stories contained within every episode, *Sapphire and Steel* completed its adventure in four, six or eight episodes. The viewer was treated to a mystery that might end quickly, or go on for an entire month of twice weekly half-hour slots.

'Adventure Two', 'The Railway Station', addressed an element of modern history not noticed by television for twenty years or more. A World War One soldier haunts the railway station, the victim of cruel fate. He was killed on Armistice Day, eleven minutes after the ceasefire, when he should have been safe to return home. Sapphire and Steel team up with a ghost hunter to contact other spirits trapped in the station who, like the soldier, were robbed of life in various unfair ways. The most commonplace things become dangerous as Sapphire and Steel deal with the Darkness of despair created by the ghosts. Or is the Darkness an evil entity, using the ghosts' anguish to further its own ends? As in all of the adventures, not all these questions are answered. Lumley ends up playing three roles at one point: Sapphire, Sapphire possessed by Darkness pretending to be Sapphire, and Sapphire as Darkness. Like Lead and the other Operators, Darkness is a capital D darkness, a monstrous entity hell-bent on wreaking chaos and death. It is all rather cryptic and confusing, and you suspect just as much so for the actors as for the viewers, but that enigmatic quality doesn't stop it from being compelling. At one point she even tries to kill Steel using the malefic energy trapped within a bouquet of flowers. The idea is that beauty becomes deadly and at every turn lies betrayal. The sobering resolution trades the ghost hunter's remaining years of life with Darkness to put right the hole in time. The ghosts of the World War One dead haunt the old railway station where a lone soldier whistling 'Pack up Your Troubles in Your Old Kit Bag' walks along the platform, fading out of our reality. It is funny how such a mundane scene can become so eerie.

Shaun O'Riorden, the director of *Sapphire and Steel*, told Rob Stanley of *Dismal Light*: 'P. J. really had this thing about death and revenge – about people who'd been "mal-killed" as it were, like the soldier who'd been killed after the Armistice, and the animals in the following story; he was consumed with this idea of revenge after you'd been wrongfully killed – this haunted P.J., and he piled these characters into the stories. That was the magic for me, in him – that he wrote from his balls. He didn't just sit down and think, "Now what can I write about this time?" – he poured it out.'

'The Creatures' Revenge' introduces a time anomaly in the form of a couple from 1500 years in the future, somehow living in an invisible apartment atop a high rise. In the future all animals other than homo sapiens are extinct, giving a particular slant to one of Hammond's

Despite its enduring popularity across a number of formats, Sapphire and Steel *has never been repeated on British terrestrial television.*

personal concerns – mistreatment of animals. The time travellers have arrived in our time to dissect living animals in what they blandly term Experimental Project ES/5/77. In their temporal conveyance, fur coats come alive and attack, and down-filled pillows can suffocate the unwary, as animal products rebel against mistreatment of their former owners. Time is thrown out of joint when a life form comprised of aspects of every living animal seeks revenge on the cruel vivisectionists. This grim adventure hints at a world of unbounded thoughtlessness without appreciation of other life forms.

'The Man without a Face' addresses paedophilia with the sepia-coloured children playing in the backyard, a horrifying topic that has only really been acknowledged with any openness in TV drama in the past decade. The inference is plain, these children have been collected by the faceless man. In a junk shop, a collection of old photographs each contains a unifying figure, the eponymous man without a face. This lurking horror has taken root in current times and traps a boarder in a flat

As Sapphire, Joanna Lumley represented a humanist counterpoint to David McCallum's often caustic portrayal of Steel.

above the shop in a photograph when she learns the truth about her faceless landlord. Sapphire and Steel save her from being burned in the photo and snare the faceless man in a kaleidoscope, which they place on a sinking ship they know will not be found for another 75 years. Whether their advice to the boarder not to be photographed again is a warning against seeking fame or simply adds to the spookiness is yet another ambiguity. There is certainly a strong indication that, because they were unable to destroy the faceless man, his evil is eternal and can never be completely defeated. This is psychologically grim stuff for any television drama.

'Doctor McDee Must Die!' is another adventure, like 'The Railway Station', where one life must be traded for many. And as in the earlier adventure, Sapphire and Steel show no compunction or remorse about making this trade. This plot is structured like an Agatha Christie murder mystery but told in reverse, as time is peeled back to reveal earlier layers of intrigue as a number of dinner guests are killed. George McDee, a geneticist, has upset the structure of time by creating a plague that will wipe out mankind. Sapphire and Steel pose as human detectives to investigate the deaths that stretch backward in time, until they reach 1930 and the horror that McDee will release is exposed. Time itself is the villain, providing the fissure through which the plague can be released, but Sapphire and Steel triumph by shooting the scientist and setting fire to his laboratory at precisely the right instant.

The nature of the plague is unclear, but the warning about unchecked genetic research came swiftly on the heels of the initial CDC (Centre for Disease Control) report in June 1981 of deaths relating to the as yet unidentified Aids. 'Adventure Five' could as easily have been intended as a cautionary tale about genetic engineering or even germ warfare when it aired in the last week of August 1981. In any case, it was timely and not the usual disposable stuff of TV entertainment.

The final adventure, 'The Trap', pits Sapphire and Steel against three opponents, who are transient beings, and answer to a higher authority. In a 1940s-style café, they find themselves caught in a time trap and unable to escape. Whether their futile attempts to get away were intended as an existentialist statement or if it was merely meant as a cliffhanger for a seventh adventure, both the operators and the series have remained suspended in the limbo of an entropy-free zone since this episode aired in 1982. Joanna Lumley, in her 1989 autobiography *Stare Back and Smile: Memoirs*, says, 'It was an absorbing show which I was sad to finish. To our dismay, the last episode had us banished in a time lock . . . We were assured we'd be released in the next series. There never was another series, and our characters are still up there, waiting to break free and continue the fight.'

Sapphire and Steel presented conundrums without easy answers – or any answers at all. In that, it was a worthy successor to *The Prisoner*, with themes that included animal rights, paedophilia, genetic engineering, the brutality and unfairness of war and, indeed, the unfairness of life itself. Later television shows – notably *Buffy the Vampire Slayer, Heroes* and *Lost* – would run with a similar format, usually completing an entire story arc in a full season while dealing with lesser stories in every episode. But every four-, six- or eight-episode adventure of *Sapphire and Steel* was a complete miniseries of its own.

STARGATE SG-1 (1994-2007)

'An awful warning is constituted by all the Velikovskys, Hubbards, von Dänikens and ufologists who erect standard SF topics – which are within fiction neutral or indeed meaningful – into "true" revelations, thereby instantly converting them into virulent ideologies of political obscurantism.'
– Marc Angenot and Darko Suvin (social theorists from McGill University, Montreal. Suvin served as editor of *Science Fiction Studies* between 1973 and 1980).

In 1975, John Brunner gave a lecture at the Institute of Contemporary Arts in London, titled 'Science Fiction and the Larger Lunacy'. Brunner expressed dismay at the manner in which Velikovsky's theories of cosmic catastrophe, L. Ron Hubbard's Dianetics and Pauwels and Erich von Däniken's alien-gods-built-the-Egyptian-pyramids notions had escaped the world of science fiction, disingenuously insinuated themselves into pop-science and morphed into quasi-religious cults. 'What,' asked Brunner, 'is the attraction in this kind of sloppy nonsense?'

The answer seemed to be distilled down to the simple notion that the 'alternative' historical and scientific fallacies propagated by Velikovsky, Hubbard, Pauwels, von Däniken, Sitchin and others seemed to offer appealing – indeed beguiling – answers to those seeking enlightenment as the new millennium approached, a phenomenon that would later be described by Lovecraft aficionado Jason Colavito as the Cult of Alien Gods, in his book of the same name.

Almost two decades later, in 1994, Dean Devlin, Oliver Eberle and Ute Emmerich produced what they intended to be the first of a movie trilogy, *Stargate*, written by Devlin and Ute's brother Roland Emmerich. In the 2003 documentary on the making of the movie, they made a point of acknowledging the influence of the popularist 'alien gods' myth. Devlin stated, 'While I don't expect everyone to go out and buy von Däniken and Sitchin's books, I want people to think about it, to re-examine the possibility.' Envisaging a second and third movie, Devlin went on to state that he also 'wanted to bridge the gap of all the creatures of legend'.

Stargate used as its premise the notion that, during prehistoric times, an alien entity named Ra came to Earth and took a human body as its host. Ra enslaved mankind, set up our ancient civilisations and had them build pyramid-shaped landing platforms for his ship. He also set up a Stargate, a ring-shaped device that, when activated, allowed near instantaneous travel to other planets. From Earth, Ra took human slaves to the planet Abydos, in order to mine an ore necessary for the running of his ships and the Stargate device. Then, 5,000 years ago in Egypt, a rebellion against Ra saw the Stargate capped and buried, preventing his return.

In 1928, a team of archaeologists discovered the Stargate. However, it's not until 1995, when Dr Daniel Jackson (played by James Spader), an archaeologist with von Däniken-esque notions, joins the military team investigating the artefact, managing to open the gate and connect to the planet Abydos.

Stepping through the gate, the exploration team encounter a human culture largely unchanged since ancient Egypt. Ultimately, the team vanquish the evil Ra by blowing up his ship with a nuclear bomb, Dr Jackson remains behind and marries the alien chieftain's daughter (a fact that would fuel much of the early years of the television spin-off), while the military team return to Earth and report that Jackson is dead and the Abydos Stargate destroyed in the nuclear blast.

Metro-Goldwyn-Mayer, who purchased the movie, immediately saw the potential of the underlying premise. Under executive producer, Brad Wright, MGM went on to develop the TV series *Stargate SG-1*. They brought on board veteran actor Richard Dean Anderson to reprise (and put his own indelible stamp on) the role of Colonel Jack O'Neill, the Air Force officer originally portrayed by Kurt Russell in the movie. Anderson also saw the potential of the series, immediately

The core cast of SG-1 – Teal'c (Douglas Christopher Judge),
Major Samantha Carter (Amanda Tapping), Colonel Jack O'Neill
(Richard Dean Anderson), and Doctor Daniel Jackson (Michael Shanks).

signing up as one of the executive producers.

Stargate SG-1, set a year after events that took place in the movie, uses the notion that Ra's death created a power vacuum between an entire race of squabbling reptilian aliens, the Goa'uld, who now vie with one another for domination of the universe. Throughout human history these Goa'uld, declaring themselves to be gods, have periodically raided Earth, enslaved entire cultures and seeded dozens, possibly hundreds of worlds – most of which bear a remarkable resemblance to the areas around British Columbia – with human slaves.

The imaginative potential of these displaced cultures with their wide-ranging myths and beliefs was unlimited. But the show didn't become an instant primetime hit, coming close to cancellation on several occasions and skipping across networks before finding a permanent home with the Sci-Fi Channel. There, it consistently produced solid ratings and ultimately became the longest-running science fiction TV series in North America (ten years and then some including the spin-offs and television movies later developed), and the second most prosperous franchise earner for MGM after James Bond. This popularity has generated licensed merchandise that includes DVDs, CDs, games, action figures, comics, theme-park rides, books and a cult following, including those like Micahel Salla, the eminent international politics scholar involved in the conflict resolution of East Timor and Kosovo. Salla has written a number of books on what he terms exopolitics, and believes the Stargate is not only real but the actual reason for the Iraq war:

'From the perspective of the Bush administration, control of the Sumerian Stargate would enable clandestine government organisations to continue their global campaign of non-disclosure of the ET presence.'

This facet, the belief by some fans that the gate is real and the government is involved in a vast conspiracy to deny it, resulted in Wright incorporating the general idea into the story arc. In its first episode, 'Point of No Return', the character Martin Lloyd (played by Willie Garson) believes he is an alien marooned on Earth and that the Stargate, which he's convinced is real, is his ticket home. The landmark hundredth episode, 'Wormhole Extreme' and the two-hundredth episode, called simply '200', revisited the arc using a 'show-within-a-show' concept, whereby Lloyd sold a B-grade sci-fi TV series based on his repressed alien abduction memories of the 'real' Stargate – all approved by the Pentagon, of course, as a form of plausible deniability.

This incorporation of the fans' beliefs into the mythos made for superb entertainment; according to Sonny Whitelaw, author of five *Stargate* tie-in novels, it's one of the cornerstones of the immense success of both this and other 'alien mythology' shows such as *The X-Files* and *Roswell*. In 2004, the UK-based publisher Fandemonium had contracted Whitelaw, an Australian photojournalist and novelist, to write her first tie-in based on *Stargate SG-1*. Whitelaw, who has a degree in geomorphology and anthropology, was aware that Brad Wright's vision for the books was to explore the archaeological aspects of alien god mythology in a way that was impossible within the budgetary constraints of a television series. Excited by the storytelling possibilities and bemused by the appeal of von Däniken's 'ancient astronaut' fallacies, Whitelaw wrote what she describes as a 'Mesoamerican mythology based on von Däniken's whacky fallacies inserted into a Stargate framework'. As a homage to the root source of the alien gods concept, the opening of *Stargate SG-1: City of the Gods* begins with same tagline that H.P. Lovecraft used in 'The Call of Cthulhu':

'Of such great powers or beings there may be conceivably a survival . . . a survival of a hugely remote period when . . . consciousness was manifested, perhaps, in shapes and forms long since withdrawn before the tide of advancing humanity . . . forms of which poetry and legend alone have caught a flying memory and called them Gods.' – Algernon Blackwood, cited in Lovecraft, 1928.

City of the Gods did so well that Whitelaw almost immediately encountered fans who believed her *Stargate* take on the history of the Aztecs and Mayans was based on actual events. While that certainly wasn't her intent ('Please note the term fiction on the spine,' is the author's frequent response), Whitelaw was so intrigued by fans buying into the 'larger lunacy' that she undertook a master's thesis on the subject, while simultaneously writing her third *Stargate* title, which moved into the spin-off realm of Atlantis, *Stargate Atlantis: Exogenesis* (co-authored with Elizabeth Christensen and nominated for a 2007 Scribe Award for best original novel based upon a television series).

'The simple truth is Devlin, Emmerich, Brad Wright, Robert Cooper and indeed all the show's writers have bottled a concept that makes a great deal of money, using a recipe set out several thousand years ago in the first recorded work of literature, Gilgamesh. I wanted to understand the reason why the ingredients produced such a successful formula so that I, and other creative industry professionals, could consciously use the same ingredients in different ways to create a wider variety of Stargate narratives. Ultimately, the question came down to why is the alien god notion so appealing?'

Whitelaw began her research by analysing the history of belief in alien gods, and discovered that it was largely a history of cosmology – our view of our place (and that of our familiar gods) in the universe. For according to ancient tradition, thousands of gods lived – and in many cultures still live – right here on Earth, in volcanoes and under the ocean, in sacred cows and in mountains, rivers and rocks. The heavens are also cluttered with gods, but, unlike their terrestrial counterparts, they are a little trickier to locate. A mountain on Earth, for instance, is a fixed, defined place, while the location, nature, and even the scope of Heaven is a shifting proposition at best. When asked where it is, most people throughout the ages would have motioned in the direction of the sky. This underscores the point of where it's not, and that's Earth. And so by inference, any gods living in the heavens are extraterrestrial.

There's no telling exactly how long these gods have been around. While oral traditions have carried them through the generations, it's easier to trace the role they played in human affairs when information was disseminated by something more durable than word of mouth.

The first known texts describing gods and the heavens are Bronze Age Akkadian clay tablets from Mesopotamia, describing what's known today as the Sumerian King List. One of the most intriguing aspects of this is its scope: the King List records over 220,000 years of leadership and draws no line of demarcation between fact and legend. The first kings were said to have been the direct descendants of the sky gods and 'gatekeepers' known as the Annunaki – or Nifilim, as they were called in Genesis VI. 'After the kingship descended from heaven, the kingship was in Eridu' – Sumerian scholar L. Finkel, 1980. Eridu or Eridug, is modern-day Tell Abu Shahrain, Iraq. It was purportedly the earliest city in southern Mesopotamia. Each king of Eridu supposedly ruled for tens of thousands of years.

This, of course, is the premise that *Stargate* uses, right down to the reptilian sky gods being 'gatekeepers' who added their essence to the more primitive inhabitants of Earth to create a slave race.

So, even at the dawn of human civilisation, mankind believed that gods were extraterrestrial in origin; they came to Earth largely as a result of wars in the heavens, and, having given mankind a primer on how to build a civilisation, treated us as slaves.

Because the Mesopotamian kings granted themselves the divine right to rule – they were the direct descendants of gods, after all – the notion of extraterrestrial deities generated a huge following that lasted thousands of years and spread to other civilisations, including Ancient Greece, where machinating gods regularly squabbled with one another and humans invariably suffered the fallout in the form of storms, volcanic eruptions, floods, plagues and other unpleasant events.

Ancient Greece wasn't simply famous for its gods, though. It was the birthplace of philosophies upon which much of the Western world operates, and this is where the evolution of alien gods and cosmology in general takes an interesting turn.

Back then, a group of Greek philosophers known as Atomists proposed that all matter in the universe is made from an infinite number of tiny building blocks – atoms – that wander around in an infinite vacuum. By inference, atoms are indestructible and eternal, and when they congregate together they do so for a meaningful purpose. The Atomists believed that a grain of sand or a planet, a bird, a human being or a cloud, each have unique attributes according to the way the atoms have congregated. When a group of atoms is broken apart or dies, the scattered atoms recombine to form new groupings. Furthermore, since atoms are infinite, they must operate the same way throughout the infinite void.

This remarkable train of thought worked on all levels, which led to the proposition that the lights in the sky were not gods, but other worlds as long-lived and yet as ultimately ephemeral in their congregations of atoms as the planet Earth. 'In other regions there are other Earths and various tribes of men and breeds of beasts' – Lucretius, *c*. 50 BC.

Being materialistic and mechanistic in nature, Atomism lacked gods. Indeed, Atomists regarded religion as a monster that should be crushed, for man's pursuit of happiness was weighted down with fear and the need to appease non-existent and largely perfidious deities. The mere fact that gods were so mercurial and atavistic was evidence of their origins within the minds of men, for no true god would have created such a flawed world.

The problem, however, was that the Ancient Greeks, and later the Romans, were very fond of their gods, and while Atomism lingered until the first century BC – along with Heliocentrism, which proposed that the earth revolved around a central sun – it fell out of favour. Instead, Aristotle's cosmology took centre stage.

Aristotle began with the assumption that the universe is made of substances that either congregate together or naturally move toward that place when they are not together. The most substantial of these elements, earth, is therefore at the centre of the universe, and so anything solid must either be on the one central spherical point called Earth or move naturally toward it. Water sits above the earthy substance and air sits above water, while fire climbs above air. Beyond air is an even less substantial element called divine ether, from which the celestial bodies – the moon and the sun, Mercury, Venus, Mars, Jupiter and Saturn – were made. Along with other objects in the sky, these celestial bodies revolved within their own individual spheres. The least substantial, the stars, existed in the outermost sphere, beyond which was the spiritual realm.

There was no room for alien worlds in this cosmology because all of the substance would already have moved to Earth. However, there was plenty of room for extraterrestrial gods in the spiritual realm.

The significance of this cosmology to human thinking cannot be overstated. The model simultaneously accommodated human egos and, unusual for a cosmology, slid effortlessly from pre-Christian pagan beliefs to the increasingly powerful Roman-Christian world. Earth was in a fixed location at the centre of things, exactly as described by the Bible; the moon and sun, the planets and the stars were, by definition, extraterrestrial, and thus formed part of the heavenly realm between Earth and God. Outside the celestial spheres was the exclusive and infinite domain of God.

The structure of this much-cherished geocentric model was expressed in sublime detail in 'Paradiso', the third cantica of Dante's epic poem, *The Divine Comedy*. Earth, Hell and Purgatory (a large island on the other side of the world, more or less where Australia is located) were mapped out in such detail as to offer inarguable proof as to the existence and makeup of the heavens.

And so any alien visiting Earth during this period, and claiming to be from another planet, would have been regarded as an angel, or God, or a dead spirit.

Enter Copernicus and Galileo, who pointed out through observation that Earth wasn't at the centre of the universe after all – an event that caused a huge furore in Rome, partly because it happened in the middle of the Reformation. The problem wasn't so much the idea that the earth revolved around the sun, but that the notion challenged Aristotle's view that the earth was the only solid matter in the universe. To Rome, the mere whiff of that possibility raised spectacularly alarming issues regarding the redemption of man through the resurrection of Christ. If the Earth was merely one of several solid worlds revolving around the sun, then the dichotomy between the physical earth and the metaphysical heavens was under threat. The moon and Mars and other planets must therefore be as corporeal as the Earth. There could be no question about redemption of any other peoples living on any of these supposed other worlds – which God, by definition of being God, was clearly capable of creating – because the incarnation of Christ was a union between God's divinity and the sons of a sinning Adam, an event unique to Earth. Even the angels couldn't partake in redemption because they hadn't committed 'original sin' – besides which, they resided in the outermost celestial sphere closest to God.

This was not knowledge that could just be packed away and ignored, any more than Adam could have unbitten the apple. It didn't matter that none of these cosmological theories were entirely correct. The mere idea that other worlds existed instantly extended God's powers and magnificence, and yet simultaneously undermined the fundamental tenets that defined Christianity.

But if astronomers threw a monkey wrench into the cosmological works, 50 years later Newton threw in the entire tool kit by mathematically proving that gravity was what made the universe tick. The Ancient Greek Atomists were fundamentally right. The universe was infinite, made up of billions of worlds, and it all hung together because of a simple notion called gravity. Which of course raised the question of where exactly God resided in this newly defined cosmological map, and naturally got people thinking about what life forms might exist on these other worlds.

On to the Age of Reason, where God was relegated to a pantheistic notion at best, and science, by definition, held the implied promise that it would be able to explain everything. God was no longer necessary.

So what has any of this to do with *Stargate*? Well, thereafter followed a chain of events that led to an entire century's worth of science fiction and horror stories.

In 1898, H.G. Wells's *The War of the Worlds* became an instant bestseller. Five years later, the astronomer Percival Lowell published his ostensibly non-fictional landmark work, *The Canals of Mars*, which declared Mars to be inhabited by a civilisation of such great scientific prowess that their canals were visible from Earth.

Thus, the notion was firmly fixed in people's minds that technologically advanced Martians could conceivably invade Earth, and the outcome wouldn't be in the least bit pleasant.

Over the next decade, H.P. Lovecraft – armed with an excellent contemporary knowledge of astronomy, including the mathematically theorised planet 'X' (when

Stargate's *military subtexts benefited from unprecedented levels of technical assistance from both the United States Air Force and Navy.*

discovered in 1932 it was named Pluto) – developed what would later become known as his Cthulhu Mythos, and began publishing his entirely fictional stories in popular pulp magazines.

Lovecraft encouraged his fans and friends to expand upon his stories, the premise of which was that an evil, alien, god-like creature (bearing a remarkable similarity to Davy Jones from the *Pirates of the Caribbean* movie franchise) invaded Earth millions of years ago and mixed the essence of itself with proto-humans to create a slave race. The aliens set up a huge city in Antarctica, and periodically returned 'when the stars were right' (see, for example, 'At the Mountain of Madness').

Lovecraft's tales ultimately became so detailed that the Cthulhu framework and its derivatives, such as the Necronomicon Grimoire, are regarded as real in some circles. 'Lovecraft's Cthulhu monsters are worshipped as devils by a group of "magick" practitioners and the Church of Satan had to issue a statement telling its adherents that the Necronomicon was not real and thus is not a Church text,' writes Jason Colavito.

This despite Lovecraft's 1934 statement, 'This pooling of resources tends to build up quite a pseudo-convincing background of dark mythology, legendry, and bibliography – though of course, none of us has the least wish to actually mislead readers.'

Again, the similarity to the *Stargate* mythos, particularly that of *Atlantis* (the plot follows the adventures of the Atlantis expedition in search of the Lost City of Atlantis. The quest to find Atlantis is the major plot arc for most of *SG-1's* Season Seven), is clear – not because *Stargate* directly uses Lovecraftian themes, but because by the 1940s alien god themes from Babylonian and Greek times that had been supplanted by Aristotolean/Christian cosmology were back in vogue. Orson Welles's 1938 radio play of *The War of the Worlds* demonstrated all too clearly the public's willingness to believe in aliens, while the 1947 incident at Roswell (along with the early stirrings of the Cold War) cemented the public's belief in government conspiracies. One alien god cult, Scientology, would eventually gain the legal status of a religion.

Still, none of this explains why people were attracted to alien god cults. Returning to her anthropological roots, Whitelaw came up with an elegant answer in the works of Joseph Campbell.

Campbell argues that our mythologies provide our social structure, our laws and mores, allow us to clearly define our place in the cosmos and provide a conceptual miscellaneous folder in which we can heap the unknowns and intangibles that cannot otherwise be explained or rationalised. Mythologies, Campbell says, fulfil a life-supporting role in society:

'Such literally read symbols have always been – and still are, in fact – the supports of their civilisations, the supports of their moral orders, their cohesion, vitality, and creative powers. With the loss of them there follows uncertainty, and with uncertainty, disequilibrium, since life, as Nietzsche and Ibsen knew, requires life-supporting illusions; and where these have been dispelled, there is nothing secure to hold on to, no moral law, nothing firm.'

When supplanted or falsified by science (which does not provide absolute truths but is an 'eagerness for truths'), the symbolic meaning of mythologies is rendered empty. 'All the old mythic notions of the nature of the cosmos have gone to pieces, and also all those of the origins and history of mankind,' leaving an ontological void. 'According to our sciences, on the other hand, nobody knows what is out there, or if there is any "out there" at all.'

In his 1973 book, *The Hero with a Thousand Faces*, Campbell concludes by reflecting on Nietzsche's oft-cited quote, 'dead are all the gods,' arguing, 'It is not that there is no hiding place for the gods from the searching telescope and microscope; there is no such society any more as the gods once supported.'

Implicit within science is that, while deriding mythology as ignorance, it promises to provide answers about the nature of the universe. And yet it continually fails to answer the same questions that myths have since the dawn of time: Where do we come from? What created the universe? Where do I go when I die? This ongoing battle between mysticism and materialism to describe the true nature of the universe is nowhere more clearly exemplified than in the character of Dana Scully from *The X-Files*, whose inability to reconcile her faith in religion and her faith in science epitomises the apparently irreconcilable gap between the two.

Sonny Whitelaw argues that, despite their opposing epistemologies, both mythology and science are attempts to articulate our world, and alien god fallacies bridge the conceptual gap by regarding mythology as literal histories. When presented in a technological framework, alien god notions appear to offer substance because they claim that science and its practical application – technology – do indeed explain all mysteries and unknowns; it's just that the passage of time has muddied the details, and we've lost touch with the extraterrestrials who created us through this 'technologised mythology'.

This is particularly true of *Stargate*. As Dean Devlin reminds us, *Stargate* was developed specifically 'to bridge the gap of all the creatures of legend'. It does so most effectively by crafting a framework that, at its core, uses the two primary elements of Campbell's life-supporting role: the creation myth and the quest for immortality, both of which are addressed in different forms in the television series.

One unfortunate by-product of this complex framework, this carefully crafted 'sloppy nonsense' that exists for the sole purpose of creating an entertaining fictional universe, is that some of the audience have (mis)read the framework as real.

As John Brunner said back in that 1993 lecture, 'All too often people become willing accomplices in their own duping, discounting or ignoring evidence to the contrary of what it suits their taste to believe.'

And as pure shameless entertainment *Stargate* is the gift that keeps giving, having branched off into *Atlantis* and, as of writing, seen Robert Carlyle and crew stumble aboard the ancient ship Destiny (by dialling an unheralded ninth chevron on the Stargate, no less) and prepared to boldly go where . . . ah, maybe not. In a move not dissimilar to *Babylon 5* retaining SF author Harlan Ellison as a consultant, *Stargate* Universe has brought in noted SF author John Scalzi to act as a 'background consultant'. Given the fact that the show promises to focus upon the characters aboard Destiny for its narrative drive (none of these guys are meant to be there, they might be brilliant but they're unprepared), and that the fan universe is buzzing with words like 'dark' and 'edgy' right now, it promises to be an interesting union. Based on the opening episodes and Carlyle's portrayal of the flawed genius, Nicholas Rush, one would expect that the boundaries between good and evil are set to blur considerably in this new live-action franchise. It certainly isn't just more of the same. *Stargate* with no Goa'uld? No Wraiths? Even the shooting style is more intimate, borrowing a lot from movies such as *The Blair Witch Project* and *Cloverfield* to make the viewer feel like they are there, on Destiny, right alongside Rush and the rest of the rag-tag crew.

Stargate is dead. Long live *Stargate*.

TRU CALLING (2003-2005)

Tru Calling is a wonderful example of one of those series which was not given sufficient time to cultivate its audience: the common refrain television critics and disgruntled fans intone post mortem over their beloved shows. Usually the blame is levelled squarely upon network executives who are vilified for their impatience and poor management; surely, the argument proceeds, with sufficient marketing support, the appropriate time slot, and just one more season, the show would pull in the ratings necessary to appease the greedy network.

The fact the network bought the show in the first place believing it to have potential is ignored.

The sad fact is that the vast majority of shows cancelled each year walk gently into that endless winter night of televisual hell justly, being trite, absurd, or unforgivably insipid. Viewers should thank the networks for this triage. Nevertheless, *Tru Calling* was one of the rare series which slid into oblivion despite its intriguing premise, a strong lead and solid supporting cast, intelligent scripts, and the initial ardent support of Fox which solicited the series as a vehicle for actress Eliza Dushku.

The time travel/rewind premise of *Tru Calling* was hardly original. *Sliders*, *Quantum Leap*, and more recently the ill-fated *Journeyman*, as well as the silver-screened *Groundhog Day* and even the cult film *Donnie Darko*, had all employed similar time-travel themes, the latter two utilising the 'rewind' motif in which a character steps backward in time to relive a particular series of events with the implied purpose of altering them. *Tru Calling*, however, took this conceit only as an instigating device for what otherwise can be characterised as a conventional mystery/detective drama. Its smart, confident and witty female protagonist Tru was clearly a precursor to teen detective Veronica Mars and is a close cousin of Allison Dubois, the psychic from the ABC series *Medium*. Late in Season One a nemesis for Tru was added (Jack, played by Jason Priestly) and rather like the conceit of Sam Beckett's guiding force, metaphysical powers were implied to be manipulating human reality to their own ends. Tru and Jack were but the human agents through which this grand contest of fates was enacted.

This radically transformed the show from primarily a procedural detective drama to one solidly grounded in fantasy with the promise in Season Two of correspondingly expanded themes and conflicts. Not all fans greeted this change warmly. Many thought that Tru – resourceful, intelligent, and an empiricist (she is a medical student, after all) – needed no mystical rivals or supernatural elements to enliven the series. Indeed, in can be argued that what distinguished *Tru Calling* as primetime science fiction/fantasy television was the centrality of the protagonist's character over the series' fantastical premise.

Stars of the short-lived Tru Calling *– Zach Galifianakis, Jessica Collins, Eliza Dushku, A.J. Cook, and Shawn Reaves.*

The show had the courage to explore the confusion Tru experiences when displaced in time. Her primary struggle is not to understand the mechanisms of her 'calling' but to fulfil her vocation by providing compassion, insight, or often just a friendly ear to those in need. In this, the drama has more in common with recent literary time travellers, most notably Harry of *The Time Traveler's Wife*, who considers his time-travelling an illness of which he longs to be cured. Tru doesn't consider her time travel fun; it is a terrible burden but it is also her duty – her calling – to help the deceased who plead with her in each episode and set her day into rewind, triggering the time-travel conceit central to the show. This again recalls *Medium*, in which the protagonist, a medium who assists law enforcement with their investigations, finds her personal life constantly disrupted by her visions. Yet she continues her work despite the trauma.

The ambivalence of Tru as reluctant protagonist is mirrored by the logistical complexity of the weekly plots which she must 'resolve'. One need only review the synopsis of any early episode to understand that while the 'rewind' motif is intrinsically disorienting, *Tru Calling*'s writers delighted in contriving elaborate plots and trajectories, littering each show with minute clues and more than a few red herrings. It was not a show one could watch while cooking dinner or ironing one's clothes: it asked its viewers to pay attention. This is hardly a fault. Tru derives as much from the concise scripting of *Law & Order* as the coy charm of *Nancy Drew*. Through observation, investigation and logic Tru reasons her way to resolution in most cases. She is also, however, compelled to answer the 'why' of each mystery, which calls upon different skills. Empathy is the signature of Tru and this 'feminine' trait radically distinguishes her from traditional detective genre conventions. She pieces together forensic clues, but Tru is as much social worker as investigator. Her combination of intellect and empathy made her complex and engaging but an unconventional protagonist. This, coupled with the occasionally convoluted plots of the show, may have demanded too much of audiences, especially considering *Tru Calling*'s dearth of traditional primetime enticements: violence and sex.

It may well be that viewers who followed Dushku from *Buffy the Vampire Slayer*, where her character, Faith, revelled in brutality and raunchy sex, were disappointed by Tru's restraint. Tru, in the mould of Hitchcock's great protagonists, is the ordinary person placed in extraordinary circumstances. It is to the credit of both Ms Dushku and the series' creators that they crafted a naturalistic character and honestly approached the problems of a young woman grappling with career aspirations, frustrated romances, and sibling conflict who then suddenly finds herself drafted into the metaphysical service of dead. Whereas the current series *Pushing Daisies* treats the return of the dead with whimsy, *Tru Calling* embraced this messy, unsavoury, and morally ambiguous notion with naturalistic realism. Tru's problems were complex, occasionally even intractable. This was true of weekly mysteries as well as larger story arcs. The latter included a substance-abusing sister, her unscrupulous but charming brother, and the lingering trauma of her mother's untimely death.

Dushku told SciFi.com what appealed to her most about the role, and indeed shows like *Tru Calling*: 'I think that there are so many stories still to be told about young women. And, obviously, young women make up a pretty large part of our society, and people want to see it, want to explore it. So there will always be an interest there, an attraction there. Because I think that girls learn a lot from watching these characters, and that's why it's important that they are portrayed as real as possible, because girls are learning from the characters they watch. Their triumphs and their mistakes. It's almost a form of therapy for some people.'

Theraputic or not, ultimately it may be that *Tru Calling* failed commercially for the most banal of reasons: bad timing. One must recall that the series began its run in October of 2003, only two years after the traumas of 9/11 and only six months after the United States' invasion of Iraq. It is certainly conceivable that a show focused upon the plight of the recently dead, often prematurely or otherwise unjustly in this unenviable state, might prove disconcerting to the Americans who would otherwise have been its target audience. We aren't talking horror fans hot for shambling dead zombies à la Romero, but what was essentially family viewing. Certainly in publishing, several of the larger houses shied away from contracting 'real horror'. This assumption is supported by the fact that the short-lived show did notably better in foreign markets, particularly New Zealand, nearly as far removed from the military action in Iraq as is possible. *Tru Calling* simply may have been in the wrong place at the wrong time. It is difficult to say for sure, of course, after all, during the Depression horror movies first became really popular, and they had a renaissance during the Vietnam conflict, but we're talking about a different demographic, and a time when the news was repeatedly, day in day out, piping in visions of death and declaring wars on terror and urging folks to support the troops and be wholesome and good and everything that a show devoted to untimely death wasn't.

Dushku went on to play a young woman named Echo, a member of a group of people known as Dolls in Joss Whedon's Fox show, *Dollhouse*. The Dolls in question, rather like Joe 90, have had their personalities wiped clean so they can be imprinted with new personas that will allow them to undertake covert assignments, commit crimes, indulge fantasies, and hopefully do the occasional good deed. In between assignments the Dolls are mind-wiped into a childlike state and live in a hidden facility nicknamed 'The Dollhouse'.

Dushku may have found herself in the right place at the right time, as after a somewhat uncertain start Whedon's undoubted magic has begun to show through and *Dollhouse*, entering its second season now, is vying for its own spot amongst the pantheon of great genre shows of the last decade or so. But with other outstanding shows like *Wonderfalls* and *Pushing Daises* falling by the wayside – victims of fickle audiences and falling viewing figures – nothing should ever be taken for granted. Remember *Firefly*?

DOCTOR WHO (NEW SERIES) (2005-PRESENT)

Christopher Eccleston as the Ninth Doctor
David Tennant as the Tenth Doctor

In its original incarnation, the *Doctor Who* television series first aired in 1963 and ran for twenty-six years. It was finally taken off the air due to a combination of dwindling viewing figures and a BBC chief in Michael Grade who didn't believe it had a place in modern programming. Grade was a more effective nemesis than Master ever had been. Curiously, even though the BBC closed the *Doctor Who* production office in August of 1990, they insisted over and over that the show had not been cancelled, but was merely on hiatus and would eventually return. There was little evidence to support this, but fandom didn't need any to sustain speculations of how and when the show might reappear, what changes would occur, and who would play the Doctor.

The BBC tried to resurrect the series several times, in several different ways, and spoke to various independent production companies about having them produce the show, including numerous American networks. Fox Network eventually took an interest and commissioned a television movie, which they hoped would act as a pilot for a renewed series. The movie starred Paul McGann, making him the Eighth Doctor to helm the Tardis, and aired on 14 May 1996 in the United States and 27 May in Great Britain. It drew strong audience numbers in the UK but fared less well in the US, prompting Fox to write off the idea of a series.

With the rights reverting to the BBC, they considered the idea of bringing the series back, but their Worldwide arm claimed they were planning to create a new film version of the series. In 2003 the BBC's interactive media branch, BBCi, produced a full-length animated adventure starring Richard E. Grant as the Doctor (though in a manner oh-so-typical of this thing they call 'fandom', many point-blank refuse to believe the canonicity of this Doctor, just as they dispute Peter Cushing's incarnation from the original feature movies). BBCi intended to use that adventure, 'Scream of the Shalka', as the first in a series, which would have made Grant the Ninth Doctor and transferred the *Doctor Who* franchise to webcasts.

By then, however, BBC One's Controller had convinced BBC Worldwide to surrender the rights to the series. They invited established TV writer Russell T. Davies, a known *Doctor Who* enthusiast, to helm the new version of the series and he promptly accepted. The return of *Doctor Who* was officially announced on 26 September 2003.

Finally, on 26 March 2005, the BBC aired the first episode of what they called *Doctor Who: Series One*. It was a complete re-branding of the franchise. This episode, 'Rose', introduced both the new Doctor – the ninth incarnation, played by Christopher Eccleston – and his new companion, Rose Tyler (played by former child pop star Billie Piper), and just like that Richard E. Grant's Doctor was relegated to unofficial status.

The new *Doctor Who* quickly earned not only impressive viewer numbers but also a string of awards, and kept the front pages of the British tabloids buzzing with speculation, demonstrating that fans were every bit as excited by the show as they ever had been. With this rediscovery of 'family entertainment', dads and mums sat down with their kids come Saturday evening, eager to watch the Doctor's adventures through space and time. During the week the schoolyards were filled with games of Doctor and Dalek for the first time in almost twenty years. In terms of a re-launch it really couldn't have gone any better.

Of course, the show had changed in more ways than just the recasting of its lead characters. The title sequence and logo were different. This was no surprise to anyone – those elements and the theme music (which had also been updated) had often been tweaked with each new Doctor. The interior of the Tardis had been redesigned, but again this conformed to the show's established conceit that the Tardis was incredibly vast and had rooms – including spare control rooms – that

Billie Piper and Christopher Eccleston – revitalising
Doctor Who *beyond the BBC's wildest expectations.*

the characters and the audience had never seen. The format shifted somewhat as well. The original series had been based on the serial model, with short episodes linked together into longer stories and offered the potential for cliff-hangers galore. For Series One the producers established a different model, using 45-minute-long standalone episodes and occasionally two-parters.

The most significant change in the series, however, was its tone. The original series had been aimed at children, and had often contained what can only be described as campy elements as well as some educational themes. The new Series One was darker, with a heightened sense of danger and in places a biting humour. In another shift, it also had more 'adult' situations between the Doctor and his companions – before this the producers had always studiously avoided any suggestion that the Doctor was anything more than a platonic father figure and friend to his various companions, even the young ladies. He was, for want of a better word, sexless. But Christopher Eccleston's Doctor flirted heavily with Rose, and smitten, young Rose returned his affections. This burgeoning relationship became much more pronounced in Series Two, when David Tennant took over from Eccleston as the Doctor. It was hard for even the most ardent fan to deny that this new Doctor had romantic feelings for Rose and vice-versa. Heck, viewers were even treated to some lip-locking.

Other characters had romantic and (heaven forbid) sexual urges as well – in Series One we first encounter Steven Moffat's creation, Captain Jack, an 'omnisexual' being attracted to men, women and good-looking aliens alike.

This new Doctor was darker as well. He was a damaged man now. As episodes revealed in brief mentions here and there, at some point between the last of the old episodes and the first of the new the Time Lords and the Daleks fought an all-out war for control of all time and space. This Time War dragged even the Doctor into its service, and ultimately he finished it, annihilating the entire Dalek race – and killing his own people in the process (the story of the Time War can be picked up in various spin-off novels produced by Virgin and Telos if anyone is interested in words instead of pictures). He was now the last of the Time Lords, and this guilt and grief haunted him constantly, making him far more brooding and solitary than his previous incarnations. He also showed more disdain for humanity than he had in the past, viewing them less as equals and more as amusing but naughty little children – or monkeys.

His villains grew darker to match. *Doctor Who* adversaries had always been driven by grandiose goals, from conquering a city to repopulating a dead planet or storming the galaxy. Now, however, they became cleverer, more sophisticated, vengeful and distinctly crueller. People died from their schemes far more often, and interestingly, those deaths became less of a major goal and more of an inconsequential by-product.

The juxtaposition is that at the same time the villains succeeded in becoming more sympathetic, preventing viewers from seeing everything in black and white.

*The Daleks returned en masse at the climax
of the June 2005 episode 'Bad Wolf'.*

Despite initial concerns, David Tennant's tenure as the Doctor maintained the series' renaissance, aided by Martha Jones (Freema Agyeman).

The Doctor fought to protect innocents, but sometimes the so-called villain was a victim of circumstance as well. Even his age-old enemies, the Daleks, reappeared revamped with new, and dare we say it, subtle nuances. No longer completely cold machines, now these fearsome creatures had desires of their own, and flaws that made them almost pitiable at times.

While the darker, edgier tone made the new episodes more palatable to adult viewers, the tone itself is not the series' most important feature. The new *Doctor Who* is notable for two things, either of which would earn it a place as a significant and trend-setting series. First, in addition to being the longest-running science fiction series of all time, it is also the only series to have survived such a long hiatus. The show was off the air for sixteen years. True, audio plays and novels and graphic novels helped fill in that gap, but the gap remains, just the same. Sixteen years between the last of the old episodes and the first of the new ones! No other series has bridged such a span. Indeed, most, once taken off the air, have never come back. Perhaps it is part of the Hollywood remake phenomenon? The few that have returned have more often than not been in the form of a spin-off series or a complete re-imagining of the original, such as the recent reboot of *The Bionic Woman*, starring Michelle

Ryan in Lindsay Wagner's role of Jaime Sommers. Despite the BBC's decision to call the first of the new seasons *Series One*, no one can deny that this is still clearly the original *Doctor Who*. It is not a successor, not a reboot, but a continuation of the old series, with the same main character, the same ship, the same basic concept, and even the same core music. Certainly, elements have changed, but the fact that it could return after so many years off the air, and do this so strongly and so successfully, is a testament not only to the efforts of fans and creators but also to the strength of the story and main character.

Steven Moffat, writer of the Hugo Award-winning episodes 'The Girl in the Fireplace' and 'Empty Child/The Doctor Dances', summed it up rather elegantly in a *Radio Times* interview in 2007: 'Adults never quite grow out of their childhood fears, they just belong in a different part of our heads. *Doctor Who* isn't a childish programme, but it is childlike: it's a programme for children. And many, many adults who watch and love it watch it as that: as something like *Harry Potter*. They watch it in that frame of mind. And that's the best frame of mind to creep people out in, because it pushes you back to a time when the shadows were scary.'

The second thing that makes the new *Doctor Who* so significant is the *scope* of its alterations. The core concepts remained but most of the details were altered, including the principal sets. *Doctor Who* went from being a campy, quasi-educational children's show to being a dark, edgy 'family' series. No other series has made such an alteration in its tone, its trappings, its format, its characters. Normally a series can endure only superficial changes before the viewers lose interest and faith. That's because most shows, once you change too much, stop being the show the viewers loved and become something else entirely. But not *Doctor Who*.

Part of that tacit acceptance must surely be because an element of 'all change' is integral to the show. The lead actor has gone through ten incarnations (eleven soon when Matt Smith steps into the Time Lord's shoes), something no other show could even imagine doing, and each time it has returned to hold the viewers' attentions and sympathies. Indeed, each faction of fandom has its own Doctor, its own favourite. That said, the fans could easily have decided that this new series was not the *Doctor Who* they knew and loved, that this dark, bitter man in the black leather jacket with his grimy Tardis could not be the same Doctor they had respected and admired. (And let's face it, on some bitter internet messageboards folk are still bemoaning the fact that 'Rusty' and his team have forever destroyed their childhood with their gay agenda and their dumb stories and by their blatant disregard for what has gone before – it's to be expected.)

The truth is that the series has become more popular than ever before, its audience suddenly worldwide.

The writing, as ever, has been sharp to the point of being clever, with the use of arcs and arc words like Bad Wolf popping up here and there ominously in Series One, even in other languages (the Welsh Blaidd Drwg, the French Mal Loup, and the German Böser Wolf), and Vote Saxon presaging the return of the Master.

These overarching stories add an element of sophistication to the storytelling that wasn't there in the seventies or eighties *Who*, and owes a lot to the influence of Joss Whedon's *Buffy the Vampire Slayer*, which proved beyond any reasonable doubt that television audiences are sophisticated enough to follow long-running storylines and that the 'adventure of the week' format used by those old shows was outdated in terms of today's television.

As a measure of the impact of this new series, when Eccleston announced that he was leaving it was front-page news, not merely the domain of the tabloids. The entire world wondered who would take his place and become the Tenth Doctor. And likewise, when word leaked out that Tennant was set to tread the boards portraying Hamlet at the RSC, rumours were rife that he was leaving the show. (Including a fake-out regeneration scene which tugged the heart strings with its cheesy-dramatic musical accompaniment of the Doctor and returning Rose running in slow-motion down a midnight street like long lost lovers heading for that 'airport-embrace'. Thankfully a Dalek death ray kept things from getting too soap-opera). Who could have imagined that when the final episode of the 'classic' *Who* aired?

Doctor Who has become a cultural icon; its name and the Tardis are instantly recognisable. The return of that blue London police box and its alien owner struck a chord deep in the hearts of science fiction and adventure fans everywhere.

In a way, the show's science-fiction premise may have helped its fans endure the long gap between seasons. After all, *Doctor Who* is about travel through time and space. To a 900-year-old Time Lord, sixteen years is barely a blink of the eye.

But the show's flexibility played a part as well. After the first Doctor left and the second one took over, fans grew accustomed to the notion that the series could continue even if its face changed completely. Subsequent years merely supported that idea. When the old series went off the air, other media continued to provide *Doctor Who* stories for the fans, and they adapted, accepting that the face had changed yet again and this time the format had as well. And thus, when the new series was announced, fans weren't puzzled. They didn't wonder how a show could possibly return after so long a hiatus. They simply accepted that it had evolved again, and that this time the change had brought it closer to home, putting it back on the television screen, where it belonged. And why wouldn't it? The writing of this new series has been nothing but strong, with some fantastic scripts from the likes of Mark Gatiss (*The League of Gentlemen*), Rob Shearman ('Dalek'), and Paul Cornell (whose 'Human Nature'/'Family of Blood' two-parter is perhaps the finest *Who* adventure ever). There's even talk of Stephen Fry and Neil Gaiman penning future jollies into time and space for the Doctor.

Doctor Who has always been well-known for its cameos, with the cream and the curd of Britain's acting talent having appeared somewhere along the way. The new *Who* is no different, with Peter Capaldi, Richard Wilson, Simon Callow, Zoë Wannamaker, Pauline Collins, Anthony Head, Roger Lloyd Pack, Don Warrington, Maureen Lipman, Marc Warren, Peter Kay, Roy Marsden, and a host of other recognisable faces joining the Doctor this time around, not least, of course, a certain one-off companion for the 2007 Christmas special, Kylie Minogue.

'If you think of *Doctor Who* as daffy and camp and funny, that's because you're an adult. To a child, it's none of those things; it's deadly serious and it's frightening. If *Doctor Who* doesn't supply a couple of decent scares and shocks, it's not doing its job.' – Steven Moffat, in the May 2006 edition of the *Radio Times*.

And of course, as of writing, the Doctor is in the middle of a 'gap year' which will see a hand-over of the reins in more ways than one. Moffat himself is set to take over the role of show runner from Russell T. Davis, while David Tennant is poised to regenerate into the rather young-looking Matt Smith (most notably seen in Ben Richards's rather excellent *Party Animals*) and the relatively unknown Karen Gillan (who played the Soothsayer in James Moran's 'Fires of Pompeii' episode) set to play his new companion, Amy Pond.

4

THE BODY ELECTRIC (WE CAN REBUILD YOU)

The Six Million Dollar Man,
The Amazing Spider-Man,
Max Headroom

THE SIX MILLION DOLLAR MAN (1974-1978)

Before running at super-charged slow-motion speed into American television history as a weekly series, *The Six Million Dollar Man* began life in 1973 as a made-for-TV movie adapted from Martin Caidin's novel *Cyborg*. Both the novel and the film chronicle the origin story of the 'world's first bionic man', beginning with the crash of an experimental aircraft and the catastrophic injuries inflicted upon its pilot, Steve Austin.

Following the catastrophic accident and with Austin's life hanging in the balance, the US government steps in, bringing with it the means to carry out a revolutionary operation to restore the stricken test pilot to perfect health. Six million dollars of top secret technology replace the legs, arm, and left eye Austin has lost. The operation is a rousing success, making him whole once more, but has losing so much of what once made him human robbed Austin of his humanity? It is a question which cannot be pondered for long, as everything comes with a price. In short order, Austin finds himself beholden to the government which has saved his life and now expects him to repay that debt by going to work for them, employing his new bionic limbs and their inherent abilities while acting as an undercover intelligence agent.

The TV-movie version of Caidin's original novel, titled *The Six Million Dollar Man*, was a ratings hit in the spring of 1973, prompting two follow-up films later that same year and ultimately spawning the weekly series which ran from January 1974 until March 1978. The series launched a spin-off, *The Bionic Woman*, which aired from January 1976 to May 1978, and returned bigger, better, and faster in 2007, as well as three made-for-TV 'reunion films', the first of which aired more than a decade after both series ended their respective runs.

While not the first or even the earliest depiction of a cyborg – the fusion of a human with mechanical enhancements or even replacements for organic components – in genre fiction, it can be argued that Steve Austin represents one of the first mainstream interpretations of the concept in American pop culture. Caidin's

Combining seventies chic and super-strength – Lee Majors
as cyborg superhero Colonel Steve Austin.

novel has even been cited as a kind of forerunner to the 'cyberpunk' sub-genre of science fiction literature so popular in the 1980s and 1990s. Given its focus on cybernetics and the physical and psychological effects on the person receiving such enhancements, *Cyborg* definitely shares some lineage with one of cyberpunk's basic recurring themes; that of society's growing dependence on technology as well as the ever-blurring line separating humans from the machines they wield. The book also features more than a bit of the cynicism against technology, the government, and society in general which would later become a staple of many cyberpunk stories. While some of this is present in the first telefilm – albeit in a somewhat watered-down fashion – such themes all but disappeared by the time the weekly *The Six Million Dollar Man* series premiered.

Naturally, there were many other changes as the concept evolved from the novel toward the heroic exploits stamped indelibly into the minds of so many children who grew up watching Steve Austin every week. Though the basic premise of Austin's crash, disfigurement, and bionic 'rebirth' remain intact, it is worth noting the distinct differences, not just in the storyline but also the characters – in including their individual motivations – as much of these underwent changes for the series.

In the novel, Dr Rudy Wells is a friend of Austin's who – along with another doctor, Michael Killian – has also been conducting experimental research into bionics. After Austin's crash, Wells is essentially given a blank cheque by the government to carry out the initial operations which will replace Austin's lost organic components with prototypical versions of the highly advanced prosthetics Wells himself has laboured to create over the years. Naturally, the government – in the form of Oscar Goldman representing a special, clandestine organisation known as the Office of Strategic Operations (later renamed the Office of Scientific Information) – has grand plans for Austin if the procedure is a success. Goldman and his superiors see great potential in what they hope might be the first of many cybernetically-enhanced agents who can be used to devastating effect in the ongoing fight against America's enemies.

Unlike the laidback Oscar Goldman whom Austin befriends as the series progresses, the character is portrayed much differently in *Cyborg*. Indeed, it is explicitly stated that the OSO has been observing Wells's work for some time and is simply waiting for the opportune moment to step in, including, apparently, the delivery of just the right 'volunteer' to act as a test subject for the unproven surgical procedures. When Goldman briefs Wells and Killian on the OSO's intentions, he is well aware of Austin's background and experiences, deeming him the perfect candidate for this new project. He is a stereotypical government bureaucrat, ever watchful of the large sums of money being spent on Austin and making sure the investment is a worthy one.

This characterisation is carried off in even more cold-hearted fashion in the first telefilm, where Goldman is replaced by a similar character, Oliver Spencer (who is never seen again). As the movie begins, Spencer is briefing a group of government officials that the notion of creating a cyborg has been on the table for some time.

Massively popular, The Six Million Dollar Man *extensively used slow-motion sequences to depict Steve Austin's prodigious leaps and other feats of strength.*

'Gentlemen, we can rebuild him. We have the technology. We have the capability to build the world's first bionic man. Steve Austin will be that man. Better than he was before. Better, stronger, faster.'

He only needs the right candidate on which to perform the costly, experimental procedure which will produce his new super weapon. When asked whether he will simply wait for a volunteer – referred to in stark terms as 'raw materials' – Spencer coldly observes that, 'Accidents happen all the time. We'll just start with scrap.' Later, he tells Austin that he would have preferred a robot to a flesh and blood man – thereby freeing him from worrying about emotions or doubts which might cloud his newest agent's judgement while on some dangerous assignment. In Spencer's eyes, being given a cyborg is a compromise he has to accept due to the limitations of current technology. At the end of the film, he even suggests to Dr Wells that Austin be kept sedated between assignments, as though he were nothing more than a tool to be returned to its storage bin until needed again.

Interestingly, Spencer's attitude and even Goldman's comparably reserved approach as demonstrated in the novel represents another common thread between *Cyborg* and the cyberpunk genre it predates: That of a cold, cruel state seeing its citizens as nothing more than tools. It was not a unique notion when the first movie was produced or even when Caidin wrote his novel, and a very similar premise drives 1987's *Robocop*. A film with definite roots in cyberpunk, *Robocop* features corporate puppet masters seeking to develop a cybernetically-enhanced police officer as a means of combating the ever-escalating crime rates of near-future Detroit. One opportunistic young executive puts the controversial plan into motion when an ideal candidate is presented in the form of Alex Murphy, a cop who is literally all but shot to pieces during an encounter with a vicious gang of criminals. Nearly all of Murphy's human body is replaced with a mechanical substitute that renders him practically invulnerable, and a computer embedded within his skull allows him to interface directly with other computer databases. Murphy is more machine than man now, but somewhere in the tangle of mechanisms and wiring lay his memories and perhaps even his soul, if only he can find it. The Steve Austin of *Cyborg* as well as the three telefilms is plagued by similar doubts, even as he and his bionically-enhanced body are drafted into covert government service.

The concept is also starkly present in 2007's re-imagined *Bionic Woman*, which borrows the title character, basic premise, and little else from its 1970s predecessor. In this version, a more sinister set of benefactors have bestowed state-of-the-art cybernetics upon the mangled body of Jaime Sommers. On the surface, the group's motives appear genuine and pure – employing cutting-edge technology as they fight to stop 'rogue organisations from ending civilisation as we know it', though at the time of this writing, the new series has only aired a handful of episodes. Still, it has already become glaringly apparent that the organisation behind Jaime's bionic rebirth is pursuing an agenda which was in place long before her actual involvement.

Perhaps the greatest changes from *Cyborg* to *The Six Million Dollar Man* occurred with Steve Austin himself, not just in the abilities provided by his bionic limbs but also in his overall character. Some things remain consistent, of course, namely that he is an Air Force colonel, former astronaut and even one of the few men to walk on the moon (in the first film, Austin is portrayed as a civilian test pilot working for NASA, though his backstory still includes being an astronaut and moonwalker). The details of the crash are largely the same, as are the extent of Austin's injuries.

The novel depicts Austin as more sarcastic and cynical, and during the missions he undertakes he uses his newfound abilities with utter, even brutal lethality. He is only assigned a single mission in the film, before which he makes it clear that he has no wish to kill anyone, though he does so before the assignment ends. It happens again during early episodes of the series, becoming an increasingly rare occurrence thereafter. As the series progresses, and possibly as a result of the character's increasing popularity with children, Austin is often shown devising means of avoiding unnecessary casualties.

Other changes for the series include the capabilities inherent in his bionic components. First, and for the simple reason that actor Lee Majors is right-handed, Steve Austin receives a bionic replacement for his right arm rather than his left. His arm is stronger and possesses a wider range of motion and sensory perception; his legs propel him faster and for longer periods, and also allow him to leap great distances and heights.

The most drastic changes are with Austin's bionic eye. In the novel, it is made clear that nothing can be done to restore the vision lost with his left eye. Instead, the bionic replacement is a miniaturised camera which can be removed from the socket, and which Austin activates by pressing a hidden control under the skin on the side of his head. The first film indicates that his new eye will allow him, in the words of Rudy Wells, 'to not only approximate, but conceivably transcend normal vision'. This is shown to a much greater degree as the series progresses, with Austin's eye possessing such features as telescopic zoom, infrared vision, and thermal imaging. While not used in the series, a laser emitter is added in Martin Caidin's sequel novels to the original *Cyborg*, a feature later incorporated into the bionic replacement eye given to his son, Michael, in 1987's *The Return of the Six Million Dollar Man and the Bionic Woman*.

Also noteworthy are the features given to Austin's cybernetic limbs in the novel which are not translated to the series. In the book, it is illustrated that the bionics can be augmented with mission-specific accessories, such as for his first assignment which requires him to manoeuvre underwater. One of Austin's legs is fitted with a self-contained oxygen tank, and collapsible swim fins are constructed into his feet. For his arm, the middle finger on his bionic hand can be removed and replaced with a dart gun capable of killing an enemy in seconds. Given the aversion to killing demonstrated by Austin in the series – he rarely is seen brandishing a firearm, for example – choosing not to incorporate this feature makes particular sense.

The Six Million Dollar Man is responsible for introducing a number of pop culture hallmarks, such as its slow-motion action sequences and the familiar sound effects that accompany Austin's bionic feats. The series' opening credits and narration are among the most recognised in television, often providing fodder for homage or parody in commercials or other series. These and other familiar tropes were formed early on and only expanded as the series progressed. Austin is portrayed as the typical seventies action hero; the 'good guy' who rarely wrestles with ethical or moral questions. We know when he enters any situation that his bionics will almost always give him the advantage.

The producers, perhaps worried about finding themselves with a hero who 'could not lose', were quick to devise ways for villains to overcome Austin's superior abilities. In 'Population: Zero', the first episode of the weekly series, we learn that extreme cold hampers the functionality of the bionic components, to the point of incapacitating Austin. Later episodes pit him against adversaries who possess comparable or even greater strength – robots, another bionic man, a runaway space probe, and even Bigfoot! Such developments may even have come about out of a desire to find yet another way of demonstrating that the superpowered Steve Austin remained – at least in part – a man, hopefully still identifiable to the very human audience watching his adventures unfold on their television screens.

Any discussion of *The Six Million Dollar Man* is incomplete without comparing the concepts introduced in the series, as well as in Caidin's original novel, to reality. The commonly accepted medical definition of 'bionics' refers to the replacement or augmentation of organs or limbs with mechanical components that provide similar or perhaps even superior function. While most of Steve Austin's bionic abilities have yet to be realised, a few medical applications of actual bionics are in use today, such as cochlear implants to assist the hearing impaired, and artificial hearts far more sophisticated than the models originally created in the 1960s. Advances in the field of prosthetics have produced artificial limbs that look increasingly lifelike and provide ever greater levels of control, comfort, and functionality, including the ability to act upon instructions from the brain. Thirty years ago, the idea of a bionic arm or leg that functioned as well as or even better than the original limb was science fiction. Thirty years from now, it may well be a common medical procedure for any amputee.

No matter the differing versions of the character as presented on the page or the television screen, and regardless of whether real-world technology has either refuted or outpaced the fictional concepts at the heart of *The Six Million Dollar Man*, Steve Austin still represents one of the iconic genre heroes of the 1970s.

THE AMAZING SPIDER-MAN (1977-1979)

While Sam Raimi's trilogy of *Spider-Man* movies has dominated the box-office every summer since the first instalment hit theatres, it's a long way from the first treatment of Marvel Comics' most popular superhero in TV or film. While various channels have aired a number of different animated Spider-Man shows, before the new films Spider-Man only had one live-action program: *The Amazing Spider-Man.*

The show debuted in 1977 and ran only fourteen episodes before being cancelled in 1979. At the time, CBS (which broadcast the show) also had shows about other superheroes – Captain America, Wonder Woman, the Hulk, and even Dr Strange – in the works or on the air, which made it seem like superheroes were finally going to become a part of the mainstream media in a way they never had before.

If that sounds familiar, it's no coincidence. In the past few years, we've seen a number of comic book-inspired films and shows, with Raimi's *Spider-Man* films firmly at the head of the pack. The surge of the seventies, though, was doomed.

By today's standards – and perhaps those of 30 years ago – the show was awful. The main problem arose from the fact that special effects technology of the seventies had no way to come close to accurately depicting a character with Spider-Man's powers on the screen. The opening sequence of the show featured Nicholas Hammond (or more likely stuntman Fred Waugh) in the Spider-Man suit, being hauled up the side of a building with wires. The actor had to paw his limbs at the side of the place in a desperate and failed attempt to make it look like he even had a grip on the thing.

Similarly, coming up with a convincing shot of Spidey swinging across Manhattan on his webs proved impossible. While the show did feature a few such sequences, they cost a great deal to create and were dangerous. Still, they should get credit for trying to pull off such feats in an era long before computer-generated imagery could make viewers believe that Tobey Maguire could flip, spin, and swing himself effortlessly throughout a gorgeously lit urban landscape.

Today, the show stands as a sparkling example of how film and TV production just wasn't ready for superheroes in the seventies. The effects were laughable, and for a TV show trying to take itself seriously, as a primetime drama, that was the kiss of death. The way Spider-Man walked up walls reminded viewers of the *Batman* TV show, which had made a joke out of the tricks used for such climbing years earlier.

If anything made the show great, it's that the producers had the guts to try making it despite the obvious hurdles.

The show didn't adhere exactly to the comic book that spawned it. The only comic-book characters that appeared in the show were Spider-Man/Peter Parker, J. Jonah Jameson, Aunt May, and Robbie Robertson, who only showed up in the pilot. Peter's Uncle Ben, who gives him the renowned line 'With great power comes great responsibility,' never shows up, nor do any of Peter's long line of girlfriends.

Despite that, the show stayed more faithful to the comics than most of the other live-action Marvel Comics-based shows of the era, like those of Captain America or the Hulk. The main character and his costume and powers were mostly the same, for instance, although the TV Spidey wore his webshooters and belt outside of his suit for some reason.

At the time the TV show debuted, Spider-Man as a character was only fifteen-years-old. That's fairly young, especially when you consider what an international icon Spidey's become. Now that he has 45 years under his belt, he seems almost as much of a classic as Superman or Batman, who have far longer publication histories.

At 45, Spider-Man is older than most of his core demographic. To the kids and young adults who follow his exploits in comics, on film, or on one of the animated shows, Spider-Man has always existed and probably always will. In 1977, though, that just wasn't so. The producers of the show, who were all far older than Spidey, didn't have as much respect for him as Raimi and his crew. Because of that, they felt comfortable tweaking the character and his setting to fit their own tastes or those they perceived in the general public.

The main thing the producers didn't change – and one of the few things that Raimi fiddled with – was the origin of Spider-Man's powers. In the comics, perennial high-school nerd Peter Parker visits a scientific research lab and is bitten by a radioactive spider. In Raimi's films, the spider has been genetically altered instead.

Criticised by character co-creator Stan Lee, The Amazing Spider-Man *was typical of the clumsy adaptations of comic-book superheroes produced during the 1970s.*

In the seventies, the public didn't understand radiation very well, and because of that Stan Lee and Steve Ditko (who created Spider-Man) could work radiation into the source of Spider-Man's power. The premise is, of course, ludicrous.

First, any amount of radiation large enough to trigger some sort of alteration in a spider would likely fry it at the same time. Second, it's absurd to think the spider could transmit its abilities to Peter through a bite no matter how much radiation it may have soaked up. Third, if the spider did somehow inject radioactive venom into Spider-Man, it likely would have killed him, much like former KGB agent Alexander Litvinenko, who was poisoned with a radioactive isotope in November of 2006.

Still, it's a comic book, and readers generally forgive such silly explanations by way of getting straight to the story. Still, Lee had created or co-created a number of heroes who'd gotten their powers from radiation, including the Hulk and the Fantastic Four. Clearly he was tapping into something in the air in the late sixties and early seventies.

What Lee tapped into was, of course, fear. In the 1940s, radiation was slated to be the saviour of the world. It promised free, clean energy, and – in the hands of the right people – an end to war. In the tests for the first atomic bomb, witnesses stood and watched it from a supposedly safe distance with little or no protection. They just didn't know any better.

As time wore on and people learned more about radiation, though, public impressions of it grew less and less rosy. We discovered that nuclear power meant nuclear waste, and the threat of nuclear war between the US and the Soviet Union meant radiation was never far from anyone's mind.

In many Marvel comics, Lee used radiation not as a horror but a trigger for the most amazing things. It became a touchstone for the origins of the superheroes of the day. Radiation became not something to fear but to study, learn from, and control. After all, if it gave these superheroes such amazing powers, perhaps in the real world we could make it do something incredible for us too.

The show debuted more than a year before the worst nuclear accident in US history. The incident at Three Mile Island happened in March of 1979. Perhaps it's no coincidence that *The Amazing Spider-Man* went off the air later that year. Even as part of a superhero's origin, radiation may not have seemed all that cool anymore.

Of course, Lee didn't go about fear-mongering. Quite the opposite. While someone else might have made a cautionary tale about radiation and its effects, he made it into a source of great power and even great fun.

As the saying goes, 'With great power comes great responsibility.' Those were Lee's words, and he might have been talking about nuclear power as much as any superpowers.

Despite all that, Lee is on record as having hated the TV show, considering it too childish. As publisher of Marvel Comics (which published Spider-Man's adventures then and still does so to this day), he had a strong incentive not to say anything, but he could not hold his tongue. Perhaps that's because it didn't fit his original vision so well.

Despite all the problems people had with *The Amazing Spider-Man*, now and then, a lack of ratings wasn't the reason the show was cancelled. In its debut season, it ranked in the top 20 shows, higher even than *The Incredible Hulk*. However, the Hulk's show rated higher among adults, making for better demographics, and it continued on after Spidey's show faded away.

CBS may have feared becoming branded as the superhero network too. With so many different superhero shows on the air at once – almost all from CBS – the executives there were wary of taking on any more.

The reason for such cautiousness comes from a number of different sources. First, there's likely a limited number of people willing to watch a superhero show over, say, a police procedural. If you've cornered the market for such an audience with a blockbuster hit (like *The Incredible Hulk*), you're tempted to chase after more people with other shows, to monopolise their time and attention as best you can.

At the same time, you have to take care that you don't cannibalise your hit show's fans by having them choose the new show over the old. If that happens, you could end up with two shows performing at only a mediocre level rather than owning one big hit.

When the time came to renew *The Amazing Spider-Man*, the executives at CBS commissioned only a series of specials to be aired at various times, filling holes in their regular schedule. This could only mean doom for the show. In the times before TiVo and the internet, shuffling a show's schedule around like that meant that even its greatest fans might have a difficult time tracking down the right time at which they might expect to be able to watch a new episode.

For all that, the people who got to see the show generally enjoyed it. The first season was a bit goofy, which made it perfect for kids. However, with CBS chasing an older demographic, they tinkered with the show in the second season, gearing it for an older audience.

If Sam Raimi and his crew ever saw *The Amazing Spider-Man*, they certainly learned from the show's mistakes. As fans of the comic, they understood the parts of the character that make him great, and they avoided making changes just for the sake of putting their own fingerprints all over Spider-Man's legacy.

The core of Spider-Man, beyond the great power and responsibility, past the webslinging, far after the nutty powers and crazy villains comes down to one thing: Peter Parker.

Parker starts out as the ultimate high-school nerd, a hero to none but his elderly uncle and aunt. He's isolated, an outcast, a loner.

When he gets his powers, he thinks everything will change, but he quickly finds out just how wrong he is. His uncle dies soon afterward, due partly to Parker's negligence, and due to his aunt's weak heart he decides to keep his superpowers hidden from the world behind Spider-Man's red mask.

The principal The Amazing Spider-Man *cast –
Ellen Bry (Julie Masters), Nicholas Hammond (Peter
Parker/Spider-Man), Robert F. Simon (J. Jonah
Jameson), and Chip Fields (Rita Conway).*

So, the powers do little to help him in the real world, other than to provide him with an escape. But it's not much of an escape. Because he is such a hero, he refuses to flee from even the greatest challenges, and he often finds himself beaten nearly to death for his efforts. Only his will to go on, his refusal to surrender to conflicts both without and within, keeps him going.

Still, he has doubts. Spider-Man was the first superhero with delusions of humanity. Rather than being a millionaire playboy or a strange visitor from another planet, he's a nerd from Queens who just can't seem to catch a break. In that sense, he's far more human and heroic than the vast majority of other superheroes. After all, if you can turn back time by flying around the planet backward, what sort of problems might present you with a true challenge? There was no kryptonite to bring him down, no super-weapons created by an industrious butler. No, Spider-Man was one of us, a fallible teenager struggling to be the superhero the world needed him to be.

The show got this right, although it doesn't nail it on the head as squarely as Raimi or the original comics do. Parker is the guy who's secretly the coolest man on the planet. He just chooses not to let anyone else know it. Not because he's ashamed or humble or shy. He just wants to make sure the people he loves don't get hurt. He puts their welfare before his own happiness, as heroic an act as punching out Doc Ock, for sure.

The Amazing Spider-Man burned bright and fast, and snuffed itself out far too soon. Given a chance and the time to mature into the show it could have become, it might have found its voice more strongly, stated its beliefs more clearly, and become the kind of classic drama it had the potential to be.

Despite its cancellation, the show proved that there was an audience out there in mainstream America for a different kind of superhero. Until then, we'd mostly been fed stories about superheroes that were nearly unstoppable, but for one, silly weakness.

With Spider-Man, we finally get a superhero whose weaknesses come from within. It isn't about meteors from dead planets or the colour yellow. He can't run away from himself.

The Amazing Spider-Man was one of the first steps in bringing this kind of superhero, this particular kind of noble character, into mass-market entertainment. It may have struggled to find itself and even stumbled along the way, but without this attempt, we likely would not have seen the highly regarded Raimi films.

Now that computer-generated special effects have finally caught up with the imagination of Stan Lee and Steve Ditko, we can have a satisfying version of Spider-Man up on the silver screen. Fortunately, in the intervening years, we've also had the time for creative souls to grow up on a steady diet of comic books. This means that they not only have the tools to create something great – something faithful to the original ideals of the comics they loved so much – but they have the love of the subject matter required to pull it off.

MAX HEADROOM (1987)

Max Headroom: the ultimate clown – or more accurately, ultimate court jester of 1980s Network Television. He never did much except show up: in the cyberpunk world created for him, no one particularly wanted him and his writers seem to have had a hard time figuring out what to do with him, while in the world of 'real' television he introduced music videos, participated in some spectacularly creepy ads for New Coke, chatted with David Letterman and generally acted like those celebrities (think Zsa Zsa Gabor or Whoopi Goldberg, or in more modern parlance, Paris Hilton and Kevin Federline) who are eternally famous even though no one can quite remember why. And yet we love him.

Was he computer-generated, or was he real – and what does 'real' mean when you're talking about these kinds of things? When New York columnist Tom Waters called Madonna and Max Headroom the Yin and Yang of the 1980s, he enunciated a genuine truth. Madonna was famous for telling everyone how great it was to be superficial, greedy and in charge (Gordon Gecko's famous 'greed is good' speech from *Wall Street* is largely a guy-language paraphrase of what she had already said for the ladies in 'Material Girl'). Max Headroom was famous for nothing – and proud of it. Madonna went on to change her looks and her message 50 times: that was part of her game. Max never changed at all – because he was perfect right out of the box, *sui generis*.

The story goes like this: back in the 1970s, popular art aspired to great things. Movie studios produced big heavy pictures filled with lots of film-school fodder: *Godfather, Deer Hunter, Apocalypse Now*. TV followed the same route with the invention of the miniseries: think *Roots*, and *Shogun*'s Richard Chamberlain striding across Japan in a kimono and clean-hippie beard. And nothing epitomised the aspirations of the seventies like rock: the concept album, the pyrotechnic concert, the multi-disc set. It more or less sums up that decade to say that it was a time when the fourth side of the two-disc soundtrack to *Saturday Night Fever* included a minor epic called 'Night on Disco Mountain'.

It all imploded in the early 1980s, and the culprit was the VHS video cassette. *Supertrain* and *Heaven's Gate*, the most expensive television show and movie ever made up to that time, were catastrophic flops. First the porn studios – those bellweathers of the movie business, whose late-seventies excesses are chronicled in *Boogie Nights* – figured out that cheap, slick and dumb would sell just as readily as expensive and artsy. Out went the film cameras and in came the flat, plastic glare of video. The major studios turned to making to one-trick hits like *Flashdance* and *Footloose*. Punk was still busy sticking its stinky middle finger in the eye of pop music's artistic pretensions, while Andy Warhol, making millions from his portraits of Hollywood celebs, famously opined that business had become the greatest form of art. The sixties generation shucked their bell-bottoms, bongs and idealism, put on power suits and abandoned higher goals for the quest of the Almighty Dollar. Selling out became the gold standard of success, and 'Video Killed the Radio Star'. MTV ruled the air waves, and the VHS tape – the true icon of the age if ever there was one – became the sign of everything slick, quick, flash, and most important: profitable.

There's a third part of the mythology: the end of the age of innocence. That's utter crap of course. The seventies were hardly innocent – just ask anyone who was there. But in the years after 1980 a person could be forgiven for thinking that so far as the world situation was concerned, the stakes had gone higher, or perhaps that the game had already been lost. In America the so-called 'double-dip' recession of 1979-82 was followed by continuing failure in all the stable old breadbasket industries: cars, steel, clothing. In Washington, Ronald Reagan was rattling the American sabre, advocating space-based missiles and famously bragging on television about nuking Russia. NATO and the Soviet armies faced each other on a hair trigger across the heart of Europe. While in Britain, the economic policies of Margaret Thatcher had brought post-industrial chaos, massive unemployment and a grim sense of terminal malaise. People on both sides of the Atlantic feared for their jobs, and consequently fetishised what Bruce Bethke – who coined the term 'cyberpunk' in 1983 – called the 'ethical vacuity and technical fluency' of the young who could hack the system:

the kids with their skills, the junk bond traders snorting coke through hundred-dollar bills off the dashboard of a Mercedes, anyone who got 'Money for Nothing', as Dire Straits so eloquently put it.

And in the midst of it all, Britain's Channel 4 wanted a new Vee-Jay.

Max Headroom was a character before he was a show. In classic eighties style he was marketed first, made afterward. Channel 4 television – only on-air since 1982 and wrestling with an uncomfortable mandate to (a) cater for minority viewers (not necessarily denoting racial minorities); (b) to produce programmes that could not be seen on the other three channels and still remain commercially viable – was trying to devise a home-grown substitute for America's MTV: a programme to celebrate such deathless British video classics as Intaferon's 'Steamhammer Sam' and Duran Duran's 'Wild Boys'. MTV – which actually showed music videos in those days – had imitated the presentation format of Top-40 radio, with the videos introduced by perky functionaries like Alan Hunter, the perpetually sweaty J.J. Jackson and the celebrated Martha Quinn.

Channel 4 wanted something a bit classier than that, but still appealing to the younger set. The only trouble was – as Rocky Morton, one of the creative team, later put it – 'What could be more boring than trying to link music videos together?' Intrigued by the newly current idea of virtual reality (a term coined by Damien Broderick in his 1982 novel *The Judas Mandala*, although tech guru Jaron Lanier also took credit for it) and recent advances in computer animation, Morton and his co-creator Annabel Jankel decided on a digitally animated host, a VR talking head who could jabber and crack jokes between the videos just like the Americans, but who looked really, radically different and somehow more upscale: clean-cut, slick, yet strange. The central irony was that in the early 1980s, nobody except the US Defence Department could afford the computer power to generate a live, interactive image of a human being on television, so Max Headroom began life as a fraud: a flesh-and-blood actor, Matt Frewer, dolled up in a latex body suit and face-hugger mask designed by a Royal Academy sculptor, John Humphreys. Max was a computer graphic in drag, so to speak.

Max had no body: his slick black suit and narrow tie – perhaps modelled on the suits then fashionable in early Eighties minimalist rock – only extended about halfway down Frewer's chest. He appeared on television, backgrounded by some Amiga screen-saver animation and 'actionated' by frenetic video editing to give him his jerky twitch and repetitive 'M-M-M-Max Headroom!' stammer. Throughout the entire run of the show, he was always played by Frewer. John Humphreys later remarked that people were so convinced Max was 'really' digital, the design team won a 1985 British Film Association award for computer animation. In fact the award was for Technical Craft, which covers the makeup; even BAFTA is not that quite that dense.

To give Max an origin and a backstory, Morton and Jankel directed a 53-minute made-for-TV film, *20 Minutes into the Future*, which premiered in April 1985.

Here the cyberpunk comes in. For no obvious reason – unless it was to justify the existence of a living, responsive animated being in a computer network – they set the story in a near-future London. The film's ambience, which would come to typify 'cyberpunk' in American minds, is really more an example of reign-of-Thatcher British social satire: dirt everywhere, the economy in a shambles, a hostile public culture, incomprehensible technology, gigantic corporations and the huge edifices they build, extremes of wealth and poverty, despair.

Timbuk 3 may have been singing 'The future's so bright, I gotta wear shades,' but in the Britain of 1985, the future did not look bright at all. In *20 Minutes* interiors and exteriors alike swim in excessive shadow, wires dangle everywhere, video screens flicker incomprehensible junk at people through clouds of haze and smoke. No one seems to know how to turn on a light, or an air conditioner. This style of setting, which more or less erupted into public consciousness in Ridley Scott's 1982 film *Blade Runner* and reached its high water mark in Terry Gilliam's *Brazil* a few years later, would continue to scream 'dystopian future' in dozens of movies and TV shows all through the 1980s, finally reaching its last gasp in those corporate-fascistic AT&T commercials that asked viewers, 'Ever tucked your child in from a pay phone? You will!'

The plot of *20 Minutes* is nothing much. Frewer – out of his Headroom mask – plays Edison Carter, a crusading television news reporter who discovers that his own network, the fictitious global media giant Channel 23, is inserting subliminal advertising called 'blipverts' into its programming, increasing market share while causing older and more sedentary viewers to spontaneously explode. Carter goes on a quest for the truth and hijinks ensue. Amanda Pays (as Carter's partner Theora Jones), does the best she can with a role that had been traditional since World War Two, when female operators watched for incoming planes on the screens of early radar: the geek girl who sits among machinery, performing technical services while her man is out in the field doing something heroic. Nicholas Grace's overacting adds amusement to the otherwise uninteresting role of network boss Grossman, whose shaggy, greasy henchmen 'Brueghel' and 'Mahler' make one think of roadies for Metallica.

Paul Spurrier plays the most interesting character in the show: Bryce Lynch, amoral teenage genius, inventor of the blipverts and apparently the only technically capable person employed by Channel 23. If it seems strange now to think of a teenage computer geek, stereotypically an anti-establishment character, working in the bowels of a gigantic corporation, remember that the 'hacker' concept had not really come to public consciousness by 1985. Lynch dresses against type: wearing a neat, private-school haircut, a crisp polyester shirt and an open sport jacket reminiscent of Don Johnson's attire in *Miami Vice*. One scene – later cut for safety (and perhaps other) reasons – shows him programming his mini-computer while relaxing naked in the bathtub. Despite the fact that computer terminals and keyboards appear everywhere in *20 Minutes* (including some elaborate scientific keyboards that

Despite its 1980s computer wizardry, Max Headroom *was portrayed by actor Matt Frewer wearing a specially constructed latex mask.*

would be collector's items today), no one ever uses a mouse. According to rumour, the show's designers thought the mouse such a clunky instrument that they decided it would be unlikely to exist in the near future.

True to form, Max Headroom himself – as the uploaded personality of Carter, recorded into a digital system designed by Lynch – doesn't make much of an appearance until the last third of the film, and does almost nothing to advance the plot. A later, 83-minute release attempted to cover this deficiency, adding in more Max footage as well as an embarrassing bedroom scene between Carter and Jones. *20 Minutes* enjoyed some modest critical acclaim, but in the end its real purpose was to explain Max's subsequent appearance as video host of *The Max Headroom Show*. That program – engagingly hosted by Max with his jittering, slack-jawed babble and wise-cracks, continued for several years, during which time Max also made the talk show rounds, appeared in a video by Art of Noise and famously shilled for New Coke – advising kids that they were now "Cokeologists" and verbally berating a sweaty Pepsi can.

This, of course, smacks of something that no one seems to want to talk about openly. The bulging, dilated eyes, twitchy mannerisms, and h-h-hyperactive demeanour all conflate to make a pretty convincing parody of a rich yuppie, deep in

In April 1987, Max Headroom *hit the cover of* Newsweek.

the throes of a cocaine jag. Whether Morton, Jankel and Humphreys realised this is pretty much a matter of supposition – and all, of course, would deny it vociferously. But, being in show-biz in the mid-1980s, was it possible to remain unaware that Max could be read as the caricature of a cokehead? There is, after all, a long tradition of entertainment people trying to slip naughty subtexts past the censor into supposedly respectable shows, and an equally long tradition of big commercial operations, ever in pursuit of the flickering attention of the young, appropriating images from the cultural fringe into the mainstream (think body piercing; think drift racing). Perhaps the dodginess of the character is one reason why Max has never had a comeback, while today's media giants scrape the bottom of their creative barrels to resuscitate old properties. Or perhaps it's just that Max's time has not yet come around. Even ardent fan James Gifford acknowledges that 'to be fair, Max Headroom is about as eighties as an eighties phenomenon can be'. Yet the accusation of drug use was never openly levelled against Max in his heyday, and perhaps we should not make it now.

In 1987 the Lorimar Corporation bought Max's contract (so to speak), and produced fourteen one-hour episodes of *Max Headroom* for US television, to air on ABC. Thus did cyberpunk come to American primetime. Frewer and Pays reprised their roles, with Bryce Lynch – played by Chris Young in huge red-framed 'smart kid' glasses – now working on the side of good. The episodes were reasonably well-written and filmed, with interesting and sometimes prescient speculations about the rise of global media corporations, medical ethics, the decay of public culture and the like, though framed in a more sentimental, more optimistic and – let's face it – more American argot. The setting shifted from London to a down tempo version of *Blade Runner*-esque Los Angeles (though the show takes pains to avoid revealing the actual location – a neat trick in a cyberpunk world of supposedly ubiquitous satellite coverage and remote sensing). Channel 23 became Network 23 and in true eighties style, its biggest client – the Zik-Zak Corporation – morphed into a Japanese conglomerate ruled by an elderly samurai. Edison and Bryce no longer pretended to speak with British accents. The smoky clouds and stacks of bulky computer monitors remained, all flickering with Amiga CGI, but the American episodes lack the sense of gloom that suffuse the British pilot. Network 23 may be a dysfunctional family but it's still a family, and one gets the impression that despite all the trouble and cruelty in their world, the characters basically like being there.

And Max? Oddly enough for the show's title character, the poor guy continued to have little to do. The first couple of episodes are largely concerned with getting him under control, and after that he pops up from time to time on whatever monitor or TV set is available, occasionally spying in remote computer systems, sometimes commenting on what's going on, or making lame jokes. The writers seem to have been under a strain to give him a place in each episode, but despite their efforts Max gets few good lines. His monologues are strictly *Reader's Digest* joke page stand-up: 'You can always tell when a politician's lying – his lips move.' Sadly, nothing much is made of the fact that Max is, in some deep Jungian sense, the alter ego of brave, idealistic Edison Carter. They interact like guys who have known each other for a long time and that's about it, though in one particularly creepy scene, Max – who possesses most of Carter's memory but none of his inhibitions – shows Bryce Lynch the memory of Carter's first kiss. This has implications of the sort that make one think, 'Don't go there.'

Yet Max is inexplicably loved: by the other characters in the show (Bryce memorably hugs the TV after Max is rescued from deletion), and by fans who have kept his memory alive down through the years. Madonna changed because she had to: obsolescence was always nipping at her heels. But Max didn't need to change or even to be good at what he did, because the thing he was is something people needed and still need. In an age when television was dominated by three or four big networks, before the Web, before YouTube, before Mystery Science Theatre 3000, an age when everyone assumed as a matter of course that the masses were entirely passive consumers of video, the mere idea of an irreverent character or avatar bouncing up in the middle of someone else's show and commenting on it had an inherently subversive quality that people found naturally loveable. Will Max have a comeback? Better to ask, do we still need court jesters? Where are you, Max Headroom?

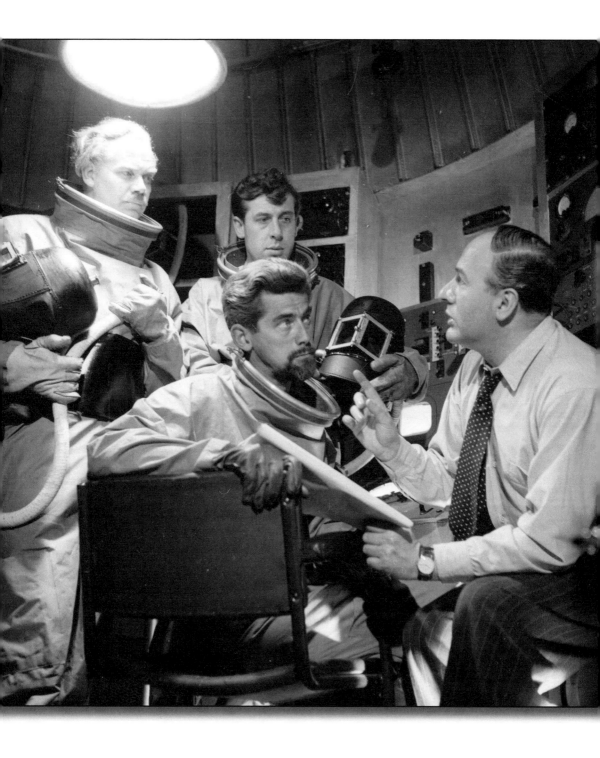

5 STRANGER THINGS HAPPEN

Quatermass, The Twilight Zone,
Kolchak: The Night Stalker, The Tomorrow People,
Charmed, Afterlife, Supernatural

QUATERMASS (1953-1955)

The 1950s were a time when television was still working out what it could *do*, what it was *capable* of. Admittedly the medium was constrained by the fact that most programmes were transmitted live, but more importantly the grammar had yet to be established: the use of cuts, of pans, of fades, of zooms. Drama on the small screen had begun by just having a cameraman pointing a single camera at a group of actors and a director saying 'Action!' – like watching a play from a seat in the auditorium. Some directors and producers on the single existing British TV channel – Auntie herself, the BBC – were content to let that be the template forever, but others – Rudolph Cartier for one – wanted to use things like cuts, close-ups, special effects and pre-recorded inserts in order to create something different. They wanted to innovate. And for that reason, the original BBC drama *The Quatermass Experiment* – produced and directed by Rudolph Cartier and written by Nigel Kneale – was, arguably, the most groundbreaking drama of its generation. It effectively set the pattern for all TV drama that was to follow it. Even now, watching *The X-Files* or any of the *Alien* movies, it's possible to see the glimmering thread that stretches all the way back to the 1950s, and a British rocket scientist in a tweed jacket fighting against incursions from a nightmarish, chaotic, almost Lovecraftian universe that would drive men mad if they ever got a good look at it . . .

The Quatermass Experiment was broadcast in six half-hour episodes during July and August of 1953, and was by no means Nigel Kneale's first TV work, but it was the one that got him noticed. Ironically, for something whose shadow would stretch so far and affect so many writers and directors in the future, the scripts were written in a hurry to fill a sudden gap in the BBC's schedule. 'I was still writing the serial when it began to be transmitted,' he told TV historian Andrew Pixley in a 1986 interview. 'I think I'd written four episodes when the first one was shown, and I wrote the remaining two while it was going out. So nobody really knew what the end was – even the production team, certainly not the actors, which made it more exciting

The Quatermass Experiment – *described by film historian Robert Simpson as*
'event television, emptying the streets and pubs for the six weeks of its duration'.

I suppose. The only people who were really in on the secret were Rudi Cartier and myself. The others had to take it on trust, which they were kind enough to do.'

The six episodes told the story of the first British space mission, and how it returns to Earth with two of its crew missing and the third, Victor Caroon, comatose. Hospitalised, he acts strangely, displaying personality traits belonging to his missing crewmates. He knocks a cactus to the floor in a fit of rage, and his body starts to absorb the plant, leaving his hand rough and spiny. Bernard Quatermass (played by Reginald Tate), in charge of the British space mission, realises the horrible truth: Victor has become contaminated by something out in space, and has somehow absorbed the other members of the rocket's crew. Victor goes on the run, with Quatermass and the Army in pursuit, but by the time he is cornered in Westminster Abbey he has changed into something truly alien, realised in a triumph of cheap special effects, by Kneale himself.

'The appearance of the monster in Westminster Abbey was my two hands,' he later revealed, 'stuck through a blow-up still of the interior of the Abbey . . . suitably dressed with gloves which I'd covered with a bit of vegetation and leather until they didn't look like hands any more and became a single monster.'

Quatermass II, two years later, was commissioned by the BBC following the success of the first serial and in a brave attempt to win viewers back from the recently launched independent TV channel (ITV). Although Reginald Tate had been cast again as Quatermass the actor died shortly before transmission, and John Robinson was thrown into the deep end instead. 'Unfortunately,' Kneale said later, 'just before we got to the second serial, Reggie Tate died, which was very, very tragic and saddened us very much, but I think if he'd continued to play the second and third and fourth and make various film versions, he would have been definitive in the role.' The 'II' of the title indicates not only that it's the second serial, but more importantly that *Quatermass* has moved on to a new design of rocket – one which has unfortunately been blowing up with alarming regularity. Disgraced, the professor accidentally stumbles across an alien plan to colonise the planet. Meteorites falling to earth contain creatures which then take over human hosts who then assist in the harvesting of more meteorites, leading to an increasing paranoia as Quatermass discovers that the people he is trying to warn are already under the control of the invaders.

'I think a number of things turned up in *Doctor Who* that have been pinched out of my stories,' Kneale later said. 'I know I switched on one day and was horrified to see practically an entire episode of one of mine stuck straight into *Doctor Who*!' He was probably referring to the first few episodes of the 1970 *Doctor Who* story 'Spearhead from Space', in which alien creatures in meteorites attempt to take over the world in a manner not dissimilar to that in *Quatermass II* – more evidence, if it were needed, that the things Kneale thought of first would crop up again and again in the history of TV and cinematic science fiction. Many episodes of *The X-Files*, for instance, deal in similar themes and images, and it was reported at one stage that

Kneale had been approached in the 1990s to write for that series, but refused.

Almost simultaneously with the transmission of *Quatermass II*, Hammer Films released their adaptation of the first serial under the title *The Quatermass Xperiment*. Though Hammer had been going since the mid-thirties it was still a relatively new British film production company and was, at the time, specialising in making film versions of popular TV serials such as *A Case For PC 49* (1951). Kneale was not pleased with the film, and particularly disliked the casting of American actor Brian Donlevy as Quatermass – a part Donlevy was to reprise in the 1957 Hammer version of *Quatermass II* (which was, at least, scripted by Nigel Kneale himself).

'The film versions that Hammer made used an American actor, Brian Donlevy, in the lead,' Kneale told TV historian Andrew Pixley (in the interview 'Behind the Dark Door') in 1986, 'because of contractual arrangements with the American distributors, and he was certainly my least favourite. He was then really on the skids and didn't care what he was doing. He took very little interest in the making of the films or in playing the part. It was a case of take the money and run. Or in the case of Mr Donlevy, waddle.'

Three years later, the BBC transmitted *Quatermass and the Pit* – unarguably the best of the serials. Although forced into casting John Robinson in *Quatermass II*, Kneale and Cartier now had more time to choose who they wanted as the urbane professor. They plumped for André Morell, a highly respected and versatile character actor who had previously appeared in the BBC's 1954 version of George Orwell's *Nineteen Eighty-Four* – adapted by Kneale and directed by Rudolph Cartier.

In *The Quatermass Experiment*, the alien force is accidentally brought back to Earth by an Earth rocket. In *Quatermass II* the alien force arrives uninvited, almost like a natural storm. In *Quatermass and the Pit* the force has been here all along – a crashed Martian craft which has been buried underground for thousands of years, only to be uncovered during the construction of a new underground train line (a topical choice at the time). And once uncovered, some remaining echo of the alien force starts to awaken buried race memories within anyone nearby.

Hammer Films adapted *Quatermass and the Pit* in 1967, commissioning Kneale again to write the script and casting bearded Scottish actor Andrew Kier as the title character (by then the fifth actor to play the role). The original TV version has been described as one of the best things ever made by the BBC, and the film version is one of the best horror films ever made full stop. The mounting sense of hysteria and the almost unstoppable nature of the Martian creatures – or what may be their ghosts – provides a textbook example of how to ratchet tension up to an almost unbearable level. Kneale's skills as a writer – helped here by Roy Ward Baker's directorial talent – have influenced at least two generations of writers since the film was released.

Kneale had intended *Quatermass and the Pit* to be the last appearance for the good professor. 'I didn't want to go on repeating because Professor Quatermass had already saved the world from ultimate destruction three times,' he said, 'and that seemed to me to be quite enough.'

But it wasn't. Kneale was approached by the BBC in 1965 to bring *Quatermass* back in a one-off TV play, and allegedly again in 1969 as a replacement for *Doctor Who*, which had just lost its lead actor for the second time (something that *Quatermass* kept surviving, of course). Kneale apparently refused, but was approached again by the BBC a few years later and finally said yes. 'I think it was commissioned by Ronnie Marsh, who was then in charge of serials,' Kneale later said, 'and Joe Waters was going to be the producer. It lingered through the summer and slowly died as a project.'

What the BBC abandoned, independent TV company Thames Television (through their subsidiary, Euston Films) commissioned in 1977, and aired in 1979 as the first programme after the end of an eleven-week ITV technicians' strike. The four-episode series, titled simply *Quatermass*, was a lavish affair costing more than £1 million (compared to the £18,000 or so that *Quatermass and the Pit* cost the BBC). As was traditional by now, a different actor was cast as Quatermass; although André Morell was still alive and still acting when production started, it was felt that actor Sir John Mills had more stature, and would pull in more viewers (Morell died before the series was transmitted). Again, Kneale decided not to repeat himself with the scripts, and derived a new way of having the alien force interact with humanity. Now it just lurks somewhere far out in space, snacking on large crowds at sporting events and other gatherings using a beam of energy.

'The major change,' Kneale revealed to Andrew Pixley, 'was that the BBC version would have been much more in the studio, whereas the Euston Films version was entirely shot on 35mm film with a great deal of it outside. Much more lavish than either the BBC or I had contemplated.' Later, he told interviewer Jack Kibble-White in 2003 that: 'It was originally for the BBC but they lost heart in it. They said it was too gloomy. Well, yes, it was supposed to be gloomy. Stripping the Earth of its population is a gloomy thought. But maybe it was just not destined to be jolly.'

Not destined to be jolly, and not destined to be cheap either. 'Euston Films spent a fortune,' Kneale said in 2003. 'For example, they built a whole entire eighteenth-century observatory when in my original version I had simply written about a bit of rather battered countryside and railway engines. But the whole production was splendidly done. I was actually surprised and a bit shaken to see it.'

One of the many things that we owe to *Quatermass* is the portrayal of the scientist as hero. We've become so used to the idea in the intervening 50-odd years that it's hard to think otherwise, but back then it was something of a shock to the audience that Quatermass was a fully rounded human being who happened to be a scientist, rather than a stereotypically obsessive and myopic supporting cast member in a white coat (examples of which can be found in films such as 1951's *The Thing From Another World*). Quatermass had authority. He had gravitas. He could throw his weight around with politicians and with the military, and come out on top. He probably had a wife somewhere in the Home Counties, and perhaps a son at boarding school. From Bernard Quatermass we can draw a line through to the

Reginald Tate (centre), who died in 1955, as the original Doctor Bernard Quatermass.

character of the Doctor in *Doctor Who* (1963-present), and arguably extend it all the way to Gil Grissom in the US crime (and borderline SF) series *CSI: Crime Scene Investigation* (2000-present).

Quatermass's underlying humanity is reflected in the other characters as well. In fact, one thing that is clear from watching the three black-and-white *Quatermass* TV series is that they are *dramas*. They are motivated by people rather than events. Characters such as Victor Caroon in *The Quatermass Experiment* are complex and troubled human beings, and we care about what happens to them because we sympathise with them. 'The stories are told through the characters and the action,' Kneale told interviewer Andrew Pixley. 'Now that is one area where an awful lot of science fiction stuff, so far as I've seen, collapses. It doesn't just weaken, it collapses, because there are very few coherent characters. Construction of the story is often rotten and is waiting to be saved by the special effects . . . All too often nowadays, expensive films do depend on them and that's why we have this increasingly dry, hugely expensive stuff coming out of Hollywood . . . I find the characters and the settings far more interesting than sparks flying.'

Another of the innovations that Nigel Kneale brought to science fiction was the concept that the universe beyond Earth's atmosphere was not at all like anything we were used to. In most written and filmed SF space is just somewhere with no atmosphere or gravity, where alien planets are more or less like Earth except for the colour of the skies and the shape of the rocks. In Nigel Kneale's vision of the cosmos, space has hidden deeps in which monsters lurk and the Earth's atmosphere is a thin skin separating us from chaos and madness. There are things out there that would drive us insane if we ever tried to understand them; amorphous life forms that do not think or act the way we do. 'The humans are vapourised by whatever the forces are that simply wants to use them as fodder,' he later said about the fourth of the *Quatermass* TV series. 'We never see what these things are because they are several million miles away and our skills don't extend to finding that.' In this, Kneale was closer to the horror fiction of H.P. Lovecraft than to the rigorously logical science fiction of Stanley Weinbaum, Arthur C. Clarke or Isaac Asimov. One cannot imagine Bernard Quatermass ever co-existing with the alien races that turn up in *Star Trek*. For *Quatermass*, all alien life is, almost by definition, beyond human understanding. That legacy is still seen now in the *Alien* movies (1979-present), whose creator, Dan O'Bannon, is an acknowledged fan of Nigel Kneale's work. A universe that spawns primal, chaotic creatures such as the Aliens is not one in which humans should be running around recklessly.

Like all good horror institutions, *Quatermass* refuses to die. Various scriptwriters and film directors have been so influenced by Nigel Kneale and his three original *Quatermass* TV series that they have attempted to either piggyback on Kneale's talent or to directly remake the *Quatermass* stories. John Landis, director of *An American Werewolf in London* (1981), brought Kneale to America in the 1980s to work on a proposed remake of *The Creature from the Black Lagoon*, which, for various reasons, never got made. John Carpenter – director of, amongst others, *Halloween* (1978), *The Fog* (1980) and *Escape from New York* (1981) – took the opportunity to ask Kneale to write the script for the third of his *Halloween* movies, but Kneale's vision was criticised as being too old-fashioned and the script was rewritten extensively by director Tommy Lee Jones. (And it can't have escaped anyone's notice that the narrative of *Halloween III: Season of the Witch* has almost nothing to do with Carpenter's slasher franchise and is, in a wonderfully perverse way, closer in style to the *Quatermass* stories.) Kneale left Hollywood in disgust, but John Carpenter, still smitten, went on to use the pseudonym Martin Quatermass on his script for the Kneale-inspired *Prince of Darkness* (1987), provoking Kneale to write, in a letter to the *Observer* newspaper, 'If this is homage who needs insults?' More recently, Dan O'Bannon (whose script for the 1979 *Alien* was inspired by Kneale's dark, chaotic vision of a space that was deeply inimical to man) wrote a script for a proposed remake of *The Quatermass Experiment* that would be set in America and have its climax shifted to a nuclear power station. Like many projects connected to Kneale's name, it never went into production. Another director, Alex Proyas, who had made the films *The Crow* (1994), *Dark City* (1998) and the blockbuster *I, Robot* (2004) has long harboured a desire to remake *Quatermass and the Pit* and co-wrote a script with writer David Goyer, but legal issues have apparently scuppered production. Then there was Tobe Hooper's film *Lifeforce* (1985), based on Colin Wilson's novel *Space Vampires* and including a sequence in which a naked female succubus causes chaos at Holborn tube station, which is spookily reminiscent of the climax at Hobbs End in *Quatermass and the Pit*.

It seems only fair that we should finish, as we started, with Nigel Kneale. In 1996 he wrote a radio documentary for the BBC about *Quatermass*, in which Andrew Kier reprised his role as the professor, and while recording an audio commentary for the 1997 laserdisc release of *Quatermass and the Pit*, he discussed the possibility of writing a script about Quatermass's early experiences in rocketry, in Berlin in the 1930s. Sadly, it was not to be. Nigel Kneale died in 2006, a year after seeing BBC4 transmit, as an experiment and an affectionate tribute, a live version of *The Quatermass Experiment* starring actor Jason Flemyng as the youngest and most dynamic Quatermass we had ever seen. The strange thing was, although the script was over 50 years old, it still worked perfectly as drama. And that, in a nutshell, is why Nigel Kneale's influence will be felt for as long as television exists.

THE TWILIGHT ZONE (1959-1964)

'There is a sixth dimension beyond that which is known to man. It is a dimension as vast as space and as timeless as infinity. It is the middle ground between light and shadow and lies between the pit of man's fears and the summit of his knowledge. This is the dimension of the imagination. It is an area that might be called . . . the Twilight Zone.'

'The place is here. The time is now. And the journey into the shadows that we are about to watch could be our journey.'

And so it all began, with a rather portentous voiceover delivered dead-pan by the series' creator and main writer, Rod Serling. Even thinking about it now, remembering that voice, those words, is enough to send a thrill of anticipation down my spine.

Pointless factoid: studio executives originally sounded out Orson Welles for the role of narrator . . .

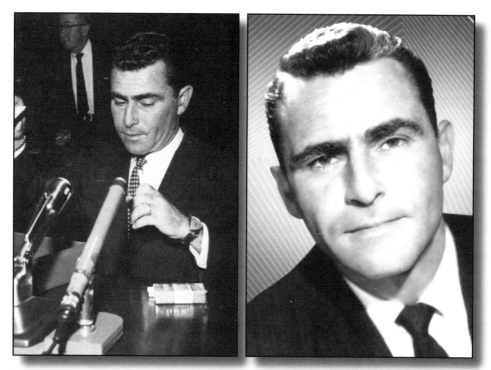

Rod Serling (1924-1975) – as creator of The Twilight Zone, *he wrote 92 of the series' 156 episodes.*

Everything that the show was and hoped to be was encapsulated in that brief opening gambit. It is easy to see the influence of those early pulp magazines like *Weird Tales, Astounding Science Fiction* and *Amazing Stories* on Serling's creativity and an absolute delight that the show never tried to explain away the *outré* with pseudo-science. It didn't hide behind maguffins and shoddy effects. It didn't need to because the secret of *The Twilight Zone* was always about the hero's journey – be it to redemption or damnation.

Add to that the fact that *The Twilight Zone* showcased a spectacular array of talent including, but by no means limited to: Robert Redford, Dennis Hopper, Martin Landau, Bert Reynolds, Robert Duvall, James Coburn, Charles Bronson, Peter Falk, and of course, Captain James T. Kirk himself, William Shatner – it is hardly surprising it was a darling with the advertisers and struck so many emotional chords with its viewers.

The format was deceptively simple, and one that has been oft copied – an anthology show, much like its televisual descendants *Tales from the Crypt,* Roald Dahl's *Tales of the Unexpected* and of course *The Outer Limits,* each episode self-contained and more often than not hiding a nasty little sting in the tail.

The stories of *The Twilight Zone* delivered the 'bang', the 'substance', the implications of the 'story' itself with consummate skill, often reducing complex moral concerns of the time, like the nuclear threat, or our rising reliance upon technology, mass hysteria, and of course the rise of McCarthyism (all subjects previously *verboten* in primetime dramas), into a succinct twenty-two minutes of entertainment. Risks were being taken, things previously brushed under the carpet were being talked about openly.

The writers of the show, the core talent responsible for what it was saying week in and week out, were part of this loose association of fellows who called themselves the California Sorcerers. Ray Bradbury, William F. Nolan, George Clayton Johnson, Charles Beaumont, Richard Matheson, they were all of them doing some clever stuff, disguising their inflammatory messages in fables and allegories, much as that grand old English reactionary and rabble-rouser, George Orwell, had with his satirising of Stalinism in *Nineteen Eighty-Four*. We are talking about a time of fuelled paranoia which the writers of the era couldn't help but feed off and react against.

It is important to consider the social mores of the late fifties to better understand the importance of what the writers of *The Twilight Zone* were trying to do. The Red Scare, the overt and subliminal threat of Communism had dominated much of US politics for best part of two decades, and the Cold War was very much still in full swing. Socially there were huge developments in music with the birth of entire genres, including the rebellious rock'n'roll which lent its voice to the young people, allowing them to be heard for the first time. The conservative values of the day were being challenged, much as they would later be challenged again by the counter-culture of the 1960s and, across the pond, the British punks of the 1970s. Up until then it had all been about conformity, a relic of the Great Depression and World War Two. Still, this latent fear of Communism was prevalent, the studio executives under the aegis of the Motion Picture Association of America, the major players in the Hollywood film industry, had gone on record stating: 'We will not knowingly employ a Communist or a member of any party or group which advocates the overthrow of the government of the United States,' and blacklisted the Hollywood Ten; screenwriters, producers and directors they believed to be acting outside the national interest. It was, of course, blatant censorship of ideas.

Not only was this open exchange of ideas via the medium of television important, it was new and exciting, emerging as it did from a time of stifled social awareness. But then science fiction in all of its various forms has always prided itself on this self-same exchange of ideas and the tackling of serious issues.

Despite this social relevance few critics at the time believed that the show could ever transcend the stigma of being 'vapid escapism' and be recognised for what it was: socially relevant drama. When interviewing Serling, Mike Wallace, a respected journalist (who later went on to helm CBS' *60 Minutes*) asked: '. . . [Y]ou're going to be, obviously, working so hard on *The Twilight Zone* that, in essence, for the time being and for the foreseeable future, you've given up on writing anything important for television, right?' which is a sad indictment of how the general public often see science fiction. Fifty years on the comment was echoed by Sir Richard Attenborough, speaking to the British interviewer, Michael Parkinson: 'I don't like science fiction. I like stories about people. About characters.' The times may change but the prejudices remain the same.

Scott Edelman, a comic-book veteran who went on to become one of the creative forces behind the *Tales from the Darkside* anthology show, explains just how wrong these prejudices are:

'He taught me things, important things, regardless of the way Wallace's question implied that the fantastic had no worthwhile message to impart. "Walking Distance" let me know that I should never lose touch with the child within. "The Monsters Are Due on Maple Street" warned me about the dangers of suspicion. "To Serve Man" reminded me that, regardless of the cliché, I should always look a gift horse in the mouth. Again and again, Serling offered messages as powerful, eternal and, yes, important as those he tried to convey when battling with sponsors over his more "realistic" scripts. I owe him more thanks than I can possibly express.'

'*The Twilight Zone* . . . was easy to imitate badly – just as it is easy to do a poor impersonation of Rod Serling's clipped delivery – but inimitable. Easily parodied, unable to be imitated. In the years since the original *The Twilight Zone*, one thing we have learned from the attempts to imitate it, to revive it, to remake it, under *The Twilight Zone* name or another, is how astonishingly difficult it is to make something like that work, and it throws back into focus something it's easy to overlook – that *The Twilight Zone* was simply one of the high water marks of television.' – Neil Gaiman, in his introduction to *Dimensions Behind the Twilight Zone*.

From a psychological point of view much of *The Twilight Zone* can be categorised as an examination of the human psyche – one that delves deep into the frailties of both flesh and spirit and the triumphs of the self same things. We flatter ourselves as being in control of our destinies, masters of our roles in this world. What the writers of *The Twilight Zone* did was show a species tempted by its darker side. Unforgettable tales like 'Nothing in the Dark', 'The Hitch-Hiker' and 'Long Live Walter Jameson' revolve around the one inescapable human truth: we are born to die. We are shown death in many guises, the suave Mr Death of 'One for the Angels', cruel death, a gentle, dare I say spiritual death, and of course, the staple of *The Twilight Zone*, the ironic demise. Sometimes death offers redemption, sometimes damnation.

Because its premise was grounded squarely in the field of science fiction, not

'There is a fifth dimension, beyond that which is known to man. It is a dimension as vast as space and as timeless as infinity . . . It is an area which we call the Twilight Zone.'

horror, it is perhaps surprising that so much of the show revolved around the supernatural – ghost stories from the recently dead, the near-dead and those in denial, refusing to go gently into that endless winter night – all of these and more cropped up again and again. Perhaps the most remarkable of all of them, certainly for me the most thought provoking, is Charles Beaumont's morally fascinating 'Long Live Walter Jameson'. Beaumont offers us an insight into death and the high cost of living, as Jameson comes to slowly realise after thousands upon thousands of years wasted as an immortal, it isn't about amassing time, it is about the quality with which that time is lived. And there is a haunting resonance that lingers into Beaumont's own life here, a prolific and talented writer whose life was cut tragically short at the age of 38 by prolonged illness.

Looking back at those early shows now, what is fascinating is just how many of these stories and themes have themselves become archetypal. They reverberate throughout decades of genre television, as telling and timeless now as they were when they were first broadcast over 50 years ago. It is one of the cultural peculiarities of the show that it is so closely linked with introducing popular scientific ideas to its early audience. More accurate would be to say that this 'science-lite' was used as a vehicle for social commentary.

From those opening episodes penned by Serling himself (and let's put it into perspective, Serling wrote twenty-one episodes during that first season) one that leaps immediately to mind is 'One for the Angels'. Lew Bookman, played by Ed Wynn, is a pitch man, a sidewalk salesman. The set-up is fairly simple, as with most of the twenty-two-minute shows. Mr Death pays Bookman a visit, arranging his 'departure'. Bookman is to die at midnight. Of course Lew Bookman doesn't want to go, so he makes a deal, to live until he has had the chance to do his masterpiece, the Big Pitch, 'One for the angels,' as he calls it. And course, just as any one of us would, our salesman tries to renege on the deal so Mr Death arranges for a replacement. It's an eloquently simple twist. A truck hits a neighbourhood kid, leaving her clinging to life. She will of course pass at midnight, Bookman's own date with Death. The way it works is that Mr Death has to be in her room at midnight to claim her. Confronted by the tragedy of a young girl being taken early Bookman does what we'd all like to think we would do under similar circumstances, he rises to the challenge by making a pitch so enthralling that Death misses his deadline to collect the little girl. Having made his one great pitch, one for the angels, Bookman is content to die and leaves with Mr Death. It is beautiful in its simplicity, haunting in its morality and powerful in its telling.

> 'As I look back at *TZ*, which I was introduced to during reruns on WPIX in the 1970s, I find the episodes that continue to resonate with me are the ones about compelling characters, more the underdogs than the heroes. My favourite, "One for the Angels", is about a decent man who does something extraordinary and selfless, for example. Or even Jonathan Winters's world-weary pool player who, despite being a ghost, seemed burdened by being the best. How people react to the odd situations and the consequences of their actions no doubt informed my writing and editing sensibilities along with Serling's wonderful gift for dialogue.' – Bob Greenberger, *Star Trek: Deep Space 9* and *The Next Generation* writer.

Another perennial favourite comes out of that same opening run, 'Time Enough At Last'. It is the simplest of all premises, a man's love of books. Burgess Meredith plays Bank teller Henry Bemis, a simple man who loves nothing more than to read. Come lunchtime he sneaks into the vault and is knocked unconscious by a huge shockwave. He awakes to a not-so Brave New World: a world destroyed by nuclear war. It's a fairly simple Last Man story, deceptively similar to the show's pilot episode in which our hero appears to be alone in a small town, trying to raise someone – anyone – but can't. In the pilot the sting in the tail is that it is all part of some elaborate governmental testing for the space program. Bemis's story is a little different. Alone in his post-holocaust world he is sure he can't go on, the only course open to him is suicide – until he sees a library and a paradise of unread books. With civilisation effectively gone, this simple book-lover has time enough at last to lose himself in all of these fabulous imaginary worlds. He begins to organise the books, planning out his reading for years to come. But just as he settles down to crack open the spine on that first book his glasses slip from his face, the lenses shatter on the hard stone steps of the library, forever trapping him in a blurry world. Brilliantly simple, heartbreakingly poignant.

In addition to featuring a cavalcade of guest stars, The Twilight Zone *also showcased original music by the legendary composer Bernard Herrmann.*

The Twilight Zone *often provided a platform for Rod Serling's liberal social conscience, dealing with such issues as death, old age, racial prejudice and sexism.*

'The original *Twilight Zone* still stands as a great tutorial on "How to write a 30-minute TV episode". Most of them in the five season series are absolute gems of writing. No matter how good the actors or direction was in any particular episode, the writers were the stars of this show.' – Raymond Benson, author of the James Bond novels *Tomorrow Never Dies, Die Another Day* and *The World is Not Enough.*

That isn't to say that *The Twilight Zone* never tackled traditional science fiction tropes, it most certainly did: time travel, voyages into space, aliens and extraterrestrial creatures, the rise of machines, and alternate universes and parallel worlds. But these were always offset against very human concerns. And that, perhaps, is the secret to the show's enduring appeal. There is a quality of escapism in stories like 'Little Girl Lost' by Richard Matheson, where we are actually treated to a glimpse of the Fifth Dimension, an unknown portal beneath a little girl's bed. Who didn't make sure their feet were properly tucked in before they fell asleep? It is that fear of the

William Shatner panics in 1963's 'Nightmare at 20,000 Feet' – the future James T. Kirk also appeared in the 1960 episode 'Nick of Time'.

unknown that grips us and holds us rigid in its grasp – be it the unknown quantity that is death and what comes after, or the noise in the night, the creak of floorboards outside the bedroom door, and yes, the monster underneath the bed.

We live lives trapped within the mundane, we get up and go to work, get home, cook, watch TV and fall asleep, wake, rinse and repeat.

Who then doesn't dream of escape?

Of something different?

Of taking that first unknowing step into the Twilight Zone where anything is possible? Where the mundane becomes the miraculous? Where as travellers we have a chance to be something *more*? Where the only boundaries are those set down by our imaginations?

In the end it distils into a single question of faith: dare we believe the magic still works or have cynicism and age battered us into submission?

Our all-knowing guide to The Twilight Zone, *Rod Serling reprised his narrator's role for 1969's* Night Gallery.

There is a concept in television known as the 'fourth wall' – this is basically the screen, the boundary between the fiction being told and the audience watching – actually it pre-dates television by quite some time, originating in the old proscenium theatres but like so much else it has been subsumed by the tube. By utilising Serling's narrator the show systematically broke the fourth wall, talking directly to the viewer to simplify the moral of the story or drive home the point, but that first time the invisible wall wasn't so much broken as it was shattered. It was in the episode 'A World of His Own' again written by Richard Matheson, another of the California Sorcerers and author of *I Am Legend* (filmed multiple times, most recently with Will Smith) and *The Incredible Shrinking Man* among others. It is a relatively unremarkable piece of television right up until Serling appears on the set and says, 'We hope you enjoyed tonight's romantic story on *The Twilight Zone*. At the same time, we want you to realize that it was, of course, purely fictional. In real life, such ridiculous nonsense –'

'Rod you shouldn't!' interrupts the maligned male lead, quite nonplussed with this summation of his story, before he walks over to his safe to retrieve a tape marked 'Rod Serling'. 'I mean, you shouldn't say things as "nonsense" and "ridiculous"!' he continues, as he throws the tape into the fire, erasing Serling from the show.

It is a moment of magic, so typical of *The Twilight Zone*'s sensibilities.

Magic.

'*The Twilight Zone* is still one of my all time favourite shows. So many of those episodes left an indelible mark on me, though I saw them in repeats. Of course there are the classics, like "Time Enough At Last" and "The Monsters Are Due on Maple Street". But that's just the tip of the iceberg. The show could break your heart with tales like the Jack Klugman starred "In Praise of Pip", or address the horrors of the Holocaust as in "Death's Head Revisited". War was a frequent subject for Serling, as was space travel. Seeing the faces of our enemies, seeing that they resembled ourselves, was a theme-bell rung to great effect over and over. "People Are Alike All Over" is one of my favourites. But to my mind, the best *Twilight Zones* – and the ones that influenced me the most as a writer – were the ones that were sad or wistful and dealt with nostalgia for the past. "Walking Distance" and "Of Late I Think of Cliffordville" are two stellar examples. The truth is that at least half of all of the episodes of *The Twilight Zone* are amongst the best hours and half-hours ever produced for television. Even a handful of episodes sampled would give a newcomer something remarkable. Spread the word. Nobody has ever done it better – nor half as well – as Rod Serling.' – Christopher Golden, author of the *Hellboy* novels, novelisations of *Buffy* and *Angel* and, along with Mike Mignola, the movie *Baltimore*.

Magic is a fundamental concept delicately interwoven throughout the show itself – much more so than nuts and bolts science – we've got black magic arcana, dead men's shoes that possess the wearer, giving him a life quite unlike his own, animated dolls and puppets that play on our most basic fears, and more mundane stuff like love potions and quick-draw potions, genies, hexes, voodoo, wish-fulfilment – indeed, it is a veritable arsenal of the supernatural. The key to *The Twilight Zone* lies in the imagery. The door to somewhere else, some place magical, where the possibilities are only limited by the imagination of the traveller. And more often than not it was the *belief* in magic that was all important, not the geegaws themselves. George Clayton Johnson's 'Kick the Can' is a wonderful example of this. Again it is an appreciably simple tale of old friends. Charles Whitley, a resident of Sunnyvale Rest Home, has worked out that the secret to youth is no more complicated than acting young. Understandably, his friend Ben Conroy is rather cynical and thinks Charles's mind is addled. As night comes Charles wakes his fellow residents for a game of kick-the-can. Everyone agrees except Ben, who runs off to tattle to the home's superintendent. All they find are a group of children playing kick-the-can – they are all young again. Ben begs his old friend for a second chance, but Charles,

In late January 1964, CBS announced the cancellation of the series – it has been consistently repeated across the globe ever since.

now a boy, tells him it's too late. The children all run off into the bushes, leaving Ben behind. And Rod Serling's parting shot tells us:

'Sunnyvale Rest, a dying place for ancient people who have forgotten the fragile magic of youth. A dying place for those who have forgotten that childhood, maturity and old age are curiously intertwined and not separate. A dying place for those who have grown too stiff in their thinking to visit the Twilight Zone.'

And there is a lovely message in that judgement, isn't there? You see, the magic is in childhood itself, that's the time when we believe all things are possible. It isn't a magic can; it is that state of mind that allows us to walk out of the every day, travellers in the Twilight Zone.

'I watched them all, sometimes one at a time, sometimes in big weekend-long marathons. You just can't get tired of the mix of creepy, humorous, science fiction, horror. Burgess Meredith with his coke-bottle glasses, rejoicing in the end of the world because he'll have enough quiet time to get some reading done . . . And then he breaks his glasses! But my favourite episode had no fantasy element whatsoever. "Dust" is set in the old west, with a travelling con-man selling the rope to hang a young Mexican man, and also selling "magic dust" he scrapes off the ground to the distraught Mexican father desperate to save his son. The old man makes a fool out of himself throwing his magic dust over the crowd to get them to forgive his son. But they hang the young man anyway . . . and the rope breaks. I loved the neat plotting in almost every episode, the surprise twists. *The Twilight Zone* was not just about ideas, but emotions, too. Good stories, well told, which shows how much you can do in a very short time frame.' – Kevin J. Anderson, author of the *Dune* prequels, and over 100 novels linked in with the *Star Wars*, *The X-Files*, and *The League of Extraordinary Gentlemen* universes.

'One of the first episodes of *The Twilight Zone* I watched was about a rich old man with a very greedy, disgusting family who had come to "visit" because they knew he was about to die. As it was Mardi Gras, he made them wear hideous, grotesque masks or they would inherit nothing. On the last *bong* of Mardi Gras midnight (as I recall) he breathed his last. You can guess the rest – now they were rich, but their faces were permanently disfigured. I was terrified. But I also realised that I, too, could make up *TZ* episodes about stuff like that because *I* had a black wig from Halloween! So I wrote two teleplays. One was called "The Monster in the Furnace" and the other was called "The Monster in the Swimming Pool". Thus began my life of crime.' – Nancy Holder, author of over 50 novels including novelisations of *Buffy the Vampire Slayer* and *Angel*.

KOLCHAK: THE NIGHT STALKER (1972-1975, 2005)

Jeffrey Grant Rice wrote *The Kolchak Papers* in 1970, an unpublished novel about an old school reporter and his encounters with the supernatural. Optioned by ABC and producer Dan Curtis, the novel was adapted into a Movie of the Week by Richard Matheson, a novelist and television veteran from *The Twilight Zone*. Directed by John Llewellyn Moxey, *The Night Stalker* debuted on 11 January 1972, earning a then record-setting television rating, with 54 per cent of available viewers watching that night.

The movie starred Darren McGavin as the seersucker suit-wearing Carl Kolchak, a reporter with a nose for news and reputation for trouble. Having been drummed out of jobs in cities across America, he wound up in Las Vegas in time to cover a series of murders that he linked to a vampire, played with hissing relish by Barry Atwater.

The ABC Movie of the Week was not where one would expect such a terrifying production. The brainchild of network supremo Barry Diller, it was a place to put people to work, as a showcase or training ground for people the network wanted to do business with. No one expected the telefilm to be such an explosive hit and the reasons behind its success are myriad. First, TV-watching habits show that people flock back to their television sets at this point right after the Christmas holidays when most programming is traditionally reruns and specials. The nation was also

Darren McGavin as newspaper hack and supernatural investigator Carl Kolchak.

growing accustomed to more intense thriller/horror films in the wake of theatrical releases such as *Rosemary's Baby*, while the bestseller lists at the time included William Peter Blatty's novel *The Exorcist*.

The American psyche was certainly ready for a jolt as social unrest and displeasure with the Vietnam War grew. The first broadcast of *The Night Stalker* preceded the Watergate break-in by only a handful of months.

People needed an outlet, and a good scare seemed to be what the doctor ordered. Curtis certainly knew how to create an atmosphere, having trolled in gothic horror with the ABC daytime serial *Dark Shadows*, which had ended its run during the previous April. Shot in a mere eighteen days, the ominous lighting and eerie music added to its effectiveness, with McGavin excelling as the cynical everyman.

The movie proved such a success that ABC asked for another story. Matheson was inspired by a vacation to Seattle to come up with 1973's *The Night Strangler*, featuring a nineteenth-century alchemist living in the bowels of Seattle's old city. Once again, audience numbers were impressive. Curtis, who cut his directing teeth on the *Dark Shadows* feature films, directed the second telefilm and proved to be something of a bully, pitting himself against McGavin. Curtis immediately set to work on a third, *The Night Killers*, featuring androids in Hawaii. McGavin, though, didn't like the development and refused to shoot the finished script.

The Night Killers exists as an unproduced television script, credited to Richard Matheson and *Logan's Run*'s William F. Nolan. The first draft was dated 15 January 1974 and went through numerous drafts that winter. It was finally abandoned by ABC when they chose instead to greenlight a weekly series. Had the ABC revival succeeded in 2005, rumour had it that this script would have been revised and used.

ABC, though, wanted more Kolchak and reached a deal with Universal, Curtis and McGavin for a weekly series. McGavin had cut a deal with Universal to produce the series and own a piece of it, something that caused tension later when the studio

Despite its short run, Kolchak's influence proved enduring, inspiring X-Files *creator Chris Carter, who subsequently cast McGavin in two episodes of the hit 1990s series.*

seemed to renege on the deal, which was never put in writing and irked McGavin until his death.

Unfortunately, no one secured the rights from Rice. When he submitted the unpublished manuscript to Matheson's agent, rights were quickly sold to ABC and the agent secured the writing assignment for Matheson. Rice tried to press this legal oversight into securing the sequel's writing assignment for himself, but once again it went to Matheson. Rice finally sued and gained a piece of the action and a 'Created By' credit. He also turned the two movies into novelisations, published by Pocket Books.

The TV series, which lasted twenty episodes during the 1974-75 season, relocated Kolchak and his long-suffering editor Vincenzo (Simon Oakland) to a Chicago-based wire service. Each week, Kolchak dealt with mummies, werewolves and automated threats. However, it quickly fell into a routine of Kolchak encountering the threat, neutralising it, and the authorities preventing any news about the exploits from reaching print.

Behind the scenes, the series was a training ground for *Sopranos* creator David Chase and featured some of the first writing work of Robert Zemeckis and Bob

Gale (who went on to write *Back to the Future* together). Chase recalled that to fill out the weekly demands of a series, they populated the newsroom with stock characters so that McGavin had someone other than Vincenzo to bounce off of. None of them worked well with the milieu and only bogged the stories down with an inconsistent tone.

Ratings were lacklustre despite the 10:00pm timeslot that allowed the production to be a little creepier. Its lead-in show, *The Texas Wheelers*, though, was a situation comedy and not ideal fodder to convince audiences to stay tuned to have the bejeezus scared out of them. After the holidays, it was switched to the 8:00pm slot and the ratings began to increase. However, by then McGavin had had enough. The actor disliked the formula and the penchant for black humour in addition to the long night shoots. Unable to produce, as promised; he clashed with Paul Playdon, who filled in when Curtis chose not to handle a weekly version. McGavin tried to produce the show, anyway, and the two fought so bitterly that Playdon left after only two episodes, replaced by Cy Chermak, who brought peace to the production. In February, despite the improved numbers, McGavin asked ABC to pull the plug, which they did, trimming its order to a mere twenty episodes.

The change in tone from the spooky movies of the week to the less threatening hour-long format showed how difficult it was to sustain horror on primetime. Prior to *Kolchak*'s debut, the only real horror shows had been in the sophisticated suspense school. The notable exception would be *Boris Karloff's Thriller*, an anthology series hosted by Karloff, the difference here though is that instead of outright horror, *Thriller*, as its name suggests, originally told 'mundane' tales of crime and mystery, rather than the supernatural. In its later episodes though, *Thriller* did became a showcase for gothic horror stories, and because many of them were based on the stories of respected horror authors including Cornell Woolrich, Robert Bloch and Charlotte Armstrong the majority of *Thriller* held to that edge of suspense over easy scare. There are exceptions of course, including the R.E. Howard story 'Pigeons of Hell', which was anything but sophisticated. The last attempt had been two years earlier, with *Ghost Story* and *Night Gallery*, both anthologies, on NBC.

Before *Kolchak*, primetime television treated their weekly spooks with a dash of humour, as showcased in *The Addams Family, The Munsters, Bewitched,* and *The Ghost and Mrs Muir*. This was to be the first dramatic colour series dealing with the supernatural, and thus proved influential on those working on the series and those watching. *The Night Stalker* clearly is the progenitor of series ranging from Chris Carter's *The X-Files* to Joss Whedon's *Buffy the Vampire Slayer* and even 2007's CBS series *Moonlight*.

Still, the influence of the TV-movies and McGavin's brilliant portrayal of the kind-hearted, cynical, muck-raking reporter reached many. Much of what made Carl Kolchak attractive to people was what McGavin brought the character. Rice initially wrote that Kolchak was covering the vampire murders in Las Vegas wearing Bermuda shorts and a Hawaiian shirt. The actor thought that unrelatable and noted

McGavin's engaging portrayal of the down-at-heel newshound was a significant factor in Kolchak's long-term cult appeal.

that the script said he'd been most recently run out of New York. Figuring the guy was too poor to buy a new suit, McGavin had him switch from Hawaiian shirts to seersucker suits. It was also a visual cue, recalling for television watchers the fictitious media's great reporters, notably Billy Wilder's *The Front Page,* made famous by Jack Lemon and Walter Matthau. Vincenzo even refers to Kolchak as looking like a stock player from a production of *The Front Page* in the second telefilm.

Frank Spotnitz, who also worked on *The X-Files*, was tapped in 2005 to rework the series for ABC. While ABC had remake rights to the original movie of the week, they did not have rights to any other story or episode. Still, that should have been more than enough for a successful updating. Unfortunately, everything Spotnitz liked about the original, including its wry humour and cynicism, was missing from the new series, which starred the charisma-less Stuart Townsend, whose Kolchak failed to act his way out of the proverbial paper bag. Now writing for the *Los Angeles Beacon*, the investigative reporter had lost his wife to a mysterious murderer. Believing that other strange deaths were all linked to some larger conspiracy, Kolchak doggedly pursued any lead. Fellow journalist Perri Reed became his constant companion, the sceptic who needed to be convinced there really was a conspiracy. His editor was Anthony Vincenzo, but the sparks between them lacked any of the McGavin-Oakland zing.

The series was scheduled for Thursday nights at 9:00pm, but it was placed opposite the dramatic juggernaut, *CSI* and the then popular reality series, *The Apprentice*. As a result, stiff competition and poor reviews kept audiences from sampling the show and it was cancelled after six airings, whereupon it was sold off to rerun on the Sci-Fi Channel complete with four unaired episodes.

The original's influence was strong, filling popular culture for years afterward. Actor/Producer Nicholas Cage cited *The Night Stalker* as inspiration for the Sci-Fi Channel's *The Dresden Files*, based on the popular Jim Butcher novels. Janos Skorzeny, *The Night Stalker*'s vampiric threat, was also named as a werewolf antagonist on the short-lived series *Werewolf*. Janos was played by the great Chuck Connors. Characters in comic books, roleplaying games and genre television series have been named or nicknamed Kolchak. An unnamed Kolchak can be seen in the 'Fearful Symmetry' episode of the Cartoon Network's *Justice League Unlimited*; fitting in that the story had fellow journalist turned crime-fighter The Question investigating conspiracies.

Cleveland Plain Dealer TV columnist Mark Dawidziak co-wrote a new Kolchak novel, *Grave Secrets*, with the reclusive Rice and later wrote *The Night Stalker Companion*. Kolchak enjoyed better creative success as a series of comic books from Moonstone Books. They also released two prose anthologies and an original novel in addition to comic book miniseries, collected into trade paperbacks.

> 'He's very, very close to Kolchak,' Kathie Browne McGavin said in Mark Dawidziak's *The Night Stalker Companion* before her husband's death in February 2006. 'The people who really love *The Night Stalker* love Kolchak because he never gives up. He's fighting, always fighting. You can take the monsters and take them to be anything you want – the government, big business, corrupt officials. Their hero comes at the end, beaten up but ready to go on fighting another day. I think Darren has a lot of that in his own personality.'

> 'I was inspired by the show *Kolchak: The Night Stalker*. It had really scared me as a kid and I wanted to do something as dark and mysterious as I remembered it to be. So I was able to say to Fox when they hired me to an exclusive deal, "This is what I want to do."' – Chris Carter, creator of *The X-Files*.

THE TOMORROW PEOPLE (1973-1992)

Dudley Simpson's distinctive theme music accompanied by the image of a gradually opening hand, revealing arcane images intercut with human faces, is as powerful a trigger for British childhood memories as the sound of *Doctor Who*'s materialising Tardis. Devised by Roger Price and produced by Thames Television, Britain's ITV network between April 1973 and February 1979, *The Tomorrow People* had

Gotta make way for the homo superior – the Tomorrow People hold court in their secret underground base.

a similar vibe to the *Doctor Who* episodes of that era, albeit rougher and with cheaper production values. Its special effects were dismally shoddy and particularly heavy on the use of now dated-looking bluescreen work, but the show remains well loved to this day because of its interesting concepts and appealing characters.

Thames Television's thinking behind the series was for it to run up against *Doctor Who* as direct competition. Veteran *Doctor Who* director Paul Bernard was commissioned to direct the first series. *The Tomorrow People*, a show starring children and made for children, featured 68 episodes in all, comprising of twenty-two stories over eight series. And despite its lacklustre production values it was a hit with its target audience.

The premise: that there exist among us those who are not human, is a popular one itself. The Tomorrow People are not homo sapiens, but rather the next step along the evolutionary ladder: homo superior, possessed of extraordinary talents such as telepathy (the ability to read the minds of other Tomorrow People), telekinesis (the ability to move objects with the power of the mind), and teleportation (referred to as 'jaunting' and performed with the aid of a special belt), as well as the odd evolutionary restriction. For example, homo superiors cannot deliberately commit murder. This limitation is known as the 'prime barrier', and is a little reminiscent of Isaac Asimov's Laws of Robotics, originally published in the story 'Runaround', which prohibited robots from causing harm to or allowing harm to befall human beings.

Tomorrow People are born to ordinary human parents and must be intercepted when they 'break out' and discover their initially confusing differences. If left to their own devices, they might unwittingly endanger themselves or others.

The Tomorrow People base themselves in 'The Lab', a secret laboratory built in an abandoned London Underground Tube station, containing their ally, the biological computer TIM. TIM is the essence of funky seventies interior design, incorporating a modular lounge arrangement, plastic tubes and swirling green blobs.

TIM is sentient and able to boost their telekinetic powers and assist them with their jaunting (which is always accompanied by cheap swirling effects and smudgy blobs).

Together they protect Earth from alien menace and keep alert for signs of more Tomorrow People breaking out. Now and then they consult the Galactic Council, a collective of telepathic alien races. At the end of Season One, two of the cast, Carol and Kenny, leave to join the Council as Earth's homo superior representatives.

While the Tomorrow People do reveal their existence to some, they operate mostly in secret, worried that ordinary people (whom they refer to as 'Saps', short for homo sapiens, not fools), will either behave aggressively towards them, afraid of their telekinetic powers, or else attempt to exploit them for sinister military purposes. Because of the prime barrier they must resort to non-lethal means to defend themselves, such as stun guns and sly ju-jitsu moves.

The leader and brains behind the team, and a definite father-figure, is John. Usually attired in a white polo-necked jumper, John was always the voice of calm and logic when things got out of hand. Played by Nicholas Young, he wore a perpetual look of extreme seriousness on his face and was the only actor to appear in the complete three seasons. Season One also featured Carol (Sammie Winmill), the 'emotional heart' of the group, often the voice of reason, her character frequently serving as a contrast to John's hard scientific nature. Her high-pitched, whiny voice and pageboy haircut was the height of chic and glamour back in the day, making her quite the siren, particularly in the white flared suit she wore in the first few episodes.

Kenny (Stephen Salmon) is the youngest member, and supposedly some sort of child genius. But his acting was dreadful, even by cheap-ass children's television standards. The show picked up a lot when, after defeating the Spidron (an evil alien who came here to mine a rare mineral directly from the Earth's core) and saving the Earth from destruction, he ran off to join Overmind, a group that advises the Galactic Council alongside Carol. (Carol eventually fell in love with an Andonesian ambassador.)

The first story sees John, Carol and Kenny attempting to connect with Stephen (Peter Vaughn-Clarke), another skinny white boy fond of polo necks, as he begins to break out. Later stories see members come and go: there is Elizabeth (Elizabeth Adare), a sensible young schoolteacher, who provides the Yin to John's sturdy Yang. Tyso (Dean Lawrence), a young gypsy boy; bad boy Mike, a teenager whose band the Fresh Hearts gets infiltrated by Satanists in a later storyline; oriental 'goddess' Hsui Tai (Misako Koba) jaunted to safety and saved from a fiery end by her Tomorrow People brethren; and the mischievous young kilted Scot Andrew (Nigel Rhodes), whose father fears the Tomorrow People might be an ungodly influence on his son. The voice of TIM is provided by Philip Gilbert, who appears in the show occasionally portraying Timus the galactic ambassador.

The bad guys are generally easy to spot, as bad guys are in cheese-fests. They tend to be either thuggish, leather pants-wearing, scruffy-haired bully boy types, or else blessed with pantomime bushy eyebrows and dramatic beards, like Jedikiah the evil shape-shifting robot. Alternatively there are the slick government types in suits (Colonel Masters and Trisha Conway) who hunt the Tomorrow People in the hope of acquiring them for secret weapons research.

Alien races including Sorsons, Kleptons and Thargons put in appearances, and the thawed Adolf Hitler is revealed to be Nebor from the planet Vashig.

The humorous episode 'A Man For Emily' features *Doctor Who*'s Peter Davison (before his stint as the fifth incarnation of the Time Lord) and his then wife Sandra Dickinson in hot-pants and silly wigs. Other episodes tackled more serious social issues. The stand out story from Season Two is 'The Blue and the Green', reminiscent of Jane Elliott's infamous blue eyes/brown eyes exercise back in 1968. In response to the assassination of Martin Luther King Jr, Elliott, a school teacher, devised an exercise to explore the impact of racism, prejudice and discriminaiton. In a class of all white children her methodology was simple: she divided by eye colour, stating that blue eyes clearly indicated a superior intellect. It didn't take long for oppression to occur, those 'superior' instilling fear and self-loathing in the brown-eyed group. The next day, though, Elliott flipped it on its head and said she'd lied the day before and actually the reverse was true. Lo and behold, the oppressed quickly became the oppressor. She chose eye colour because she believed it was one of the defining factors in whether Jews were sent to the gas chambers by the Nazi regime. As a new Tomorrow Person, school teacher Elizabeth M'Bondo breaks out, violence around the world is increasing, due to blue and green badges being distributed by an alien species, the D'henagali, that needs large amounts of violent energy in order to metamorphose into their energy-based adult phase and leave the planet. According to TIM, this happened before, in Ancient Rome. (The Nika riots, Constantinople 532, where the Blues and the Greens destabilised the empire, leading to its long-term collapse. The idea of aliens harvesting human emotive by-product is also similar to one used by Nigel Kneale in 1978's *Quatermass*.) To prevent widespread destruction, the Tomorrow People turn the Skylab satellite into a giant stun gun, putting the populace to sleep in order to resolve violent dreams in safety. The D'henagali are able to harvest the energy they need and leave Earth without further incident.

The Living Skins, featuring ameboid aliens human-controlling bubble skin jump suits (that can hang themselves up) to invade Earth presents a comment on the mindlessness of fashion and mass consumerism. Mike, Hsui Tai, John and Elizabeth are all taken over, albeit temporarily, by the alien invaders. Other issues tackled include racism, espionage, Nazism and violent death. In 'The Dirtiest Business', Pavla, a young Russian telepath, escapes from her Soviet intelligence minders in central London, prompting the Soviet Intelligence Service to raid the Tomorrow People's headquarters. The Tomorrow People set out to find Pavla before either the KGB or the SIS do. The episode ends violently with a bomb implanted within her exploding as Pavla throws herself out of a window in order to protect the Tomorrow People from the blast.

Dramatic Moog synthesiser music often – ahem – enhanced the action, entrenching *The Tomorrow People* firmly in its seventies time zone.

1992 witnessed a revivial of the series, produced by Tetra Films in association with the US company Reeves Entertainment, Thames TV and Nickelodeon.

Roger Price served as executive producer alongside a new cast and modern special effects. The cast: Adam, Lisa, Ami, Kevin, Megabyte and Jade, operated from a crashed alien spaceship buried on the shore of a remote island. Jaunting, telepathy and telekinesis were still very much in place, but these kids relied more on their wits than gadgetry. This series ran for three seasons. In 2001, Big Finish Productions, best known for their new audio adventures of *Doctor Who*, reunited members of the original series to produce further audio adventures of *The Tomorrow People.*

CHARMED (1998-2005)

Charmed, created by Constance M. Burge, is a show that follows the exploits of the Halliwell witches: Prue (Shannen Doherty), Piper (Holly Marie Combs), Phoebe (Alyssa Milano), and Paige (Rose McGowan). The concept is simple enough: the sisters, first Prue, Piper and Phoebe, and later Piper, Phoebe, and Paige, wield the Power of Three. This, we are told, makes them the most powerful witches of the age. Their destiny has them fighting demons in nearly every episode, as well as other creatures who would use, abuse, or destroy them. The sisters are watched over and protected by Leo, a human turned Whitelighter. Whitelighters are akin to angels and charged with protecting witches as they fight the forces of darkness. The series first aired in 1998 and ran for eight seasons. The show was nominated for seventeen awards and won four, including an ASCAP award in 1999 for Top TV Series.

The show was significant for several reasons. First, in its initial season, the writers sought to reconcile magic and witches with mainstream religion. Second, the show was able to survive the loss of a key character, replace her, and go on to greater success. Third, the show managed to combine hip, modern women with storylines that are as old and tired – sorry, ancient – as storytelling itself.

The show's representation of magic and mainstream religion in the first season was fairly unique. A coming-of-age story arc introduced the viewer to Piper as she struggles with her witchly identity. In the second episode she enters a church, but is afraid of what will happen to her. Will a furious and vengeful God smite her? Piper needn't have worried. The *Charmed* universe managed to quickly incorporate angels, demons, heaven, hell, and concepts of God and Satan into the mythology of the series. Given that the show revolved around three witches, it was

Charmed's Halliwell Witches – Phoebe (Alyssa Milano), Piper (Holly Marie Combs) and Paige Matthews (Rose McGowan).

an interesting, and curious, choice to make the surrounding universe more dependent on Christian concepts than on Wiccan or Pagan ones. The practical result was that many people who might have rejected the concept of the series ended up pulled in as faithful viewers. Piper quickly fell into a relationship with a Whitelighter (played by Brian Krause), and Phoebe ended up in a relationship with a demon (played by Julian McMahon). Of course, the animosity between the Whitelighter and his traditional demon enemy occasionally reached Biblical proportions. Witches became the central figures in the battle between good and evil on earth and were held up as protectors of innocents and destroyers of demons.

Being able to blend the magic with mainstream religion was only one obstacle that the show would face and overcome with apparent ease.

Shannen Doherty as Halliwell sister, Prue.

Most television shows never recover from the death of a major character. Yet *Charmed* managed not only to recover, but also to flourish after one of the three witches was killed off. At the end of the third season, Shannen Doherty left the series and the character of Prue went with her. Rose McGowan came on board to play Paige, a previously unknown half-sister, who had been given up by the girls' mother and her Whitelighter lover for adoption. The character of Paige was decidedly nothing like Prue, which is probably what ultimately saved the show. Fans warmed quickly to the family's new addition and *Charmed* went on to continued success. This can be attributed to several factors. One factor that almost certainly aided the transition was the richness of the universe that the show had built up around itself. There had always been a real sense of danger, but with the death of one of the Charmed Ones, that was only heightened. The idea that these core characters weren't untouchable added a sense of jeopardy that went against the initially cosy concept of the show and its reassuring 'charm'. More tellingly, it showed the reactions of all the other characters, giving them time to mourn the loss of Prue along with the audience. Ultimately the audience is bound to accept Paige when the sisters do. Rose McGowan portrayed the troubled, quirky newcomer in such a way as to allow for more growth on the part of the original characters.

The sisters consult the Book of Shadows, an ancient compendium of magical lore.

One traditional flaw of many a television show is that it remains static. The characters don't evolve, every episode is encapsulated in its own little bubble, and all within it remain the same week after week. With *Charmed*, the strength of the show was that the characters did change. They grew, they backslid, they took on new responsibilities and responded to their emotions in realistic ways. The contrast between seasons is sometimes very marked as far as the personalities of the characters go. That's only fitting for a show that manages to embrace different worlds and different times.

Another interesting aspect, in terms of storytelling ethic, was its ability to combine the old with the new. *Charmed* put itself across as very hip and modern, and – rarely for a major show – was helmed by strong, young and independent women. Much of the soundtrack music was derived from the San Francisco club scene, which grounded the mythic nature of the show's central narrative in the here and the now.

Despite this hip-to-be-cool nature, the storytelling itself was rooted very much in tradition, particularly fairytales.

The Alpha and Omega of *Charmed* is that the show presents a modern-day fairytale.

It has all the classic components that would be recognisable to the viewer: damsels in distress, white knights, monsters, magic galore, and the power of love. Several of the more whimsical episodes featured actual fairytale characters including mermaids and leprechauns. However, it is the overarching themes that really resonate with the viewer.

The Charmed Ones, although dynamic and powerful women who tackle demons head-on, are still very much your run-of-the-mill damsels in distress. They are constantly overwhelmed by the pressures of trying to hold jobs or go to school and keep up with their magical duties. Much like Susan from the 1985 Madonna film, each woman here is desperately seeking something – in this case a man who will sweep them off their feet and make them feel like a princess. Needless to say, they are forced to rely heavily on the aid of men, not only as lovers, but also as protectors of their secrets and investigators. The many men in the series, both magical in nature and drab and mundane, often find themselves having to rescue the women – more often than not from themselves. The sisters are universal, to hear them complain about trying to find a good man or the difficulties of motherhood is to hear every woman from every walk of life and every era voice the exact same complaint. Just as fairytale princesses are trapped in castle turrets, the Charmed Ones are just as effectively trapped in their attic with their mystical Book of Shadows, waiting for their lives to somehow become 'normal'.

With so many damsels in distress, the show also offers a strong selection of white knights. There's Leo, the Whitelighter who watches over them and eventually marries Piper. On the opposite side of the equation, Cole, the demon who married Phoebe and co-incidentally became the Source of All Evil, served as the black knight masquerading as something nobler. Throughout the series each woman had multiple suitors, most of whom wanted to rescue them from something. Even though not all of the men were aware of their loved one's powers or magical responsibilities, they all sensed strength, and beneath that, great vulnerability. What guy wouldn't want to save the girl from a monster? It's the white knight syndrome. Unfortunately in this case the monsters are real.

Here be monsters, a staple of fairytales. They parade through Halliwell Manor with frightening regularity. Every shape, size, and level of malevolence. Some, like Cole, even come disguised. Sooner or later, though, they are all vanquished by the witches, with occasional assistance from one of their white knights. While some monsters were laughable, both in design and execution, others, such as the one who killed Prue, posed a genuine threat to our spell-slinging sisterhood. But even the strongest had its fairytale heel; the trick was identifying it and exploiting the monster's weakness. Alas, death or banishment came in the rather repetitive form of an incantation, usually read hunched over the Book of Shadows, wind machine in full force. It is fair to say that magic, one of the central themes of almost every fairytale, is also the central theme of *Charmed*. Magic, of course, takes many forms. There is the good stuff used by the sisters and other witches and then there's the bad stuff, the dark magic

Paige marries parole officer Henry Mitchell (Ivan Sergei) in Season Eight's 'Engaged and Confused'.

used by demons and villains of the peace. Of course it is magic that means the sisters have more in common with their enemies than they have with the innocents they protect. Lots of storytelling panders to the deep-seated need in all of us to experience a true sense of wonder, that's what drives us to consume escapist television, so it's no surprise that our need for wonderment is fed by the arcane in this story.

Charmed succeeded in making the viewer feel that magic was happening, just around the corner, out of sight but there, haunting our peripheral vision. Thanks to the dozens of original *Charmed* novels that were published, it was a feeling readers could keep alive during the week while waiting for the next episode.

The other overriding theme of the series, though, its *raison d'être*, is another lifted straight from fairytales and bad power ballads: the power of love.

The power of love is seen as *the* great emotion that justifies all else. Not just one type of love but several. Familial love, romantic love, and love for mankind were all thoroughly explored in the course of the show.

Family love, of course, was at the very heart of the concept of *Charmed* and was a key idea in the pilot. Prue, Piper and Phoebe haven't always gotten along, but they are family and they love each other despite their differences and their pasts. It's this same sense of sisterly love that Piper and Phoebe eventually extend to Paige when they welcome her into their home and lives. Through the years the Halliwells adopted other friends or family members into this circle of love and acceptance – perhaps subconsciously to remind the audience that 'family' doesn't have to have a strict interpretation. Piper, always portrayed as the more loving, motherly sister, is the epitome of familial love.

Romantic love, the illusive one that drives rom-coms straight to box-office busting, is one of the more commonly portrayed types of love. With three women as its central cast, it's hardly surprising – if a little disappointing in terms of the blatant reinforcement of gender stereotypes – that the writers would choose to focus upon romance as a prevalent theme in *Charmed*. Each sister is in turn glorified and nearly destroyed by it. Phoebe, wearing the crown of most passionate sister, is the one who is most closely allied with this type of love. Indeed, her romance with the demon Cole is, right up until the end of days, almost identical to that of Beauty and the Beast. Both Beauty and Phoebe were thrust into a relationship with a creature that was not what he appeared. The Beast needed Beauty to fall in love with him so that he could return to his human form. Cole wooed Phoebe in an attempt to make her fall in love with him. Cole's motives, though, were a little less honourable than the Beast's. Cole wanted Phoebe to fall in love with him so that he could use her trust to destroy her and her sisters. A real heartbreaker, that demon lover. When Phoebe eventually found out that Cole was half-demon, half-human, she struggled just as Beauty to see only the humanity and the goodness in the man she loved. Eventually Cole won Phoebe's heart and her love transformed him, turning him into a better 'demon', just as the Beast won Beauty's love and was transformed from a monster to a prince. At first, just like the Beast's transformation, Cole's transformation was an internal one, but ended in a physical change as well when his demon half was vanquished, leaving him fully human. Love conquered all and tamed the monster. However, Phoebe's story then took a turn for the far more interesting (and thankfully less sappy). Demon boy became the Source of All Evil. This was right about the time Cole became Phoebe's husband – not surprisingly he didn't mention his deep, dark secret. In almost Shakespearean fashion, tragedy, love's best friend, took centre stage. Phoebe lost him, their baby, and nearly her life.

Just as Phoebe stands as the character with the strongest connection to romantic love, Paige stands as the character with the greatest love for humanity.

The Power of Three, Three Witches, Three Great Loves, it's all wrapped up in a neat little package. Because of their gifts, the girls feel a need to protect the innocents who go about their day to day in McDonald's, down at the library, working out at the gym, and all those other gloriously normal pursuits, blissfully unaware of the supernatural struggle taking place all around them.

Characteristically, Paige would be the sister who stands as the archetypal embodiment of this aspect of love. For a start, she is a social worker when she is first introduced, and something of a bleeding heart. As the show's arc develops she begins to take on other aspects of this social conscience, becoming a leader and a teacher.

Being half-human, half-Whitelighter, there is a part of her that *needs* to help.

The most charming aspect of this show, though, is reflected in the diversity of its audience. People from all faiths, ages, and walks of life enjoyed the story of the *Charmed* sisters, and who's to say whether or not they found a little inspiration amongst the entertainment?

AFTERLIFE (2005-2006)

Before *Afterlife* (2005-2006), writer Stephen Volk had already terrified Britain, quite literally it seems.

In 1992, BBC TV aired a special Halloween programme called *Ghostwatch*. As scripted by Volk, it purported to be a 'live' journalistic investigation of a haunted house, a claim given credibility by the presence of Michael Parkinson and other familiar TV personalities. With Parkinson in the studio co-ordinating field reports, expert opinion and ring-in comments, the programme told of a classic haunting, gradually 'uncovering' new information and 'witnessing' an escalation of poltergeist activity in the haunted residence. At the end, the 'ghost' invades the studio itself, and by implication uses the broadcast to spread virally into homes throughout London. Parkinson is left in peril, possessed by the angry spirit.

Just as Orson Welles's radio adaptation of *The War of the Worlds* had created a panic across the US in 1938, *Ghostwatch* in 1992 is supposed to have done the same for London. Viewers rang up in a lather of fear. They made all sorts of claims, which, even if intended as mischief, had the effect of adding to the frenzy. Afterwards thousands of letters and phone calls protested against the perceived deception – and it was even claimed (apocryphally, no doubt) that one unstable viewer killed himself to avoid the spectral apocalypse he believed was taking place. The BBC apologised and the show was never repeated.

Given that there was abundant indication that the show was a fiction, it should be surprising that it was taken so readily as fact. But somehow it's not very surprising. Parkinson's involvement, the slow build-up, and the accurate tone – which included the sort of technical difficulties you'd expect from a live broadcast – were all cleverly marshalled by Volk's script, which played on one obvious fact, foreshadowing *The X-Files* rather nicely: people want to believe. Fiction relies on the propensity of readers and viewers to lower their mental barriers if encouraged to do so, so that – on one level anyway – they accept the events of the story as 'real' and allow themselves to experience suspense, fear, exhilaration, love and whatever other emotion is required. Ghost stories traditionally evoke a sort of urban legend credulity that this happened to the friend of a friend – really, it did. *Ghostwatch* simply adopted this approach to tell its tale and worked it with aplomb.

Another thing *Ghostwatch* showed was that Volk had a knack for pushing the right horror buttons. It's not a question of believing in ghosts (though that would no doubt help), but a question of blurring the line between fiction and fact. It's a borderland that ghost stories love to explore – both as a methodology and as a theme.

The theme rather than the methodology is what Volk explored in his next ghostly fiction, the series *Afterlife*. The result, though less deceptive in its relationship with reality, was just as compelling.

Afterlife is about the relationship between Robert Bridge (Andrew Lincoln), a lecturer in psychology, and Alison Mundy (Lesley Sharp), a psychic medium. Bridge is still grieving over the loss of his son Josh, but it is his Houdini-esque fascination with explaining, and explaining away, the belief that psychics can communicate with the dead that draws him to Alison. In Alison, he sees someone who genuinely believes in the reality of her irrational abilities and is able to manifest them in a way he finds puzzling; she is thus a perfect subject for his study. He wants to get to the psychological roots of her belief. Alison, on the other hand, is interested in Robert because she is aware that his dead son is trying to communicate with him – and it has been her compulsion to help the dead to resolve their issues and move on. Both are increasingly drawn to wanting to help the other for their own sake.

Alison agrees to let Robert write a book about her and so he becomes involved in her life. What he sees, though often ambiguous and open to alternative interpretation, starts to threaten his certainties. At the same time, however, Alison finds her own emotional stability increasingly hard to maintain. Through each episode we get their opposing view of events and as tacit participants find our own certainties continually undermined. Volk gets us to take Alison's side, but then shows how fragile her hold on reality really is, thus putting what we see in question. By the same token, he appeals to our rational scepticism as manifest in Robert, only to reveal the psychologist to be clutching desperately at his own set of delusions. We veer uneasily from one side to the other.

The tactic of placing opposites together in order to generate conflict and intense dramatic interaction is hardly a new one. Even in the realm of supernatural thrillers it isn't new; it was enthroned as a successful strategy when Chris Carter placed the belief/scepticism dichotomy at the forefront of *The X-Files*, with the roles of believer and sceptic split between the two FBI agents Mulder and Scully. The interplay between them, driven by a strong degree of unresolved sexual tension, goes some way toward explaining the popularity of the show.

But in *Afterlife* the interaction and developing complexities of the relationship between Robert and Alison provide a strong central narrative arc. Volk has described the fourteen-part series as a sequence of short stories that form a novel. Continually he plays with our grasp on the show's apparent realities until all we can do is accept

Afterlife *protagonists Robert Bridge (Andrew Lincoln)
and Alison Mundy (Lesley Sharp).*

the two extreme possibilities at once, holding them suspended in an emotional tangle that represents the reality of human life. In this, it feels remarkably unified.

The line between what is in our heads as a belief and what manifests in the objective world is blurred and broken and often uncertain. As the study of our internal world and how it affects our behaviour, psychology tries to define that borderland so that we can safely exist on the right side of the tracks. But perhaps it is continually in danger of missing the signs, of getting too myopic, of defining its own rules too rigidly and forgetting that subjective experience is not merely in the imagination, but can impinge on the real world in very real ways. Sometimes indeed what lies on the far side of the borderland might want to pop over and say hello – but in doing so will take the form of a psychological, emotionally evoked delusion. The clear-cut line between truth and delusion, the objective and the subjective, becomes scarily uncertain.

This is the methodology that drives Volk's spooky tales of restless ghosts, vengeful spirits and unresolved conflict. Unlike *Medium*, the US foray into the 'psychic investigator' genre, *Afterlife* does not dwell on the legal aspects of Alison's investigations into the mysteries surrounding supernatural phenomena. It is supernatural drama, rather than supernatural crime-solving. The emotions that lie at the heart of the hauntings are the real focus – and it gains in power from that. Volk also gives his protagonist no emotional validation – no supportive family or accepting DA. Instead she is isolated from society and, sometimes, even herself.

Not that the show neglects the more standard methods used by filmmakers to scare their audience. Strange sounds, weird imagery, occasional bloody violence, gruelling moments of threat, insane outbursts, phantom perceptions, faces seen in mirrors or at the periphery of vision, flickering lights, poltergeist intrusions – they're all there, but marshalled with a conviction that is much rarer. The conviction arises from the close attention given to the main characters and our engagement with their problems.

As played by Lesley Sharp, Alison Mundy is the driving force behind the success of the show. She is strong yet emotionally damaged; someone who is able to deal with experiences way outside the norm, but who has become isolated and conflicted as a result. Sharp allows Alison's essential strength and equally essential fragility to show through her every action. Half the time we as viewers are inclined to agree with those who see her as a crackpot or even as a danger to herself and others. Yet at heart we believe in her and, like Robert, we respect her, even against our better judgement. She can be intense, uncontrolled, unsettling, dangerous, and fragile – yet we are drawn to her. Sharp has won two awards for her work on this series (the Monte Carlo TV Festival, Outstanding Lead Actress in a Drama Series and Royal Television Society UK, Best Actor – Female) and the accolades are well-deserved. Her portrayal could have become a genre stereotype, but instead her Alison is both utterly unconventional and totally believable.

Not that Andrew Lincoln lets down the team. His Robert Bridge seems simple enough to get a handle on, but beneath the relatively calm and rational surface there are emotional issues that he persistently avoids coming to terms with. Lincoln lets us see the conflict, but subtly, and he conveys the gradual undermining of Bridge's entrenched certainties with great conviction. He also gives a strong sense of how based in fear his character's earnest rationalism really is.

Over the course of the two series of *Afterlife* the relationship between these two characters is not only affected by what they experience, but also by the growing complexity of the emotional bonds that come to exist between them. They fight, they bicker, they frustrate each other – but they grow to respect each other, too. This progression could have been handled in a clichéd manner if not for the subtlety, intensity and conviction that Sharp and Lincoln bring to their respective roles.

Because we can believe in these characters as real people rather than as genre stereotypes, the horror can be even more affecting. The combination of excellent writing, intelligence, strong characterisation and emotionally compelling stories – not to mention good work from the various directors assigned to particular episodes – means that the result is often terrifying and dark. Of course, for those who gauge scare-factor by levels of violence and bloody threat, the show probably isn't so frightening. Indeed as often as it provokes tingles by way of suspense and moments of shock and frightening revelations, it also often involves the viewer in the drama as drama, without attempting to scare. But when it does scare, it does so well.

One of the best examples, both dramatically and as a work of horror, is the episode 'Daniel One and Two'. Recognising Alison's intuitive ability to empathise with people in trouble and wanting her to face up to her past, Robert brings her to a psychiatric hospital. There she meets Daniel, a young man displaying signs of violent schizophrenia. Daniel claims that he has a spectre on his back, an invisible friend who has been with him from childhood and is now attacking those he feels threaten his hold over Daniel One. Daniel trusts Alison, though she admits that she can't 'see' Daniel Two. The boy's parents and attending psychologists, however, believe that Alison is merely exacerbating his delusions. Robert almost convinces Alison to see that what Daniel suffers from is an emotional dysfunction caused by a severe chemical imbalance, and unsettles her belief in her own visions. However, when Daniel Two makes an appearance to Alison, attacking her, Alison realises she must find a way to help Daniel One before his invisible friend totally destroys him.

The episode builds to an emotional climax in which Alison forces Daniel's mother to face up to an uncomfortable truth, even at the cost of her marriage: that Daniel Two is the angry remnant of an abortion she had prior to marrying her morally rigid husband and giving birth to her living son. All the dead Daniel wants is recognition.

The power of Sharp's performance here is nothing short of stunning, as she loses her emotional equilibrium through the desperation and frustration she feels trying to defend Daniel against the spectre and the doctors, who are totally resistant to anything she says, determined that their patient's psychological trauma is physiological and can only be handled with drugs. The climactic scene is positively sweat-inducing, after a gradual build-up in which director Charles Beeson unsettles us with glimpses of Daniel Two and one particularly frightening sequence in which the dead spirit's claw-like fingers appear from behind Daniel's head as a herald of the spectre's manifestation.

This episode works well on two levels. First there is the sheer terror of the story; then we have the issues boiling away between Alison and Robert. These are woven with intricate precision through the events and become the narrative drive of the story. The conclusion of the episode (with Daniel Two's need for recognition) resonates strongly with Robert's own failure to recognise that he must come to terms with his son's death in order for the boy's spirit to be at rest. There's a power to this kind of storytelling that goes beyond the supernatural, right to the core of what it is to suffer and lose, be it yourself, your ghostly bully-companion, or your own son.

Afterlife is a particularly intelligent and brilliantly effective part of the apparent post-millennial upsurge in ghost stories. Always popular, ghosts of all persuasions have undergone a massive renaissance over the past decade, producing not only significant books, but more films than all the others combined – not to mention TV series such as *Medium* and *Supernatural*. Central to the upsurge in major ghost films has been the influence of Asian, and specifically Japanese, horror. When *Ring* (1998) hit the scene it re-energised horror films generally, and dragged them into the mainstream box-office in a way not seen for a long while. *Ju-on: the Grudge* and its many progeny followed, and brought with them successful ghost films from Hong Kong, Thailand and Korea – the Hollywood remakes inevitably followed. Somewhere in the early inspirational mix, though, there was *The Sixth Sense* (1999) with its 'I see dead people' plotline, which itself echoes the T.M. Wright novel *A Manhattan Ghost Story* (a million-seller boasting the cover copy 'Soon to be a major motion picture with Sharon Stone' that never materialised) – one of the original inspirations for *Afterlife*. The enormous and unexpected success of that film worldwide was as influential as the *Ring* cycle. These films arguably created an aesthetic that is still functioning, despite signs of stagnation, and has led to the rule of the ghost.

In their Asian form these films brought into the ghost story the sort of viral fears more commonly found in apocalyptic zombie stories, without that subgenre's visceral contempt for the flesh. Traditionally ghosts were very limited in their influence, usually seeking revenge on specific guilty individuals or the progeny of those who had brought about their deaths or otherwise wronged them. Either that or their spheres of influence were localised, restricted to the environment in which they had lived or died (the classic haunted house scenario). Gradually, however, ghosts have come to take a wider vengeance, spreading their influence from one victim to the next in an expediential progression. Volk foreshadowed this movement – so prominent in *Ring* – in *Ghostwatch*. Unfairly referred to as a hoax, *Ghostwatch* was always a drama, as its broadcasting as part of the Screen One series on BBC One would suggest. What was unique about it was the presentation, selling it to the viewer as a genuine unscripted Halloween ghost hunt *à la* the more modern *Most Haunted* and *Ghost Hunters*. Based at least loosely upon a genuine haunting in Enfield, just outside of London, everything about *Ghostwatch* was fiction. Still, Volk worked hard to maintain the illusion, right down to plastering the standard BBC Live call-in number across the screen so viewers could call in to report activity or to discuss ghostly shenanigans. Plotwise, *Ghostwatch* was an on-air investigation of a house in Northolt, Greater London, where poltergeist activity was believed to be taking place. The set-up utilised plenty of interviews with neighbours and the haunted family, introducing the viewer to the malevolent ghost 'Pipes' (so called because of his habit of knocking on the house's plumbing). Its choice of presenters in Michael Parkinson, Craig Charles, Sarah Greene and her husband Mike Smith, added a credibility to the proceedings that really served to sell the drama as a documentary. As the drama unfolded, viewers were told that Pipes was actually the spirit of a psychologically deranged and dangerous individual, Raymond Tunstill. The twist upon the twist was that Tunstill supposedly believed himself to have been a victim of haunting (by a child killer from the nineteenth century, no less). As the 90 minutes rolled on the ghostly manifestations grew increasingly terrifying, until, right at the end, the frightened reporters realised that the programme itself was acting as a sort of 'nationwide séance' through which Pipes was gaining horrific power.

The *coup de grace* was Pipes possessing Sarah Greene and the show having to break away from the studio. It was nothing short of brilliant.

Of course the ghost story is classically about the persistence of the influence of past events. Metaphorically the subgenre explores guilt and the knowledge that the past lingers as an influence we have to deal with – one we may not be able to deal with. *Afterlife* is very much in this tradition, whether seen as psychological drama or ghostly thriller.

Of course, the popularity of ghost films also reflects current conflicted attitudes to traditional matters of life, death and the 'eternal truths'. TV shows such as the interminably insipid *Ghost Whisperer* perpetually reassure the viewer that death is not the end. Ghost films generally offer this reassurance, of course, but more commonly it is hard to find solace in the knowledge, as the afterlife proves to be as conflicted as life and more often than not offers hellish vengeance and demonic confrontation as an eternal truth. In *Medium* the conduit of ghostly communications might have found a legalistic niche as well as a structure of support via the family and the DA's office, but in *Afterlife* seeing the dead leads to pain, alienation and emotional dysfunction. Not very comforting.

But of course, that is not the end of it. *Afterlife* does offer a sort of emotional resolution by the concluding episode of the second series, even if it's not quite the one we expected. Robert and his son are re-united – which might be seen as sentimental and a source of traditional solace, if we ignore what it takes to get there.

SUPERNATURAL (2005-PRESENT)

'Star Wars *in truck stop America.*'

The tagline doesn't immediately bring to mind the spooky urban legends and folklore that inspired creator Eric Kripke, but that's right there in the title: *Supernatural.* And, as Kripke explains, the tagline is just 'a way to shorthand it to attract viewers to the show – Han Solo and Luke Skywalker with chainsaws in the trunk.' It's an apt description, seeing as how many people who have worked with Jensen Ackles (*Dark Angel, Smallville*), who plays lead Dean Winchester, describe him as 'a young Harrison Ford'. And Sam Winchester, as played by Jared Padalecki (*Gilmore Girls, House of Wax*), is similar to Luke Skywalker in many ways, most notably that he's a reluctant hero with father issues and the potential power to play mind tricks on people.

Like *Star Wars, Supernatural* explores motifs found in most Westerns. As Kripke puts it: 'More than anything, this show is kind of a Western and the Impala is their horse. They ride into town and they fight the evil and they kiss the girl and they ride out of town again. The mythic tropes of the Western really serve us and makes it feel bigger than it is.'

And in Season Two they added a roadhouse, which Kripke likens to the cantina in *Star Wars.* 'There's this sort of gunslinger breed of [monster] hunters out there dealing with the supernatural and people were hip to the truth and so the notion was, alright, let's have a place where organically these people can bump into each other . . . a place that's owned by hunters, where hunters would go and they'd pick up a hunt or exchange information or just grab a drink and brag about their latest kill.'

But despite the show's action and adventure spirit, it's a family drama at heart. As illustrated in *Life & Style*, the Hollywood gossip rag. 'Ackles and Padalecki act like true brothers, watching each other's back as they trade barbs.' And Kripke is quick to point out that getting the brotherly dynamic right isn't always easy to write. 'It's very challenging because you have to tell twenty-two effective relationship stories a year between two characters. It forces us to go psychologically deep.'

Yet, if the brothers' melodrama is indeed the heart, it's horror and humour that pumps the blood through it. (And there's a lot of blood on this show.) 'My favourite movies are *Poltergeist, Evil Dead II*, and *An American Werewolf in London,*' Kripke reveals. 'Those are my touchstones. That's the tone I love to do. It's a way to say to the audience that we're not taking ourselves too seriously. But you have to use the humour carefully. We say keep the scary parts scary and the funny parts funny. The boys are living in the real world. The threats are real. These monsters are real and they're scary and they're killing people. During the scare sequence, no quips, only fear. Then when it's over you can take a breath and their coping mechanism is to make a joke.'

'What's fun about *Supernatural* is it's a popcorn movie,' states the show's executive producer John Shiban (who also wrote and produced a number of episodes of *The X-Files,* its spin-off *The Lone Gunmen* and episodes of *Star Trek: Enterprise*). 'It can be a lot of fun and actually liberating to write the quippy dialogue and do the big set pieces that are just meant to be *fun*.' So it's no surprise that Kripke says, 'The very first version was to combine all these urban legends into one feature film.' There's already been a movie called *Urban Legend*, but it contains no supernatural elements – no urban-legends-are-real revelations – only a standard slasher killer who uses the legends as his modus operandi.

But Kripke quickly realised that there were too many great legends to squeeze into one movie, so he switched gears and began outlining a TV series, one that featured 'a bunch of tabloid writers in a van driving around the country'. But fortunately for him, this idea was shot down when he pitched it, because it turned out that ABC was already working on a revamp of *The Night Stalker*, a horror series about reporters investigating supernatural activities. Ironically, that show debuted the same time as *Supernatural* and failed to survive its first season.

In fact, of the six new shows with paranormal themes that debuted in the fall of 2005, only one other, *Ghost Whisperer*, lasted an entire season. Tim Goodman explains why in the *San Francisco Chronicle*: '*Supernatural* manages what few of this season's trendy phenomena series can't – the drama immediately finds its identity, then tears off without looking back.' And in *TV Guide*, Tracy Phillips gives a good reason why the show will continue to satisfy viewers: 'Unlike some paranormal shows that torture you by dragging out their mysteries indefinitely, *Supernatural* is moving along at a deliberate, satisfying pace.'

So once Kripke settled on the simple idea of two brothers on a road trip hunting down monsters of legend, everything fell into place. It allowed him to do a mini horror movie-of-the-week, in which he's regularly played homage to all his inspirations. Sometimes it's just a scene, like the *Jaws*-style opening of 'Dead in the Water', the *Ring*-flavoured ghoul climbing out of the mirror in 'Bloody Mary', the skin-ripping transformation inspired by *An American Werewolf in London* in 'Skin', or *The Shining* allusions in 'Playthings'.

And other times there are strong plot correlations, such as between 'Asylum' and *House on Haunted Hill* (both involve ghostly goings on and psychiatrists performing cruel procedures on their patients), 'Benders' and *Deliverance* (both feature antagonists from psychotic backwoods families), 'Roadkill' and *The Sixth Sense* (both have lead characters who are ghosts that don't know they're dead), and the *Hell Hazers II* movie being filmed within the 'Hollywood Babylon' episode has many similarities to *The Evil Dead* trilogy.

Kripke points out that in 'Children Shouldn't Play With Dead Things' 'Dean even has the line, "C'mon, didn't you see *Pet Sematary*?" because if we're gonna make an homage to another horror flick, we have the good manners to overtly reference it in the dialogue.' Indeed, there are other movies, TV shows, novels, and comic books referenced in every episode, with *Star Wars, The Shining, Ghostbusters, The Exorcist*, and *The Evil Dead* getting the most frequent tips of the hat.

There's another shtick going on here as well; riffing horror culture references in the naming of the episodes. *Hell House* being the title of Richard Matheson's classic novel, *Children Shouldn't Play With Dead Things* Bob Clark's 1972 horror comedy. Episode Eighteen, 'Something Wicked', is a definite reference to Ray Bradbury's novel *Something Wicked This Way Comes*. Other titles include 'The Usual Suspects' and 'Crossroad Blues' – they've all got their roots in horror culture.

Week in and week out, *Supernatural* hits that big-screen horror-movie vibe. As Barry Garron of the *Hollywood Reporter* professes, 'It is as close as TV has come to importing the kind of horror associated with theatricals, but it combines those spine-tingling moments with camaraderie and mystery.'

But *Supernatural* doesn't just draw inspiration from movies. The original incarnations of *Kolchak: The Night Stalker, The Outer Limits*, and *The Twilight Zone* are all obvious influences. Looking at more contemporary shows, Tracy Philips of *TV Guide* asserts, 'Not since *The X-Files* has a show revelled so successfully in giving us goosebumps.' And Eric Kripke's *Supernatural* directorial debut, 'What Is and What Should Never Be', was inspired by an episode of *Buffy the Vampire Slayer*. In fact, one of the most quoted lines from the show is when two amateur ghost hunters caught in a tough situation (in 'Hell House') tell each other to be brave, and ask, 'WWBD? What would Buffy do?'

'We're writing a show that is every bit as sophisticated as *Buffy* [*the Vampire Slayer*] or *The X-Files*,' Kripke proclaims proudly. Indeed, *Supernatural* has the great creatures and wit of *Buffy the Vampire Slayer* (and *Angel*), yet with more realistic scares. And it has the dark moodiness and chills of *The X-Files*, yet with a more uplifting undertone. As Ben Edlund (*The Tick, Angel*) puts it, 'The standard is pretty high here.'

Recurring star Jeffrey Dean Morgan (*Watchmen*), who plays the brothers' father, John Winchester, feels that 'between Eric Kripke and [executive producer] Kim Manners they've set a tone that's never been done on television before. And I think every episode Jensen and Jared bring something more to the table as actors and as characters. I'm duly impressed with them.' What's also impressive is that while Morgan was working on *Supernatural*, he was juggling recurring roles on the critically acclaimed *Weeds* and the hugely successful *Grey's Anatomy*. And in its second season *Supernatural* was moved from its post-*Gilmore Girls* timeslot in America to follow *Smallville* on Thursdays, opposite *Grey's Anatomy* and CBS juggernaut *CSI*, which was quite *scary.*

'We loved being behind *Smallville* because we thought that was a really good companion piece to us,' comments executive producer Robert Singer (*Lois and Clark, TimeCop*, and 1973's *The Night Strangler*). 'Having said that, we didn't

Supernatural's demon-hunting siblings, Sam and Dean Winchester (Jared Padalecki and Jensen Ackles).

realise that this was going to be a battle of the titans between CBS and ABC . . . Given that *CSI* and *Grey's Anatomy* were our competition, we were really pleased with the audience we got. But our audience is a really hardcore, loyal audience.'

As of this publication, *Supernatural* is in its fifth season, and as recurring star Samantha Smith (*Transformers*) enthuses, 'It only gets better!' It could have settled into that adventure-of-the-week routine that it started out with, but with a definite shift to the darker the brothers have found themselves caught betwixt and between the angels and the demons with all hell quite literally breaking loose (thanks in no small part to Sam and Dean). This 'bigger' story has taken the show in an entirely new and very welcome direction with the introduction of Castiel, played by Misha Collins. Angels and Demons in the *Supernatural* mythology need to occupy vessels – a euphemism for possessing humans. This possession can be voluntary, such as when Jimmy Novak offers himself to the angel Castiel and becomes his host, or involuntarily, being just about every demonic possession we see in the show. With Armageddon well and truly underway Sam, Dean and the rogue angel, Cas, find themselves going toe-to-toe with Lucifer himself, destiny seeming to suggest that, like Cain and Abel, these two brothers are destined to come to a rather bloody end. Dean, it seems, is the sword of Michael, or Michael's vessel, while Sam is Lucifer's chosen vessel. As mum used to say, 'It's all going to end in tears.'

JUST BECAUSE THEY'RE OUT TO GET YOU, IT DOESN'T MEAN YOU'RE PARANOID

The Prisoner, The X-Files, Torchwood

THE PRISONER (1967)

> Number Two: 'Are you going to run?'
> Number Six: 'Like blazes. First chance I get.'
> – 'Free For All'

On 1 October 1967, the first episode of *The Prisoner* ('Arrival') aired on ITV, immediately becoming one of the most original and progressive television shows ever created. Brought to life by co-creator and star Patrick McGoohan, many dismissed the lead's new show as just another spy series. After all, McGoohan had just come off a 39-episode stint as the star of the popular super-spy drama *Danger Man* a scant four years before (in fact, in the US the show spawned the hit song 'Secret Agent Man', where it was re-titled *Secret Agent*). Few people at the time would have guessed at the show's far-reaching cultural impact and its eerie ability to prognosticate many Orwellian facets of our modern life.

The show was originally envisioned quite as it appears: an allegorical statement on personal liberties and those in charge of such liberties. McGoohan, despite a personal dislike for the works of Ian Fleming and his dashing James Bond hero, was able to catapult the success of that franchise to get *The Prisoner* made. Secret agents were cool. And while many fans of Number Six will tell you that he was 'cool', McGoohan had a unique and singular vision for the show that often engendered conflict with the network and his producers.

The Prisoner has a simple enough conceit – a British government operative (a spy by any other name) decides enough is enough and quits his job. Was he John Drake from *Danger Man*? ITC certainly seemed to think so, though McGoohan himself was of course non-committal. He writes a resignation letter, gives it to his employers, and goes home, readying himself for a nice vacation. Not content to allow their employee to leave of his own free will, his former employers capture

Trapped in The Village – Patrick McGoohan
as The Prisoner's *Number Six.*

McGoohan's character and sequester him off in a remote township called the 'Village', where he is put through a number of different treatments, all in the hope that he will divulge information, such as why he quit. All this is shown in one of the more memorable opening sequences of any show in television history and is capped with the following famous dialogue.

> Number Six: 'Where am I?'
> Number Two: 'In the Village.'
> Number Six: 'What do you want?'
> Number Two: 'We want information.'
> Number Six: 'Whose side are you on?'
> Number Two: 'That would be telling. We want information . . . information . . . information.'
> Number Six: 'You won't get it.'
> Number Two: 'By hook or by crook, we will.'
> Number Six: 'Who are you?'
> Number Two: 'The new Number Two.'
> Number Six: 'Who is Number One?'
> Number Two: 'You are Number Six.'
> Number Six: 'I am not a number, I am a free man.'

The information Number Six holds is never divulged – but not through lack of trying by the various Number Twos that are brought in for the job. These individuals employ a number of questionable techniques, some even tantamount to torture. Number Six is subjected to hallucinatory drugs, brainwashing, live action roleplay, seduction, battles of wits, and scientific experiments. He's treated like a prisoner of war. His every move is scrutinised while at the Village. He can't read the paper, listen to the radio, or have a conversation without it being analysed by the mysterious leader of the group, Number Two. But Number Six remains resolute in his silence. In the first episode, 'Arrival', he tells his captors, 'I will not be pushed, filed, stamped, indexed, briefed, debriefed, or numbered! My life is my own.' It is this overlaying sentiment of rebellion that McGoohan sought to make with the show. That without rebellion of some degree by the people, institutions such as the Village become all-powerful.

> Assistant: 'He doesn't even bend a little.'
> Number Two: 'That's why he'll *break*. It only needs one small thing. If he will answer one simple question, the rest will follow. Why did he resign?'

While the show made bold, broad statements on personal liberties, civil disobedience, government desperation, and the importance of 'self', McGoohan kept fans of the show in the dark with his refusal to be pinned down on certain

Although many fans of Danger Man *found* The Prisoner *baffling, its mix of allegory, post-modernism and Orwellian themes has proven enduringly popular.*

important plot aspects. Who was Number One? Why was it so important to discover why Number Six quit his job? What was up with the Butler (played by Angelo Muscat) and his umbrella? Was the Village some sort of secret agency that has its hands in most world affairs? Who the heck was Number Six? Was he *really* John Drake from *Danger Man*?

Interestingly enough, it was such oblique storytelling that has fed the popularity of *The Prisoner* over the past four decades. During that time, the show has bled into the fabric of pop culture. Its influence can be felt on both sides of the Atlantic Ocean, be it with direct references in music, television, and movies, or more practical in nature, such as its narrative structure, high-minded metaphorical plots, and general distrust of 'those in charge'. Satirical television shows such as *The Simpsons* routinely make *The Prisoner* references. British rock bands the Clash and Iron Maiden have released songs based on the series. There are numerous online fan clubs. Dozens of websites exist that analyse every episode, seeking meaning in every image.

Three television shows come to mind that owe much of their roots to *The Prisoner: Lost, Twin Peaks*, and *The X-Files*. The most recent of these three shows, J.J. Abrams's hit series *Lost,* shares many traits with its sixties predecessor. First and foremost, there's the locale. The geographical location of the Village was never divulged in *The Prisoner*. Several vague references were made that could theoretically place the Village somewhere in the Mediterranean region of the world. Certainly the Village could pass as a small Mediterranean town. But one common theory is that the Village *is* a representation of the world. That would mean that we, like Number Six, are those wild exultant choruses of joy and freedom in our world, whether we choose to be or not. We are not numbers, despite technology's drive to reduce us to such. We crave, we quest, we seek, we grow, we explore, and in doing so, we escape. Likewise, the island where the stranded members of Oceanic Flight 815 land is located in a shadowy geographical nexus, akin to the Bermuda Triangle. Is the island a manifestation of higher powers, such as the Village? The castaways are treated as pawns in a larger game that is never explained to them.

Lost and *The Prisoner* also share likeable but ultimately flawed and fallible heroes. Number Six refuses to break under the torture of his captors. He even makes the bold statement that he will seek his revenge when he returns.

Number Six: 'I'm gonna escape and come back.'
Number Two: 'Escape and *come back* . . . ?'
Number Six: 'Ah, yes – escape, come back, wipe this place off the face of the earth, obliterate it . . . you with it.'

Compare this to *Lost*'s own intense hero, Dr Jack Shephard. In Season Three, he promises to exact revenge on those running the island just as he is on the verge of escape (and after having endured mental tortures similar to those suffered by Number Six).

The X-Files explores political ground akin to that presented in *The Prisoner* and can be considered one of its closest cousins in terms of plot and metaphor. Again, shadowy government agents focus their machinations on one man for their own needs. Yet, that one man fights back despite the odds. *The X-Files'* creator Chris Carter shows us that society needs rebellion against those in charge to keep them in check. Time and time again, Fox Mulder puts his own life on the line (or has his life put on the line for him) to expose the cabal of dangerous men in charge (and who are doing nefarious deeds). Mulder is a neutral anti-hero, much like Number Six. In general, both have little need for the opposite sex. Both are clever, and sneaky when necessary. Both are single-minded in their goals. Thus driven, they believe that the trouble with science is that it can be perverted. And most importantly, both know to trust no one.

Perhaps the only other show as obtuse as *The Prisoner* was David Lynch and Mark Frost's *Twin Peaks*. Lynch and Frost employ similar storytelling techniques: difficult to decipher metaphors, bizarre characters, a setting seemingly removed from the rest of the world. They are less concerned about any political statements and more interested in dealing with the unknown. What you see isn't necessarily what it seems. This happens time and time again to Number Six, especially in his many attempts to escape the Village. Like Number Six and Fox Mulder, the hero of the show, Dale Cooper, is an agency man.

Number Six: 'You still have a choice. You can still salvage your right to be individuals. Your rights to truth and free thought! Reject this false world of Number Two . . . reject it *now*!'

Will we ever receive answers to some of *The Prisoner*'s deeper questions? It would spoil things if we did, don't you think? After all, the beauty of the show and the key factor that has allowed its longevity is the impenetrable enigma surrounding it.

THE X-FILES (1993-2002)

'Trust No One. The Truth Is Out There. I Want To Believe.'

Appearing in the opening montage of Chris Carter's groundbreaking television series, *The X-Files*, these three phrases perfectly reflected both the mood and tone of the show as well as the consciouness of a nation. As Chris Carter said on the *Vicki Gabereau Show* in May 1995: 'I think when people are pursuing the truth, the conscience is built-in. There's no political message being delivered, no social message being delivered, but I think there is sort of a universal, scientific, religious message that can be extrapolated. I think that's not a conscious decision to do that. People who see the show oftentimes feel the show is actually a very religious show, which is funny because when I've thought about this, I think of myself as a non-religious person looking for religious experience, so I think that's what the characters are sort of doing too.'

First airing on 10 September 1993, *The X-Files* would go on to win 141 awards from 24 different organisations, including sixteen Emmys, three Golden Globes, and a Peabody Award, before showing its final episode on 19 May 2002. In those nine seasons, *The X-Files* would capture the heart of a nation and become a pop culture beacon. Before it was over it would spawn myriad tie-in projects and merchandise, including two feature films (1998's *Fight the Future* and 2008's *I Want to Believe*), multiple novelisations, official and unofficial guide books, an official magazine, a comic book series, mugs, jackets, caps, and not one, not two, but three soundtracks. Hundreds of fan sites haunted the internet and its fans – known as X-Philes – were among the most obsessed in popular culture. At the time of its final episode, *The X-Files* was the longest-running science fiction series ever to air on American television and the thirty-seventh best TV show of all time according to *TV Guide*. More recently, *Time Magazine* included it in their 2007 list of the 100 Best Television Shows of All Time.

The series centered on the exploits of Fox Mulder and Dana Scully, two agents with the Federal Bureau of Investigation who were tasked with investigating the 'X-Files'; those strange, unsolved cases that no one else wanted to touch, cases that usually involved the paranormal. Originally filed under 'U' for unsolved, the cases grew in number until they had to be moved to the less-used 'X' drawer of the filing cabinet. It is from here that the series drew its name. Fox, played by David Duchovny, was the believer, the one who was convinced of the existence of extraterrestrial life, who knew that the government was hiding something, and who had absolutely no doubt that there were creatures out there that man was never meant to understand. Dana, on the other hand, was the sceptic, determined to find a rational, scientific explanation for everything they encountered. Played by Gillian Anderson, Scully was initially assigned to the X-Files to debunk Mulder's more outrageous claims, but would slowly fall into his orbit as she experienced her fair share of unusual encounters.

The programme's focus on alien abductions, paranoid government conspiracies, religious mythology, and bizarre monstrosities hiding among us, not only in the dark stretches of lonely countryside but in the heart of the city and in the depths of the human mind, were a perfect mirror of the American cultural attitude in the midst of the 1990s. Disgusted with the government, distrustful of the growing spirit of religious fundamentalism pervading the world, and convinced more than ever before that there were 'more things in heaven and earth, Horatio, than are dreamt of

The X-Files agents Dana Scully (Gillian Anderson)
and Fox Mulder (David Duchovny) – uncovering
conspiracies one blade of grass at a time.

in your philosophy', the American public was primed for a show that captured this sense of discomfort, that made us examine our belief systems in a new light and that brought previously separate issues crashing together on centre stage. Chris Carter gave it to them. In an insightful comment, Carter himself once said, 'The show's original spirit has become kind of the spirit of the country – if not the world,' and he was right.

Of course if we are considering the zeitgeist, and the influences driving Carter, we can't ignore Adam Parfrey's endlessly fascinating and often deeply disturbing millennial non-fiction anthology, *Apocalypse Culture*. Indeed, Carter himself has often cited it as not only one of the main formative influences for *The X-Files*, but also as one of the most important books ever.

Carter, interviewed by Alex Strachen in the *Vancouver Sun* on 25 July 1996, laid it out for us: 'I think it has a lot to do with the global, political climate, the lack of a clear enemy and a certain amount of navel-gazing. But I think it also has to do with science. We are living in a world where technological and medical advancements are making quantum leaps. We don't quite know how to fathom those things, and it gives us a feeling that, in fact, we may not be in control.'

One of the ways that *The X Files* differed from previous television programmes centered on the structure of the show itself. Previous one-hour dramas tended to be character-driven. *The X-Files* was the exact opposite – more plot- and idea-driven than its competitors. Carter went so far as to combine serial drama elements, more often found in miniseries or soap-opera style programming, with individual stand-alone plots that did not require a viewer to understand the show's history prior to watching. In this fashion, Carter was able to exploit the loyalty of fans who were following the show's complex mythology while at the same time not alienating new viewers before they had the time to understand what was going on. Executive Producer Frank Spotnitz summed it up quite well when he said, 'One of the interesting things about *The X-Files* is it defies conventional wisdom about what a

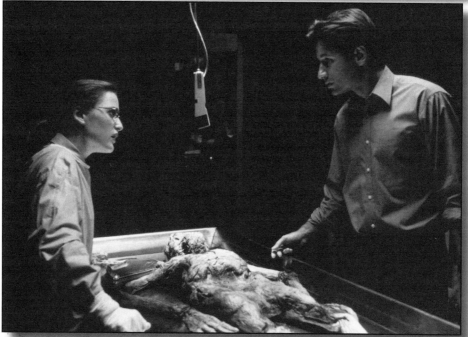

*Scully's medical background and innate empiricism
regularly tempered Mulder's desire 'to believe'.*

The sexually ambiguous nature of Mulder and Scully's relationship provided fans with intrigue throughout the series' long run.

drama is supposed to be. The wisdom in the television industry in America is, "Give them the same thing every week, only different." *The X-Files* said, "Forget that. We're gonna give you a different type of show, a different situation every week. As different as we can make it.'"

Another major difference from contemporary dramas of the time was the mythology – or mytharc, as it is sometimes called – that Carter developed for the series. Mulder becomes a believer in extraterrestrial life when he witnesses the abduction of his younger sister by alien visitors years before the show's current timeline. It is his quest for answers that drives his character to continue even in the face of seemingly insurmountable odds. Slowly, over time, he begins to uncover the truth of a conspiracy within the US government that stretches back to the famed (and quite possibly apocryphal) Roswell saucer crash of 1947. (After all, the US military did attribute the sightings to an experimental aircraft.) Not only is the government aware of the existence of alien life, but it has co-opted alien technology for its own use and has seemingly agreed to collaborate with the aliens in their plan to re-colonise the earth. The Syndicate, as the cover group is now known, works not only to help the aliens create a virus designed to infect the Earth's entire population, but also covertly develops a counter agent, though whether this was to be used by select Syndicate members or to be made available to all humans was never made clear. The abduction of Fox's sister, an event that motivates his actions throughout much of his adult life, wasn't truly an abduction at all – the Syndicate agreed to have one of their family members live under alien control and William Mulder surrenders his daughter, Samantha, as part of this agreement.

The standalone episodes, which, in fact, comprised the majority of the nine seasons, did not disappoint in their energy or creativity either. Carter skillfully made good use of genre styles, moving throughout a huge range of tastes from horror to comedy, which delivered a series unlike any other. Each episode started with a teaser, designed to pull the viewer into the mystery right from the beginning, and would then cut to the show's opening, complete with its well-recognised catch phrases. Mulder and Scully would then be called in to solve the mystery hinted at in the show's teaser opening. The monster of the week, as standalone episodes came to be called, ranged from miracles of a religious nature, such as Season Three's 'Revelations', where a young boy displaying the gift of stigmata is marked for execution by a deranged killer, to the presence of supernatural creatures straight out of myth and legend such as the killer sea serpent highlighted in the 'Quagmire' episode. Yet even here the writers avoided the audience's typical expectations, continually bringing something new to the series. 'Jose Chung' is the story of Scully's abduction by aliens, but it is told entirely through her point of view as she relates it to a journalist, the episode's title character. 'Post-Modern Prometheus' was filmed entirely in black and white. Season Four's 'Paper Hearts' blended the mythology storyline with a stand-alone plot, effectively merging the two styles and once again springing something new on the unsuspecting audience.

Indeed, the show's writers were adept at turning conventional expectations on their heads, simultaneously confounding the audience while keeping the show fresh and original. *The X-Files* took the typical cop-buddy drama made famous in shows like *Starsky and Hutch* and twisted it just enough to be both recognisable and completely different. In most previous crime dramas, FBI agents had been presented as paragons of moral virtue, walking the straight and narrow path, incapable of bending the rules, never mind breaking them. Mulder shattered that stereotypical image; he seemingly never encountered a rule he didn't take delight in breaking and seriously considered explanations for events that the average FBI agent wouldn't be caught dead thinking about, never mind discussing aloud; from voodoo sorcery to little green men from outer space. In similar fashion, casting Gillian Anderson as Mulder's methodical partner with advanced degrees in physics and forensic pathology was a brilliant move, putting a woman into a typically male role and providing a strong female lead who would appear in all but three of the show's 210 episodes.

The X-Files not only featured unusual detectives, it also featured unusual detective work. A conventional detective drama would move inexorably to the unveiling of the mystery – by the episode's end all that was unclear at the beginning would be revealed and explained. By comparison, many episodes of *The X-Files* ended in ambiguity, with several different possible explanations presented to the audience, leaving it up to the viewer to determine just what might have happened.

This change also extended to the way the show was presented. Most of the contemporary dramas of the time took place in limited settings – the characters' homes, their places of work, a local restaurant. Sets were re-used repeatedly, until the locations became as familiar as the characters. *The X-Files* turned this pattern on its head, often having four or five new settings in each episode. The writers constantly took the central characters out of their familiar surroundings and by doing so, helped to better focus the viewers' attention on the characters themselves.

Certainly one of the major reasons the show gathered such a loyal following

In addition to encountering unearthly and supernatural threats, the duo often found themselves at odds with their own government.

was the chemistry and sexual tension that developed during the course of the series between agents Mulder and Scully. During the first few seasons, that relationship was built upon Fox's driving need to prove the existence of supernatural and paranormal events weighed against Scully's equally passionate devotion to science and reason. In a way it was faith against science, but without the religious trappings. Yet as the series progressed, the two individual views began to blur into one, as the duo sought to find the answers to the questions that plagued them and to which the easy solutions were never quite applicable.

Sticking with their unspoken intent to confound the viewers' expectations, the writers made sure to hold off on creating anything other than a platonic relationship between the two heroes for as long as possible. Season after season came and went, with nothing more than a few shared looks and moments full of unrealised potential happening between the two. For all that, it maintained the complexity of love, substituting conversation for sex.

At its heart, *The X-Files* was a series that looked for meaning in the world around us. Whether that meaning dealt with the existence of extraterrestrials or the existence of God, it was still a search for order, a quest to understand just how it all works, how A connects to B and so forth. By stepping outside the norm, by showing us that search through the eyes of two fundamentally different characters, *The X-Files* gave us a chance to examine our own fears, our own search for meaning, and to try and make sense of it all, just as Scully and Mulder were trying to do. The show structure, the actor selections, the mixing and mashing of separate genres into one singular series – all of these things had an impact on the show's success. Taken together, they added up to a show that stirred our thoughts while at the same time firing our imaginations. And it is for that reason, above all others, that *The X-Files* carved a niche for itself within our cultural references and is as loved today as it was on the day its final episode aired.

In Chris Carter's own words: 'All I can do is speak to my own paranoia, which is great. So if my paranoia has inspired more paranoia, I think I'm a happy man.'

That says it all.

TORCHWOOD (2006-PRESENT)

Conceived by *Doctor Who* producer and chief writer Russell T. Davies and widely heralded by the BBC as a groundbreaking new science fiction series, *Torchwood* was devised to appeal to a more adult audience. Airing initially on the BBC's digital network rather than on terrestrial TV, the series spun off from *Who* and featured John Barrowman reprising his role as Captain Jack Harkness, former Time Agent and loveable con-man from the fifty-first century.

For *Torchwood* – the name derives from an anagram of *Doctor Who* – the staggering success of its parent franchise proved something of a double-edged sword. Captain Jack's popularity ensured that a vehicle for the character would stimulate interest, while the post-watershed slot and mature themes served to marginalise the younger viewers who made up the bulk of the mothership series' audience.

Russell T. Davies described his intentions thus: '*Torchwood* will be a dark, clever, wild, sexy, British crime/sci-fi paranoid thriller cop show with a sense of humour – *The X-Files* meets *This Life*.' Whether the series lived up to Davies's concept is debatable – the first season was undermined by an unsympathetic and oversexed cast for whom 'dark', 'clever', 'wild' and 'sexy' too often translated to the screen as smutty or banal.

Torchwood's basic premise follows a group of misfits brought together under Captain Jack's leadership, who are ostensibly unified by the common goal of saving the world and obtaining all of the alien technology they can get their hands on. Relationships within the team are often frayed or fraught with supposed sexual tension – which regularly resulted in a dysfunctional unit that alternated between conflict and clinches, often to the detriment of the plot.

Given that the series was, to a large extent, devised to be character driven, it's

Torchwood's Captain Jack Harkness,
portrayed by the ebullient John Barrowman.

As Torchwood's 'new girl' Gwen Cooper (Eve Myles) was conceived as a sympathetic character aimed at introducing viewers to the top secret institute.

ironic that it was the characterisations that frequently let *Torchwood* down. The devil-may-care qualities that served to make Captain Jack such a hit in *Doctor Who* only shone through intermittently as the writers struggled to square his maverick nature with his responsibilities for holding the unstable team together. This resulted in Jack's depiction as an almost schizophrenic character, switching between delivering polysexual innuendo and coyly withholding information as a means of demonstrating his leadership status.

The character of Gwen Cooper was introduced as the gateway through which viewers discovered *Torchwood*. As the new girl, seconded to the team from the local police, Gwen represented a dramatic device whereby viewers could share her wonder at being pitched into a world of alien visitations and otherworldly occurrences. Initially, this was successful, as Gwen was inducted into the team and her domestic relationship with her sweet-but-dim partner, Rhys Williams, was established. However, any sense of Gwen being the series' sole sympathetic character was fundamentally derailed by her gratuitous affair with the eminently dislikeable Owen Harper, which began in Episode Six, 'Countrycide'.

Arrogant, cocky and usually in the grip of some kind of hissy-fit about nothing in particular, Harper was presumably devised as the series' 'edgy' character. At best, he comes across as a poor man's Dexter Fletcher; more often he's simply annoying. Evidently, these flaws were recognised by Davies and his team of writers (which included *Life On Mars*' Chris Chibnall) and attempts were made to soften the character through a doomed love affair with a temporally displaced 1950s pilot played by Louise Delamere, a former flatmate of David Tennant, best known for her role as Lia Costoya in the medical comedy-drama *No Angels*.

Throughout the first series, the rest of the team were little more than dramatic ciphers; Doctor Toshiko Sato tended to conform to gender and ethnic stereotyping – being portrayed as a quietly efficient Japanese boffin who only saw any genuine character development toward the end of the series. Despite having hidden his part-android girlfriend in the basement, Ianto Jones fails to deliver as the series' mystery man, tending to come across as a slightly autistic gofer.

Despite being a part of the *Doctor Who* phenomenon, *Torchwood* makes every effort to stand out on its own – a brief that could be seen as counter-intuitive in terms of cashing in on the success of its core franchise. The series has a slick, high-camp take on life, death, sex and aliens. It is also unique in two ways, in that it is perhaps the only spin-off to ever purposefully distance itself from its parent show, and features a leading man who is an immortal, omnisexual action hero.

Spin-offs are an increasingly commonplace part of television, normally targeted at the same audience as the original show from which they are derived. When *Angel* first aired, *Buffy the Vampire Slayer* fans were identified as its natural audience. When *Frasier* first aired, it was aimed at *Cheers* fans. The makers of *Torchwood* have gone out of their way to break with this tradition, aggressively distinguishing the show from *Doctor Who* in terms of its broadcast time, advertising and overall content. Finally, they declared that the Doctor himself would never show up on *Torchwood*, as that might encourage younger fans to watch when they should perhaps abstain from doing so. This, of course, doesn't stop other characters from crossing back and forth – Barrowman appeared in *Doctor Who* for the finale of Series Three, while the Doctor's companion Martha (Freema Agyeman) joined the *Torchwood* team in Series Two. In an apparent balancing act, the BBC offered up a second spin-off – *The Sarah Jane Adventures* – in an afternoon kids' TV slot.

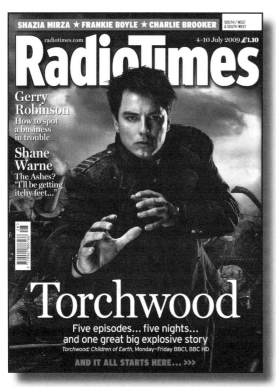

The Radio Times *heralds* Torchwood's *third season – which aired nightly and drew in a highly creditable six million viewers.*

By targeting *Torchwood* at an adult audience, it was hoped that the same children who grew up watching the original *Doctor Who* and who are now introducing their own children to its current incarnation may have found the series to be the obvious next step in the development of the franchise.

Torchwood's much-heralded 'adult themes' manifested themselves with varying degrees of success. The issues brought into play by Captain Jack's bisexuality were at best enlightened and at worst juvenile. 'It wasn't me sort of dying to get a bisexual character on screen,' said Russell T. Davies. 'Yes, I'm a gay writer, but I was thinking: Jack's from the fifty-first century so of course he's going to go out with men and women. To get hung up on it is too sad for words, frankly.'

Despite its inherent flaws, the debut series was nominated for two BAFTA Cymru Awards (Welsh BAFTAs): Barrowman for Best Actor and Eve Myles for Best Actress. Myles won for her performance in the episode 'Everything Changes'. Interestingly, this is her second outing in the *Who*-niverse. Her first was as Gwyneth in the *Doctor Who* episode 'The Unquiet Dead'. Myles isn't the only double-dipper, Naoko Mori also migrated from the main *Who*, her character Toshiko Sato being the same Doctor Sato that wrestled with pig aliens in 'Aliens of London', while Freema Agyeman's popular Martha Jones turned her back on the Doctor at the end of Series Three to do a stint in Cardiff for the second series of *Torchwood*.

While *Torchwood* was initially uncertain about its direction and identity, and consequently bore the brunt of numerous critical maulings, some good moments were provided by writers Cath Tregenna (the episodes 'Out of Time' and 'Captain Jack Harkness' are as close to exquisite as the show could ever hope to get), P.J. Hammond (of *Sapphire and Steel* and *Ace of Wands* fame, with his episodes 'Small World' and 'From Out of the Rain') and Helen Raynor ('To the Last Man').

Many of the very best episodes seem to revolve around wartime Britain: the family stranded in their future, unable to cope and hopelessly out of time, the boys on their last night of freedom before they go off to war to die, and the shell-shocked lad trapped between then and now in a loop of temporal flux where the residents of the wartime hospital bleed through as ghosts into today. With all of these episodes the focus is on the characters, not genre tropes or the gimmicks modelled by the special effects team at The Mill. Here the show explores existentialism, the value of human life and the corrupting nature of power. Just the kind of adult themes that Davies presumably had in mind.

While the first series was neither as groundbreaking nor original as its creators obviously intended, and somewhat inevitably wasn't a patch on *Doctor Who*, its climax enabled an overhaul ahead of Season Two. This meant that *Torchwood* was able stop fighting against its all-ages-welcome origins and come home. Not only was the swearing done away with, but the second run of thirteen shows also offered child-friendly episodes for screening earlier in the evening on the terrestrial BBC2. This made sound sense – if you create a show with such strong ties to the most popular family programme on British television, you can damned well bet the kids are going to be begging to stay up to watch Captain Jack. Audience figures bore this out, after drawing 2.4 million viewers for its pilot episode, Season One stabilised at a healthy-for-digital 1.3 million. The transfer to BBC2 pulled in an average audience of 3.1 million.

This reboot did much to address many of the previous season's flaws. It ceased being a profane version of *Doctor Who* for grown-ups, and episodes such as the climactic 'Exit Wounds' (which featured Tosh's death) were genuinely affecting. Gwen marries long-suffering boyfriend Rhys, Captain Jack's charm returns, Ianto is promoted to a full, active member of the team, and Owen Harper is killed off.

By the start of Season Three, in July 2009, the BBC's confidence in the series had grown to the extent that the network gambled with taking the show into the realm of 'event television' – commissioning a five-part series, 'Children of Earth', to run across consecutive nights at the beginning of that month. The miniseries, described by the *Radio Times* as 'an epic, frantic political thriller – with aliens', begins with chilling scenes of children across the world stopping what they are doing to stand and chant 'We are coming' in unison.

Although it raised the series' profile, this change in format (in addition to the nightly scheduling the series ran for only five episodes rather than the customary thirteen) disappointed John Barrowman. 'Personally, I felt like we were being punished,' he declared. 'Other shows move from BBC3 and 2 to 1, and they don't get cut. So why are we? It felt like every time we moved we had to prove ourselves.'

Despite Captain Jack's misgivings about the series' length, the promotion to BBC1 and the star billing the series received across that week's *Radio Times* demonstrated the network's faith in its sometimes awkward offspring, and it appears that *Torchwood* may well fulfil Russell T. Davies's original hopes and establish itself as a unique part of the *Who* mythos.

7 A NEW KIND OF HERO

Wonder Woman, Xena: Warrior Princess,
Buffy the Vampire Slayer, Ultraviolet, Angel,
Smallville, Lost, Heroes

WONDER WOMAN (1975-1979)

*'In terms of Wonder Woman, I've never really had a woman
not identify, or identify in a negative way. At least they haven't come up
to me and said anything. That was always a goal of mine, sort of
that sisterhood thing from Paradise Island.'*
– Lynda Carter, 2006

Sex sells. It's one of the most obvious reasons for television eclipsing radio. It's hard to lust after a voice carried on the airwaves – though not impossible, obviously – but there is a reason television is called the goggle-box: legs, lips, hips, the swagger, the swoosh and the sway, the smile, the pout, the eyes – and, of course, the breasts. Cue *Wonder Woman*.

On the back cover of the 29 January 1977 issue of *TV Guide* was an ad for Virginia Slims cigarettes, picturing a good-looking (but not so good-looking as to be threatening to her sisters), fashionably dressed young woman, cigarette between her fingers, beneath the celebratory slogan of solidarity: 'You've Come A Long Way, Baby.'

On the front cover, in all her Lichtenstein-esque glory, was Wonder Woman, cartoon bullets bouncing off her cartoon bracelets. 'From the Comics to TV: Lynda Carter as *Wonder Woman*,' the copy-line read.

Above the magazine's logo ran the promise: 'A Startling Survey: What Criminals Learn From Television.' The corresponding lead article was 'When Television Is a School for Criminals', wherein 'a surprising nine out of ten [criminals interviewed at Michigan's maximum security Marquette Prison] . . . actually learned new tricks and improved their criminal expertise by watching crime programmes. Four out of ten said that they have attempted specific crimes they saw on television crime dramas.' It's a staggering concept. (*Starsky and Hutch* as a criminal blueprint? *Really?*)

Lynda Carter as Wonder Woman – bringing William Moulton
Marston's Amazonian princess to life for 1970s TV audiences.

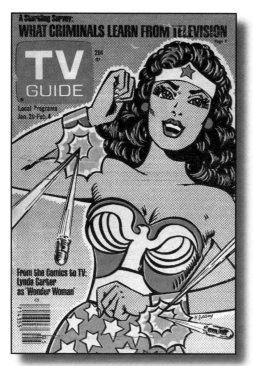

TV Guide *showcases the climax of* Wonder Woman*'s first season – January 1977.*

Thankfully, the other leading article was about someone who fought television criminals with television justice: 'From the Pages of Comic Books . . . Comes "Wonder Woman" Lynda (Wham!) Carter, Who Is Scoring A Hit (Zap!) With Children And Their Fathers (Crash!)'

Lynda Carter and Wonder Woman were the media darlings and punch-line *du jour* of 1977. After a couple of uninspired and insipid pilots and TV movies, *The New Original Wonder Woman* debuted on 18 December 1975, on ABC. The series was set in the days of World War Two, copying the look and feel of the original comic book by Charles Moulton (aka William Moulton Marston) and H.G. Peter. The villains were Nazis, Fifth Columnists and war profiteers. The tone was campy, though not high-camp, a few notches down from the over-the-top approach which worked so well on *Batman*, the show that, even a decade after it had gone off the air, continued to provide the TV audience's perception of comic-book superheroes. *Wonder Woman* was played with unconscious cool and retrospective irony, but the appeal was (unavoidably) sexual.

Readers were made to wait until the end of the third paragraph for information about the 'spectacular six-foot dimensions' of the 'ex-Miss World USA', and to learn that, in the line-up of ABC's most comic-bookish TV shows (*The Six Million Dollar Man*, *Happy Days*, *Welcome Back, Kotter*, *The Bionic Woman*), no other star could hold a candle to Ms Carter in the bosom department: 'Lynda's is an impressive size 38.' Against which the likes of Lee Majors, Henry Winkler, Gabriel Kaplan and Lindsay Wagner could hardly compete; the inclusion of this tidbit smacked of studio-approved pandering, and it would be surprising if all of Lynda's supposed measurements were not included in producer-approved press material. All of this was in support of the only sure conclusion one could reach about a mid-1970s TV show starring a tall, attractive woman costumed in a star-spangled bathing suit and red, knee-high, high-heeled boots: 'It is not only nine-year-olds who are watching.

The Nielsen evidence is that their fathers are also impelled to steal peeks at this particular comic-strip show.'

Undoubtedly.

TV Guide critic Judith Crist wrote in November 1975: 'Produced with taste and fine period feeling by Douglas S. Cramer, with a screenplay by Stanley Ralph Ross (one of *Batman*'s better writers) and directed with wit by Leonard Horn, this introduction of Wonder Woman and her role in beating the nasty Nazis is indeed an animated comic strip, but done with intelligence and verve.' The cast was 'fine' and Lynda Carter was described as 'luscious'. (In all fairness to the visual appeal of her co-star, Lyle Waggoner was credited for playing 'handsome Major Steve Trevor'. But where 'handsome' can be a value-neutral description, 'luscious' is plainly sexually suggestive – especially when attached to the actress herself, rather than to the character she plays.)

The New Original Wonder Woman garnered respectable enough reviews and ratings – when viewers could locate it on their dials. (This was back when TVs still had radio-like dials.) For instead of giving the Amazon Princess a regular berth on the weekly schedule, ABC used the first season's eleven one-hour episodes as specials to counter the competition on CBS and NBC. Clearly, it was the costume and the spectacular six-foot dimensions of the former beauty queen who filled it that drew its particular demographic: kids and adult males eighteen to dead. Junior came for the comic book goofiness; dad stayed for the size-38s. John Leonard, television critic for the *New York Times*, reviewed the 1977 premiere of *The New Adventures of Wonder Woman* on CBS (Warner Brothers, the studio that owned Wonder Woman, had grown tired of ABC's lack of commitment to the programme, picked up their size-38s and took them somewhere else): 'Obviously none of this is meant to be taken seriously. And I won't. Using comic strip exaggeration, the producers are offering another of those escapist fantasies in the mode of grim bionic creatures and camp cartoons that once transformed *Batman* into an electronic success.' It was a bit of a cliché, but a fun, harmless one. 'As an actress,' he could not help but add, 'Miss Carter creates the impression of a sweet little girl disconcertingly trapped in the body of a potential Fellini sexuality symbol.'

Yeah, you've sure come a long way, baby.

'Not even girls want to be girls so long as our feminine archetype lacks force, strength, and power. Not wanting to be girls, they don't want to be tender, submissive, peace-loving as good women are. Women's strong qualities have become despised because of their weakness. The obvious remedy is to create a feminine character with all the strength of Superman plus all the allure of a good and beautiful woman.'
– William Moulton Marston (creator of *Wonder Woman*), 1943

In 1972, Gloria Steinem recruited Wonder Woman as the symbol of the growing women's liberation movement, by putting the Amazon Princess on the cover of the first issue of *Ms Magazine*. She was depicted (drawn by a middle-aged male artist) as a colossus striding Godzilla-like over a small town, brushing aside attacks by the military while preserving the peace. She is carrying what appear to be those things that are good and giving and encapsulate the American Dream: jobs, cars, houses, a safe family environment, and all that is supposedly representative of female nurturing and strength, bound up protectively in her gold Lasso of Truth.

Wonder Woman – created by William Moulton Marston, psychiatrist, inventor of the lie detector and feminist, so that little girls could have a 'funny-paper heroine to root for' – had survived the highs and lows of publishing to be one of only three pre-existing superheroes to stay in print (Superman and Batman were the others) through a seven- or eight-year dry spell, comics having been commandeered by other genres: Westerns, romance, crime, humour, the supernatural, funny animals. The popularity of *The Adventures of Superman* on TV kept DC's core heroes afloat, but titles such as *All-Star Western, Girls' Love, The Adventures of Dean Martin and Jerry Lewis, Tomahawk, Mr District Attorney, House of Mystery, Animal Antics* and *Mystery in Space* far outnumbered the dozen or so superhero titles.

Wonder Woman came about as the response to a challenge made by Dr Marston in his role as educational consultant to All-American Comics (later known as DC). Disturbed by the overwhelmingly male world of superheroes, he asked where the role models were for little girls who read comics.

All-American publisher Max C. Gaines (whose middle name, Charles, was combined with the doctor's to come up with the 'Charles Moulton' pseudonym he employed on *Wonder Woman*) turned the challenge back on Marston, offering him the opportunity to create a 'wonder woman' to stand with the 'super men'. Marston responded with the first baby born in aeons to the Paradise Island-dwelling race of Amazons, blessed by the gods with the gifts of Aphrodite's beauty, Athena's wisdom, Hermes's speed, and Hercules's strength. She was, of course, the feminine archetype in Joseph Campbell's monomyth ideal.

The monomyth, Campbell's unifying theory, is a basic formula repeated in many universal narratives. In his book *The Hero with a Thousand Faces* (1949) Campbell coined the term, or more accurately borrowed it from James Joyce's *Finnegans Wake*.

Campbell's contention was that the myths we remember today, no matter where they are from geographically, all share the same fundamental structure:

A call to adventure, which the hero has to accept or decline

A road of trials, regarding which the hero succeeds or fails

Achieving the goal or 'boon', which often results in important self-knowledge

A return to the ordinary world, again in which the hero can succeed or fail

Applying the boon, in which what the hero has gained can be used to improve the world.

In the introduction to *The Hero with a Thousand Faces*, Campbell explained it as: 'A hero ventures forth from the world of common day into a region of supernatural

Critics often cited Wonder Woman's use of her 'magic' lasso as evidence of the character's innate sexual subtexts.

wonder: fabulous forces are there encountered and a decisive victory is won: the hero comes back from this mysterious adventure with the power to bestow boons on his fellow man.'

The classic examples he utlilised included the Buddha, Moses, and Christ stories, although Campbell does go into Greek, Roman and other more obscure mythologies which rely upon this basic structure.

Whatever inspiration *Wonder Woman* may have provided to a young female readership, it was believed that even the readers of this 'girl's' comic were likely to be as much as 90 per cent boys. Sheldon Mayer, Marston's editor at All-American, said in Les Daniels's *Wonder Woman: The Complete History* that he felt Marston 'was writing a feminist book but not for women. He was dealing with a male audience.'

Daniels observed, 'Marston always felt that males were the ones who needed his message most. If he really did succeed in altering the social climate, it might have been by exposing millions of boys (who would become men by the 1960s) to the ideals of feminism. After all, it's not much of a surprise that women might want to assert themselves, but it's quite a different matter when many of the supposed oppressors agree to go along with the idea.'

Not everyone agreed to go along with the idea. Some mocked it with a vehemence that revealed mid-century man's deep fear of the equalitarian or – heaven forbid!

– dominant woman. In 1954, *MAD* (then a comic book; it would later evolve into the magazine format more familiar to today's readership) offered up the parody 'Woman Wonder', by Harvey Kurtzman and Bill Elder. In it, Woman Wonder is every bit the strong, capable, dominant woman. Her boyfriend Steve Adore is a little weenie of a man, constantly needing rescue by his bigger, stronger Amazon girlfriend. They can't even make out without his complaining, 'Ooh, dearest! When you crush me so hard in your strong, sinewy, hairy muscular arms . . . I . . . I . . . I . . . I . . . break . . . something in the side of chest . . . something broke, sweetheart!' Diana Banana, this relationship's obvious lead, is oblivious to Steve's pain as she demands, 'Give me another kiss!' over and over through his discomfort. Steve fakes his own abduction to draw Woman Wonder into a trap, where he first psychologically berates her for being dumb enough to believe her great powers are even possible 'both physically and mathematically', before he and his muscle goons beat and torture her for two pages of non-stop hilarity – ending with his stomping on her face 'raised so tenderly in tearful supplication' with his hob-nailed boot. 'I've been planning for years to beat

Former Playgirl *centrefold Lyle Waggoner provided Wonder Woman with romantic interest in the form of army intelligence officer Steve Trevor.*

you to a bloody pulp!' he screams as jumps up and down on her, kicking her 'back in the kitchen where you belong, sweetheart!' And so we see, in the final panel, Steve and Diana in stereotypical comic-strip domestic bliss, complete with a houseful of screaming, misbehaving children (including a little girl in a Woman Wonder outfit who is setting fire to her brother), a haggard Diana with baby in one arm, burning dinner with the other, while Steve reclines with a cigar and racing form in the living room. 'Diana Banana is now content with the normal female life of working over a hot stove!' the caption reads, leaving the reader with: 'And Steve can even knock her down in boxing!'

In all fairness, *MAD*'s mission statement (as much as one ever existed) was to twist and subvert the conventions and pretensions of the subjects it parodied. *Superman* and *Batman* both received earlier, similar skewering in *MAD*, both equally honest in their own ways, but the sheer brutality and misogyny of 'Woman Wonder' is, especially in retrospect, disturbing. This is what happens to a dame who thinks she's better than a man: she gets stomped into submission.

Gloria Steinem actually worked for Harvey Kurtzman, writer of 'Woman Wonder', in the early 1960s, when she was a contributing editor to his humour magazine, *Help!* There is no indication – anecdotal or otherwise – that Kurtzman, creator of *MAD* and *Playboy*'s 'Little Annie Fanny', was himself in any way a misogynist; indeed, for all the strip's overt sexuality, the harassed Annie usually came up the winner in the battle of the sexists. Perhaps it's simply a matter of chalking it up to the 1950s zeitgeist: when domestic violence was looked at as an understandable and sometimes necessary disciplinary action; when the punch-line of every episode of Jackie Gleason's TV series *The Honeymooners* was, 'Bang, zoom, to the moon, Alice!', as bellowed by his character Ralph, with his clenched fist in her nonplussed face. Yes, viewers knew – the apologists now contend – that Ralph was all bluster; that Alice could and would kick his ass if he ever dared strike her. But how many simply heard the stated message without its comedic nuance? The mass media was selling the then socially acceptable belief that conflicts in the home could be settled at the end of a fist.

Television was rife with this subliminal message (as were comic books and movies) from the 1950s onwards, continuing through to the present. Sometimes, when Ricky lost his temper and loomed menacingly over his wife, the eponymous heroine of *I Love Lucy*, berating her in machinegun Spanish, she would cower, literally in a corner, under his verbal assault. His eyes bulged, veins throbbed in his forehead, he flailed about with clenched fists and the thought is sometimes unavoidable: *Oh, my God! Ricky beats Lucy! Why else would she be so fearful of his fiery Cuban temper?*

Edith Bunker in *All in the Family* was another victim, verbally stifled by Archie's bigotry, hatred, and stupidity. Yes, Edith was smarter than Archie – but 'Woman Wonder' will tell you what happens to girls who don't hide their superiority from the boys. Even *Charlie's Angels* would answer to Charlie.

So Wonder Woman was a symbol waiting to be discovered, both on TV and as a political icon. Steinem, like most kids during the 1940s, read comic books but was bothered that the women in them were relegated to getting into trouble so that the superhero could rescue them. 'I'm happy to say that I was rescued from this dependent fate at the age of seven or so; rescued by a woman,' Steinem recalled in the 1995 introduction to *Wonder Woman,* Abbeville Press' 1995 collection of Wonder Woman covers. Wonder Woman was the woman that girls who followed the muscular world of comic-book heroes wanted to be when they grew up; someone worthy, unlike 'a Technicolor clotheshorse, getting into jams with villains, and saying things like, "Oh, Superman! I'll always be grateful to you!"'

In her TV incarnation, Steinem found Lynda Carter to be 'a little blue of eye and large of breast' for the role, 'but she still retained her Amazon powers, her ability to convert instead of kill, and her appeal for many young female viewers'.

'Wonder Woman is this enigma within the world of superhero comics. No one seems to ever "get her". One moment, she is this completely powerful and independent character that stands just as strong (and often stronger) than her male counterpart. Then, she diverts to this out of touch ditz who doesn't even know how to pump her own gas, then sways into a ball-busting man-hater who thinks us dudes are nothing but disgusting sperm banks. Suddenly, she is the leader of an entire race of warrior woman, [and] finally she becomes Superman with ovaries. So, what gives? Which Wonder Woman is the correct Wonder Woman?'
– Aaron Duran, 'What Is So Hard About Wonder Woman?', 2007

'When I assumed editorship of the *Wonder Woman* comic book in early 1994,'explains DC editor Paul Kupperberg, responsible for writing around 600 comic strips and for unleashing the plague that was *He-Man* upon the world, 'the character was in what could only be described as a slump. The character was 50-plus years old and showing, not her age, but the inability of the boys' club that is the comic book industry to fully comprehend the needs of a complex, older woman. Girls stopped reading just about anything other than *Archie* comics sometime in the 1960s; that left the next few generations of comic book creators an almost exclusively male domain.'

Writing any character with any subtlety or nuance is difficult in the often limited scope of mainstream comic books. For a male writer who grew up on the testosterone-soaked comics of the last three decades, it was probably asking a lot of him to write convincingly about a character of the opposite sex who is supposed to embody everything good and virtuous and – above all – peaceful in womanhood, and yet stands for the personification of the invincible warrior class. How is a man who probably doesn't even understand his girlfriend or wife supposed to decode the exemplar of the female gender? George Perez managed to come close, in a popular and critically successful run of *Wonder Woman* starting in 1987; Dennis O'Neil, the

Like The Six Million Dollar Man, *the* Wonder Woman *TV series utilised slow-motion sequences to dramatically enhance the character's feats of strength.*

writer who kicked off a controversial 1968 storyline in which she was 'de-powered' and depicted as an Emma Peel karate expert in a white jumpsuit, readily admitted to the weakness in a 2006 online interview: 'You have to understand, writers like me, we have the best of intentions. We simply don't always know how to do things well.'

O'Neil, one of the most respected writers in the medium, would seem to have been shown the error of his ways. As he recalled in a subsequent online interview: 'Gloria Steinem, bless her, without mentioning my name, wrote an article about that and after the fact I saw her point, absolutely. At the time I thought I was serving the cause of feminism by making this woman self-made and then I immediately undercut that by having her have a male martial arts teacher. [I Ching, a wise little blind man.] My heart was pure, but I now see Steinem's point. To take the one really powerful [female] character in the comics pantheon, and take away her powers was really not serving the cause of feminism.'

And yet, almost three decades after that fact, Wonder Woman, under the auspices of a talented editor and inventive writer, was reduced to working in a fast food taco franchise in stories published under covers depicting her in various poses of humiliation and defeat. As Paul Kupperberg explains, 'Several years later, down the line of my editorial tenure, a storyline by writer/artist John Byrne elevated Wonder

As with similar sequences in the comic book series, scenes depicting Wonder Woman in bondage drew criticism from the feminist lobby.

Woman to the level of a god in the Greek pantheon. A large segment of fans were outraged; how dare anyone suggest Wonder Woman could be the equal, or [that troubling concept again] superior, to Superman? He was the male, naturally superior. Wonder Woman would, in the estimation of some, be allowed second place on the superpowers scale. Others busied themselves compiling lists of all the male heroes who are stronger and why; roleplaying games have given the hardcore accepted standards for the quantification of magical and superpowers to bolster their arguments, which generated considerable heat on the internet before subsequent editors and writers returned her to the comfortable, familiar status quo.'

So, what *is* so hard about Wonder Woman?

Is she, in the end, just a fungible fictional character responding to the personalities of whoever happens to be creating her adventures? Or is she merely the sum total of the reader's interpretation? After all, every argument for William Moulton Marston being a proto-feminist can be rebutted with quotes from his writings that blatantly espouse the psychological benefits of bondage and domination, the proof of which can be found in its comically obvious presence in all of his *Wonder Woman* stories: spankings – boy-on-girl and girl-on-girl alike – were routine, covers depicting the title character astride or bound to missiles hurtling through the air were plentiful, and lots of characters spent many panels trussed up by ropes and chains in a variety of bondage poses. As a dramatic device, Marston claimed, 'binding and chaining are the one harmless, painless way of subjecting the heroine to menace and making drama of it'. Besides, he said, 'women enjoy submission'.

Which carries more creative weight: the original intent of the creator, the judgement of the individual reader, or the interpretations of later creative contributors? Comic-book characters are kept fresh through the illusion of change; readers and fans want their favourites to go through six different kinds of hell on a monthly basis – just as long as they emerge exactly as they've always been.

More people know Wonder Woman from the television show than have ever read the comic books, but the influence of the creator's original intent was hard to ignore. Network television standards and practices kept it clean – there would be no straddling of phallic symbols on NBC – but every review couldn't help but reference the true star of the show: Lynda Carter's breasts.

Wonder Woman: Feminist icon. BDSM poster girl. Enlightener of the malleable minds of impressionable little boys. Smartass broad who needs a smacking around. Role model for girls. Goddess. Harmless TV entertainment. Jiggle-TV.

Because, in the end, everyone reads into *Wonder Woman* the qualities they need to satisfy themselves. Lynda Carter needed a higher meaning for her role as a comic-strip character. Gloria Steinem needed a symbol for feminine equality. Harvey Kurtzman needed a strong woman to victimise, reflecting the era's misogyny. Dennis O'Neil needed a reminder of how art intersects with politics. William Moulton Marston needed a spanking.

And the writers find what they need to make *Wonder Woman* work for them: Robert Kanigher took over scripting *Wonder Woman* after Marston's death in 1947, taking the character off into light romantic comedy mixed with fantasy and high adventure. Fantasy novelist and *Wonder Woman* writer Jodi Picoult told Newsarama.com in a 2006 interview: 'My thoughts are to sort of give her some mother-daughter issues – because I think all women have those, and to beef up the relationships that she now has in the world of man, as she's assuming an identity given to her.'

Assuming an identity given to her. That's something Wonder Woman should be used to by now.

XENA: WARRIOR PRINCESS (1995 - 2001)

As this section of the book focuses on subverting archetypes, it seems apt to follow the road paved by *Wonder Woman* with another statuesque warrior. From John Norman's *Gor* through the bestsellerdom of Terry Goodkind's *Sword of Truth* books, science fiction and fantasy has certainly been guilty of portraying women as sex objects. Think Lynda Carter, think Jeri Ryan, think Jessica Alba – think just about every good-looking woman who has found her way into a television show, or – God forbid! – onto the covers of any novel graced by Chris Achilleos, Brom, Frank Frazetta or Boris Vallejo's artwork. SF movie history is full of women wearing diaphanous gowns and glitzy miniskirts posing as futuristic attire: Valerie Perrine in *Slaughterhouse-Five* and the delectable Jenny Agutter in *Logan's Run* spring immediately to mind. But the concept of women as helpless pawns of powerful male characters is one of the most despised – and despicable – female stereotypes in fantastic fiction.

At first glance, Xena of Amphipolis appears to be the epitome of this stereotype. She sports a curvaceous figure and often wears minimalist armour reminiscent of the 'chicks in chainmail' stereotype. She moves through a patriarchal society and receives the greatest of her powers (the ability to kill gods) from a male figure (the Archangel Michael). During her warlord days, she often achieved her ends through the use of sex and seduction, hitchhiking on the authority of male characters. When she first encountered the warlord Borias, she seduced him away from his wife and children and persuaded him to help her form an army ('The Last of the Centaurs', Season Six, Episode Seventeen). In 'The Rheingold' (Season Six, Episode Seven), Xena seduced the Norse God Odin into telling her the location of the mystical Rheingold, which she then used to forge a ring that gave its wearer godlike powers.

Dig a little deeper, however, and a wise viewer might well argue *Xena: Warrior Princess* represents a turning point in the portrayal of women in fantasy television. One of the primary appeals of the show is the usurping of male roles by a strong female protagonist. Xena's armour is actually comparable in body coverage to that worn by her male counterparts. More importantly, she does not sit around in it waiting for the male lead to come to her rescue. She's a dynamic character, a mighty warrior who regularly defeats men, armies and even gods in battle. Like Jeanne D'Arc, she has led armies on multiple occasions, and even overpowered her male counterpart, Hercules, in their first battle. Hercules won the battle in the end, but only because his cousin distracted Xena at the moment she was about to kill him ('The Gauntlet', *Hercules: The Legendary Journeys*, Season One, Episode Two). She is also portrayed as the first person (male or female) to ever successfully run the gauntlet of soldiers beating their unarmoured victims with clubs. Heck, she even usurps the stereotypically male right to promiscuity and sleeps with kings, priests and gods, and all throughout the show's run remains independent, never marrying or settling down.

It is worth noting, in passing at least, that *Xena* utilised some of what made the *Buffy/Angel* dynamic so interesting in a televisual sense, with characters from one show, *Xena*, appearing in episodes of the other, *Hercules*, and storylines developing across both.

But before we start thinking about Xena as simply a manifestation of penis envy, it should be noted that she's far from it. Throughout the show her character is used to explore aspects of the female condition, and succeeds in retaining a strong sense of femininity. The pseudo-historical setting allows for a close symmetry with the trials faced by modern women. After all, suffrage aside, women are still moving through a male-dominated world, so in effect Xena is an embodiment of their struggle. She achieves her ends not through rank imitation of male methods, but by exploring and

*Lucy Lawless as Xena: Warrior Princess – widely credited
with inspiring a new generation of female action heroes.*

expressing her own natural strengths.

While she is a formidable fighter, Xena is not mystically blessed with the incredible strength of her male counterpart, Hercules. Instead, she wins battles through speed, skill and resistance to pain. Xena is also a mother. She gives birth to two children over the lifetime of the show, and demonstrates strong maternal instincts by protecting them and making sacrifices in their interests. During her warlord days, Xena bears a child to Borias. Touched by Borias's display of commitment to her and the baby shortly before his death, she gives the child to the Centaurs to raise rather than subjecting it to her own dangerous influence ('Past Imperfect', Season Four, Episode Nine, and 'Orphan of War', Season Two, Episode One). Shortly after her resurrection, Xena became pregnant without sexual intercourse ('Fallen Angel', Season Five, Episode One). We're talking divine insemination. In order to protect the child, Eve, from the wrath of the Olympian gods, Xena was granted the power to kill gods and angels via Michael the Archangel. She wields this power in Eve's defence ('Motherhood', Season Five, Episode 22). Her relationship with her travelling companion and soulmate Gabrielle emphasises the importance of human contact and the strength that friends can lend one another.

When viewed in comparison to its contemporaries, the *Xena: Warrior Princess* series is a progressive step towards confident, powerful female characters in fantasy television. Other shows may have portrayed assertive female protagonists, but most of them had used superpowers or other abilities, or a male partner (usually a mentor), to explain the protagonist's successes. *Wonder Woman* and *The Bionic Woman* are prime examples of the former, Emma Peel (of *The Avengers*) of the latter, although all are still noteworthy characters in their own right. Yet even so, no show had dared to place female protagonists in the male-dominated world of hand-to-hand combat and physical prowess. Like the Amazons depicted in the series, Xena makes a point of fighting for women's rights. As an athletic, gutsy female character, she is the natural predecessor of female action heroes such as Buffy, Max of *Dark Angel*, Sydney Bristow of *Alias* and the Bride in Quentin Tarantino's *Kill Bill*.

At its heart, the tale of Xena is a touching story about sin, redemption, and the bonds of sisterhood. Xena, vengeful after an attack on her village and the death of her younger brother Lyceus, sets foot on the path of murder and treachery at an early age. This path puts her at the head of armies, in the beds of kings, and face-to-face with gods. She is treacherous, murderous, and seductive. After being defeated by Hercules, she is inspired by his example: Hercules had suffered losses similar to hers, yet he followed a path of integrity and only raised his sword in honour of his dead relatives. Xena decides to follow that same path, and sets out to make amends for her bloody past ('Unchained Heart', *Hercules: The Legendary Journeys*, Season One, Episode Thirteen).

Along this journey, Xena meets Gabrielle, who becomes her most devoted companion and, according to a scary amount of fan fiction posted across the internet, her lesbian lover. Gabrielle acts as an anchor for Xena, holding her to the path of goodness and representing everything that is worth fighting for. Near the end of the series, Xena rescues Gabrielle from an enchanted sleep by passing through a ring of fire and kissing her. Although Gabrielle grounded Xena and in many ways functioned as her opposite (sheltered, innocent, a thinker as opposed to a woman of action), over the course of the series she in turn began to mirror Xena, the two meeting somewhere in the middle as the warrior princess softened. Thematically, we return again to Joseph Campbell's *Hero Quest*, *The Odyssey* this time utilised as a universal myth about the desperate search of the lost for a home and being forced to wander through more and more perilous foreign lands – with the insinuation that Gabrielle was in fact Homer, the legendary author antiquity

Hudson Leick as Xena's arch-enemy Callisto.

attributed with writing the universal myth that resonates within us all.

Xena's story ends with the ultimate sacrifice. She gives up her chance at a second resurrection in order to allow the souls of 40,000 people she had once killed to be released into a state of peace. The implication is that she will one day walk the world again with her soulmate Gabrielle, an image which appeals to the romantic in all of us.

Xena's story is tied to one of the most fundamental of human dreams: the belief that you can overcome your past, surpass your own abilities, and achieve your full potential. A major factor in the show's appeal is the idea that mortals can rub shoulders with gods, angels and demons, even defeating them in battle. In this vein, Xena and her male counterpart Hercules tap into the same well of potency as Conan and other barbarian protagonists. Their stories are enthralling not merely because of the characters' brute prowess and skills in battle, but because they embody the idea that humanity can rise above itself, overcome obstacles formerly viewed as insurmountable and set foot in the realm of divinity. The idea that mortals can battle the gods is an old one as far as mythology goes – as expressed in novels like David Eddings's *Belgariad* series and his *Elenium* books, and of course the resurgence of *The Lord of the Rings* – but not commonly explored in television.

One of the show's more daring aspects was the combination of multiple mythologies, placing Xena squarely in the middle of the action and, occasionally, allowing her to usurp the roles of religious figures. She helped David kill Goliath ('The Giant Killer', Season Two, Episode Three). She was resurrected and bore a child through an immaculate conception. She killed Mephistopheles and tricked the archangel Lucifer into becoming the new King of Hell. She stole the Rheingold from the Norse god Odin. She lived continually in conflict – and in romantic tension – with the Greek god Ares. In India, she conversed with the Hindu god Krishna and battled Indrajit.

While the combination of mythologies is itself unusual, even more so is the bold manipulation of the Christian mythos, which, thanks to the influence of the 'moral majority', is generally left alone by the mainstream media. Xena was shown encountering the Virgin Mary and Joseph with baby Jesus; Gabrielle even gave them the donkey on which they rode ('A Solstice Carol', Season Two, Episode Nine). Indeed, Xena assumes several of the roles that Mary and Jesus hold in the Christian mythos; she bears a child without sexual intercourse, and is also crucified and resurrected. Her daughter Eve takes on the role of Jesus, being a miracle baby born through an immaculate conception, intended to bring about a new order. This freewheeling rearrangement of traditional mythos is audaciously uncommon in the media circus that is television.

Xena is one of the most widely travelled and widely adored personalities in televised fantasy, able to rub shoulders with kings, gods, archangels and demons, and virtually unparalleled in the history of fantastic TV. She has battled Centaurs and Amazons, instituted the custom of Santa Claus, and was present at the formation of Stonehenge. She has acted as a role model for modern women of all sexual orientations, and her name has become a synonym for 'tough, warrior-like woman'.

How many other characters in fantasy fiction – scantily clad or otherwise – can claim such a rich heritage?

BUFFY THE VAMPIRE SLAYER (1997– 2003)

Creatures of the night, and those who grab their silver candelabra to wrestle them into submission: It's the age-old story of boy meets girl, girl falls for boy, but this boy's a bloodsucking fiend with a heart of gold . . .

We're talking one of the oldest dogs learning new tricks in terms of set-up, presentation and delivery. Our slinky slayer comes from a long and glorious (or occasionally inglorious) tradition of horror stories harking back to gothic romance and those primal campfire fears of the dark we've harboured since time immemorial. So, where does *Buffy the Vampire Slayer* really come from?

A lot of places, as it turns out.

Ask Buffy herself, and she'll tell you that she's the daughter of Joyce and Hank Summers. When she was a teenager, Hank and Joyce divorced. Joyce took her daughter to the town of Sunnydale, where the cute, witty little blonde teamed up with some friends to kill demons – some of which were already technically dead, or undead, depending on your definition.

Ask Rupert Giles, Buffy's Watcher (a combination of sagacious sorcerer and fussy Jewish mother), and he'll say – at great length and with a touch of pomposity – that Buffy's one of a long line of vampire slayers who for aeons have saved mankind from bloodsuckers and other demonic types.

These answers are good enough in terms of understanding Buffy herself, but her literary and cinematic lineage descends much deeper. Whether Buffy creator Joss Whedon knows them or not, her precursors run into the dozens – and some of them bear a striking similarity to the girl with the stake.

Folk legends about creatures who stalk the night and drain the innocent of blood have long been prevalent in the Balkans and in Slavic nations like Romania, Bulgaria, Hungary and parts of Russia. In the late 1600s and early 1700s, people in these areas believed these stories so strongly that some of them started digging up graves to stake suspected vampires. There's nothing like a little yokel paranoia to inspire the literary imagination.

By the mid-1800s literary voices were taking over the telling of these stories from whispering, superstitious villagers. Lord Byron's 1813 poem 'The Giaour' was probably the first formal composition to spread the news:

> . . . *On earth as Vampire sent,*
> *Thy corse shall from its tomb be rent:*
> *Then ghastly haunt thy native place,*
> *And suck the blood of all thy race;*
> *There from thy daughter, sister, wife,*
> *At midnight drain the stream of life;*
> *Yet loathe the banquet which perforce*
> *Must feed thy livid living corse:*
> *Thy victims ere they yet expire*
> *Shall know the demon for their sire.*

'Sire', in *Buffy* lore, is a vampire who turns a mortal into a vampire. Byron was almost certainly the first to ascribe the word to a vampire's love bite, but his wasn't the only literary light to shine on the bloodsuckers. In addition to plenty of works by writers once famous but now forgotten, there's John Keats's poem 'The Lamia', Alexandre Dumas's play *Le Vampire*, and H.G. Wells's story 'The Flowering of the

Strange Orchid', all of which deal with an inhuman being draining a vital force from his or her mortal victims.

In 1867 came *La Ville Vampire* (which translates simply as *The Vampire City*), French author Paul Féval took real-life gothic novelist Ann Radcliffe – who by this time was too dead to object – and made her into a dauntless heroine out to stop Monsieur Goetzi, a powerful and vicious vampire. (Féval was almost certainly being playful in his selection of Goetzi's name, with *gosier* being the French word for 'throat'.) Like Buffy, Féval's Ann Radcliffe had her own version of the *Scooby-Doo* gang. And like *Buffy*, *La Ville Vampire* had its fair share of parody and humour to go along with its scares.

On and on the precursors go – John Polidori's 'The Vampyre' (based partly on Polidori's friend Byron), Sheridan La Fanu's 'Carmilla', Samuel Taylor Coleridge's poem 'Christabel' (and his 'Kubla Khan', in which 'As e'er beneath a waning moon was haunted / By woman wailing for her demon-lover!'). Most important, of course, is Bram Stoker's *Dracula*. Indeed, Whedon himself has gone on record saying, 'I always think Van Helsing – the vampire hunter in *Dracula* – inspired Buffy.'

And at least one real-life scholar would have agreed with Miss Summers when she tells unbelievers that vampires are real. He made his case in books such as *The Vampire: His Kith and Kin* (1928) and *The Vampire in Europe* (1929). His name: Montague Summers.

A coincidence?

Obviously not, as the Reverend is remembered primarily for the translation of the Witch Hunter's Handbook, *Malleus Maleficarum*, and wrote extensively about bloodsucking fiends, werewolves and other supernatural enemies which all pop up around the Hellmouth. And let's not for a moment think that Whedon was unaware – he's proven himself far too savvy over much more obtuse things, after all.

But *Buffy* is not a book, it's a TV show, and if works of literature are its ancestors, then movies and TV are its parents.

One of the first and most famous vampire movies, the original 1922 *Nosferatu*, has a vampire who resembles Big Bad, the Master, from *Buffy*'s first season: ancient, pale, big-eared and creepy as hell. The 1931 *Dracula*, with Bela Lugosi, popularised the most famous pop-cultural folklore: the fear of crosses, the non-reflection in mirrors, the aversion to sunlight and garlic, the wooden stake. Hammer films such as 1958's *Dracula* pumped a bit more blood and flesh into the vampire movie, which until then had shied away from pushing female cleavage or kinky grotesquerie into the viewers' faces. And then there's a nearly forgotten film from 1967, with a title that even sounds like a slice of *Buffy* dialogue: *The Fearless Vampire Killers, or: Pardon Me, But Your Teeth Are in My Neck.* (In a weird parallel to *Buffy* and *Angel*, the film's director, co-star and co-writer, Roman Polanski, would later become infamous – even, if you'll pardon the expression, demonised – for his relationship with a young girl. And the leading lady who became his wife – the lovely, doomed

Redeemed vampire Angel (David Boreanaz) and serial
vampire slayer Buffy (Sarah Michelle Gellar) cuddle up.

Series creator Joss Whedon conceived Buffy to subvert the cliché of 'the little blonde girl who goes into a dark alley and gets killed in every horror movie'.

Sharon Tate – would be bloodily slain by the evil Manson family. Though, of course, no one could have had the slightest inkling of all this back when Polanski's horror-comedy came out.)

In the comedic *Love at First Bite* (1979), a chatty young blonde, shallow but likeable, falls in love with a vampire. The vampire's mortal enemy, Dr Jeffrey Rosenberg, is brilliant but not always able to handle the conflicts that face him – much like Buffy's sidekick, Willow Rosenberg. (Another coincidence?)

In 1987's *The Lost Boys*, a divorced mom moves her family to a small California town that turns out to be a magnet for all the young, good-looking vampires. If that's not *Buffy*-esque, then what is? As critic Caryn James wrote in the *New York Times*, 'These lost boys are not Peter Pan-like innocents, but teenagers who dress like rock stars, roar through town on motorcycles and happen to fly through the air and drink blood.' Sounds like Buffy's nemesis and sometime lover Spike (except for the flying part). One of the divorcee's kids has to stop the vampires, and a couple of kids in a comic book store help him do it – who could easily have been Buffy's geeky pal, Xander, and her very geeky enemy-turned-follower, Andrew.

A few words on comic books are in order. Joss Whedon loves comics, not only as a fan but also as a comic-book writer. The medium has also presented its own share of Buffy forebears. In 1973, writer Marv Wolfman and artist Gene Colan introduced the vampire hunter Blade in their Marvel Comics series *Tomb of Dracula*. Like *Buffy*'s vamp-with-a-soul, Angel, Blade is a vampire who hunts other vampires. Fittingly, he would eventually win his own series of movies and TV shows.

Then there were the X-Men, who, like Buffy and her friends, started out as a group of misunderstood teenagers who fought evil under the direction of a somewhat formal and cerebral older man. Whedon has said that another of his inspirations for Buffy was Kitty Pryde, created by *X-Men* writer Chris Claremont and artist John Byrne in 1980. Initially a young and easily spooked teen, Kitty became a superhero known variously as Sprite, Ariel, and Shadowcat. Like Buffy, Kitty acquired a tall, dark and brooding boyfriend, the hero Colossus. (Some other members of the X-Men, popular superheroes Cyclops and Cable, share the last name Summers with Buffy.) In a fitting turnabout, Whedon has also ended up contributing to the *X-Men* comics as a writer.

In the 1950s and most of the 1960s, TV was too tame and censorship too tight for vampires to do much killing. And without killing, a vampire doesn't have much purpose. Soap operas, however, have often bent TV conventions with maze-like plots full of sex and scheming. So it makes sense that a soap opera would first bring vampires to television in a big way.

Writer-producer Dan Curtis created *Dark Shadows*, a gothic soap, which hit the tube in 1966. It started out with a big fog of mystery but not a lot that was actually supernatural. A few months later, ghosts entered the story, as, in 1967, did the vampire Barnabas Collins. 'Actor Jonathan Frid played him as a sad, cursed being who yearned to be human again,' pop-cultural journalist Joyce Millman has written on Salon.com. 'The writers obliged the burgeoning Barnabas cult with a back story recasting Barnabas as a victim of a vengeful witch.' It's a nearly perfect parallel to the story of *Buffy*'s Angel, cursed by vengeful gypsies and doomed to live on in sadness.

Another precursor was a cartoon. *Scooby-Doo, Where Are You?* premiered in 1969. Like *Buffy*, *Scooby-Doo* featured a team of young monster-hunters that included a gorgeous girl, a goofy guy, and a nerdy girl. Unlike Buffy and her pals though, the *Scooby* gang never found a single vampire, werewolf or witch. Anything that seemed supernatural was the work of some perfectly human greed-head trying to scare people away from a house or some other place he wanted for himself. Otherwise though, the show is so similar to *Buffy* that even Buffy and her friends sometimes called themselves 'the Scoobies'.

In 1972, *Dark Shadows*' Dan Curtis went bloodsucking again. He produced the TV movie *The Night Stalker*, in which Darren McGavin put on the squashed hat of grumpy investigative reporter Carl Kolchak. The stalker was a vampire, and Kolchak had to track him down despite the protests of nearly everyone around him that vampires don't exist. The movie was so popular that it spun off another, *The Night Strangler*, and finally a regular series, *Kolchak: The Night Stalker*. (It probably didn't hurt that one of TV's most popular shows of the time was about a police investigator named *Kojak*.) The series, launched in 1974, lasted for only one season of twenty episodes, but fans of supernatural stories loved it, and the format of a mortal snooping into the world of monsters set a precedent for *Buffy*.

Kolchak also inspired *The X-Files*, in which two investigators hunt down monsters and sometimes kill them. The investigators are FBI agents rather than *Buffy*'s high-school students, but, like *Buffy*, *The X-Files* features a smart redhead and her sometimes goofy but always devoted partner. (One of *The X-Files*' last writers was Tim Minear, who later wrote for *Buffy* and became an executive producer on the *Buffy* spin-off *Angel*.) It's reasonable to extrapolate from this that the show's popularity opened TV executives' minds to the idea of another series about a team of monster hunters.

So vampire hunting is an old tradition, but what about Buffy herself? She didn't come out of nowhere, of course. Her name, for instance, is nearly synonymous with superficiality. (In one of *Buffy*'s final episodes, a wise ancient asks the slayer to identify herself; when she says that her name's Buffy, the sage says, 'No, really.') For instance, the 1980 bestseller *The Official Preppy Handbook*, a satire on the WASPy upper crust, included a list of 'most popular nicknames for girls' – at number three, between Missy and Bitsy, was Buffy.

And Buffy's precursors in the heroine game are many. Nancy Drew, the most famous teenage investigator, is an obvious one, with her own TV series starting in 1977. Before that show hit the tube, however, there was *The Avengers*. From 1965 to 1968, the show starred Diana Rigg as high-kicking amateur adventuress Emma Peel. Her sidekick, Patrick Macnee as John Steed, was something of a proto-Giles. Nearly a caricature of the ultra-proper Englishman, he guided his young heroine into adventures and carried much of the show's exposition. Around the same time, Anne Francis starred in *Honey West* as a blonde, witty, well-armed and gorgeously dressed investigator, and Stefanie Powers was secret agent April Dancer in *The Girl from U.N.C.L.E.*

A few years later, from 1976 to 1978, the original *Bionic Woman* series centred on a super-strong blonde who fought evil. The show didn't dig much into the supernatural, but its star did encounter her share of robots and aliens. *Wonder Woman* kicked the hell out of bad guys, too, and so did *Charlie's Angels*.

In 1990, the Luc Besson film *La Femme Nikita* starred Anne Parillaud as a reluctant martial artist and assassin (or slayer, if you will). Her dark looks and even darker character – she started out as a criminal – are reminiscent of Buffy's sometime enemy, the rogue slayer Faith. The film spawned American remake *The Assassin* with a blonde Bridget Fonda, and a TV series with the even blonder Peta Wilson.

And while we are talking about her cinematic antecedents, let's not forget that Whedon himself gave his golden girl of vamp-dusting an outing as early as 1992, five years before the first episode of the television show aired. This time our hellion with a stake was played by Kristy Swanson, who was, according to the movie's tagline, 'Pert. Wholesome. Way Lethal.' With Donald Sutherland and Rutger Hauer headlining as Buffy's mentor and vampiric nemesis respectively, and Luke Perry fresh out of his *Beverly Hills 90210* fame, the movie played it for laughs (doubt it? Check out Paul Reubens's protracted death scene, which goes on for a good ten minutes and deep into the end credits) and had cameos from none other than Hilary Swank, Ben Affleck, Thomas Jane and Ricki Lake. Very little of the original ethos or style of this incarnation of the slayer

'Buffy the Vampire Slayer *showed the whole world, and an entire sprawling industry, that writing monsters and demons and end-of-the-world is not hack-work, it can challenge the best.' – Russell T. Davies*

made it to the small screen – it was a parody aimed at lampooning a lot of the trite clichés of the horror genre. Whedon himself has gone on record time and again, including an interview with entertainment journalist Clint Morris, to state that the television series was a much closer rendering of his vision than the movie, which was compromised by commercial demands and artistic differences.

Buffy's not just an ass-kicker, though. In addition to its heroics, her show is full of verbal wit. Whedon inherited a legacy of TV funny women from his father, writer-producer Tom Whedon, who worked on the sitcoms *Alice*, about a wisecracking waitress, *It's a Living*, with more wisecracking waitresses, and *The Golden Girls*. (Is *The Golden Girls*' sexy, self-centred Blanche a model for *Buffy*'s beautiful but snotty Cordelia Chase?)

Joss Whedon himself wrote for *Roseanne*, while his grandfather, John Whedon, wrote for *The Andy Griffith Show* – like *Buffy*, a series about a small town where odd things happen.

So what do we have here? Is *Buffy* just the latest show in a long tradition, or is it more than the sum of its heritage?

As its list of forebears indicates, there have been a lot of vampire hunters, hard-hitting heroines, and smart-mouthed gals. Every year, writers and producers pitch TV shows, movies and other projects that combine and recombine these elements in various blends. The concepts behind *Buffy* are not blindingly original. It's their execution that makes *Buffy* work. The characters have depth; they're funny and emotional and heroic and weak. The stories follow a classic form – they present a character or characters who go through a revelatory experience that makes them grow or change in some way. The characters' motivations are clear. Their dialogue is sharp. Their reactions are touching and hilarious, or even meaningful.

Buffy will be – or possibly already is – an inspiration for other much-loved TV shows. It might inspire a comedy, or an action-adventure, or a shot of raw horror. In any event, *Buffy* is taking its place alongside *Dracula*, *Nancy Drew* and other favourites in the timeline of great entertainment.

What's left to say, apart from, 'Go get 'em, Slayer!'?

'The internet, you know . . . The bitch goddess that I love and worship and hate. You know, we found out we have a fan base on the internet. They came together as a family on the internet, a huge goddamn deal . . . it's respect for storytelling. People just don't have it. But you know what? Not everybody reads spoilers, not everybody lives that way. Those are the people that really love the show. I cannot conceive of a person who wants to know what happens. People who turn to the last page of a book – what universe did they come from? I don't understand it. That drives me crazy, but I think the internet is beyond important in terms of fans communing, becoming a community and growing. People writing each other and writing fiction, and writing, well, porn. All of these things that do what I always wanted Buffy to do, which was exist outside of the TV show. Enter people's own personal ethos. The internet has been a big part in how that has happened.' – Joss Whedon

ULTRAVIOLET (1998)

It's safe to say that *Ultraviolet* was a product of its time – the vampire show that went to extreme lengths to avoid ever using the 'V word', unlike Whedon's Buffyverse, which revelled in Hellmouths and bloodsucking fiends. Broadcast on Channel 4 in late 1998, *Ultraviolet* crept onto the UK's cathode ray tubes with little fanfare. Of course, 1998 was hardly a boom time for British SF TV. Between the cancellation of *Doctor Who* in 1989 and its re-launch in 2005, it's fair to say that the genre was in something of a crisis. The BBC tried variations on the theme – *Bugs*, *Neverwhere*, *Crime Traveller* and *Invasion: Earth* – with a startling lack of success. Only *Bugs'* episode count made it into double figures, and there was no critical acclaim to offset the poor viewing figures.

Across the pond, however, science fiction was growing both in quantity and quality on American television – a trend started by *Star Trek*'s reinvention as *The Next Generation* from 1987 – while in the movies the genre had been going strong since the mid-seventies boom. The general shift was toward bigger budgets, for series with a more serious tone, and, especially after the debut of *Babylon 5* in 1993, for multi-episode storylines. Vampires, meanwhile, had been resurrected from the grave, with big-budget Hollywood movies such as *Interview with the Vampire* and *Bram Stoker's Dracula* keeping the mythology alive in the public consciousness. Their common thematic red line was an underlying desire to take the subject matter seriously, with the absurdities of the monster either played straight or ignored.

On television, the two most significant recent dark fantasy series had both been American. *The X-Files*, which had debuted in 1993, took the tropes and trappings of various horror and gothic traditions and dragged them into the real world. When government-sanctioned law-enforcers Mulder and Scully investigated vampires, ghosts and men who could squeeze down chimneys, they did it in midtown, blue-collar America. Likewise, *Buffy the Vampire Slayer* set its fantastic creations in an average Californian school. And although both series carried a healthy dose of humour – *Buffy* in every episode; *The X-Files* in occasional kooky stories – they always treated the threat of the monster seriously. At a grassroots level, both series instinctively understood that the audience needed to sincerely believe in the endangerment of the main characters.

While writer Joe Ahearne started to formulate his ideas for *Ultraviolet* before the impact of the American series, he leant towards the same sensibilities. Vampires, he argued, would have a greater impact if seen in a modern-day context. Where Hammer's vampire movies had used castles, Victoriana and garlic, a vampire show for the 1990s should feature city sprawl, modern culture and technology. Out went aristocratic angst; in came a street war for survival.

Ahearne prefigured *Buffy*'s spin-off series, *Angel*, by several years, with his concept of vampire as detective, a crusader of questionable motives helping the vulnerable and victimised. However, knowing that a series set and filmed at night would be prohibitively expensive, he changed his tack and developed the idea of a team of vampire hunters who would use modern methods and gadgets, guns and all, to catch their prey.

The premise was simple enough: police detective Michael Colefield's best friend, Jack, goes missing on the eve of his wedding. Michael is soon visited by a mysterious team of investigators – Father Pearse Harman, Vaughn Rice and Dr Angie Marsh – who believe that Jack has fallen victim to a global conspiracy of vampires. Slowly, Michael begins to realise the horrific truth: the undead walk the streets of London, and a covert union of the British government and the Catholic Church has vowed to defeat them.

The programme's cast was led by two stars of iconic BBC drama. Susannah Harker had shone as political journalist Mattie Storin in 1990's *House of Cards*, and, in a cute piece of casting coincidence, is a descendent of Joseph Harker – a friend of Bram Stoker, after whom the author named *Dracula*'s hero, Jonathan Harker. Jack Davenport, as law graduate Miles Stewart, had helped define mid-nineties British culture in BBC Two's sleeper hit, *This Life*. Ahearne had both written and directed episodes of *This Life* while his ideas for a vampire show were bubbling away. Impressed by Davenport, Ahearne cast him as Michael despite initially fearing that the 25-year-old was too young. Rounding out the regulars were Philip Quast – fresh from his appearance in the only filmed version of stage musical *Les Misérables* – as Harman and Idris Elba as Rice.

The plan had initially been to bring other writers and directors on board to fill out the six episodes. However, Ahearne ended up writing the whole series, then directing all six parts during a five-month shoot in the first half of 1998.

Ultraviolet was shot through with a rich vein of tension, helped by Sue Hewitt's astonishing incidental music. The tone was grim and gritty – some would say unremittingly so. Unlike *Buffy* and the more recent resurrection of *Doctor Who*, this wasn't a world where characters traded banter and referenced popular culture. The 1990s were typified by entertainment that wore its post-modernity on its sleeve. But *Ultraviolet* didn't fit into the pop-culture-spouting style of *Pulp Fiction* or *Friends*. It came along just as Britain was on its comedown from Britpop, Cool Britannia, the doomed euphoria of Euro '96 and the optimistic sweeping to power of New Labour. *Ultraviolet*'s tone – serious, sombre, tense – chimed with an audience hungover from the party. There was no more apt a time for a dark, pessimistic series about an eternal battle with evil.

Taking its lead perhaps from previous British serials such as *The Edge of Darkness* and *Chimera*, *Ultraviolet*'s dialogue was story-driven and to the point. Ahearne has admitted that he thinks of himself more as a plot-based writer rather than one to whom character is central, and this shines through. Which is not to say that the

The Ultraviolet *team – Detective Sergeant Michael Colefield (Jack Davenport), Doctor Angela March (Susannah Harker), Vaughan Rice (Idris Elba), and Father Pearse J. Harman (Philip Quast).*

characters are one-dimensional, but they are – in the grand tradition of all thrillers – subservient to the story.

Ultraviolet features a clash of technology versus nature. Whereas the vampires are the victims (or, as they would say, beneficiaries) of biological mutation and constantly need to feed on blood, Harman's team of detectives uses every mod con they can lay their hands on, including video cameras, advanced weaponry and containment systems. The vampires too rely on technology. Car windows are tinted to protect them from sunlight; they talk over the telephone using vocoders.

Also at play is the dichotomy between the fantastic and the real – as noted, *Ultraviolet*'s breed of vampire lives in modern-day urban settings. They look, dress and often act in such a way that they seem no different from humans. This clash

In the tradition of Quatermass, Ultraviolet *showcased the use of science as a means of overcoming supernatural menaces.*

of the bizarre and the ordinary, as pioneered by *The X-Files* and *Buffy*, makes for fascinating stories and character dilemmas. What the three shows have in common is that those characters whose points of view we share are simply normal people facing huge odds, rather than the military might of the Enterprise or the advanced technology of a sonic screwdriver-carrying Time Lord.

But most potent is the classic vampire story's clash between modernity and mythology. Bram Stoker imbued *Dracula* with heavy religious overtones, but, even with the presence of Catholicism, *Ultraviolet* dismisses much of that. The idea of a crucifix repelling a vampire is used in many stories as a never-failing tool; in *Ultraviolet* the process is referred to as a 'matter of faith'. The cross is only a representation of the barrier, not the barrier itself. (This idea has been used before, perhaps most successfully in the 1989 *Doctor Who* serial 'The Curse of Fenric', which featured a Soviet character who substituted religion with his faith in the revolution.)

There's also the literal fight between the hunters and the vampires. Famously, the V word was replaced in *Ultraviolet* by the preferred terms 'leeches' and 'Code Five', a sly nod to the Roman numeral V. Over six episodes – mostly standalone, but topped

'At the end of six episodes you find out categorically what the vampires are up to and that's it.' – Ultraviolet writer/director Joe Ahearne.

and tailed by multi-episodic stories, all with Latin titles – we follow Michael as he learns more about the war with the leeches. There is also the bubbling-under story of Jack's disappearance, and Corin Redgrave's appearances in the final two episodes as a vampire leader intent on wiping out humanity. The penultimate episode, 'Terra Incognita', features probably the series' high point: an unbearably tense sequence of Rice trapped in a locked room with a casket due to open and reveal a vampire. The acting, direction and (especially) the music combine to produce marvellous television.

Ultraviolet was seen by its producers as a limited format – the show was designed to run six episodes, with seemingly little desire from either Channel 4 or the production team to do more. Indeed, when Fox bought the rights to produce an American adaptation, Ahearne declined to be involved. A full series was planned for 2001, but a pilot episode – made with only Idris Elba from the British cast – was never broadcast and no series followed. Producer Howard Gordon, who'd previously written for *The X-Files*, *Buffy the Vampire Slayer*, *Angel* and later became a screenwriter for *24*, admitted that the pilot had been a failure.

The British series, however, can claim its part in a twenty-first century legacy.

Four years after *Ultraviolet* was screened, Ahearne created a further modern-day take on gothic mythology. BBC One's *Strange* – piloted in 2002, with a six-part series in 2003 – also focused on the battle between evil and the religious establishment, but was not as well-received as its Channel 4 antecedent.

But *Strange*, a primetime, Saturday-night genre series on BBC1, paved the way for a true television success. Starting in March 2005, a revamp of *Doctor Who* became one of British TV's most popular dramas. Five episodes of the first season were directed by Joe Ahearne, including the return of the Daleks in an explosive two-part finale.

Science fiction was back on the agenda.

ANGEL (1999-2004)

'There's a reason you have Angel do his own show,
because you can only play out the variations of "What if Romeo and Juliet lived?"
for so long. He's in her heart, but he will be used sparingly.'
– Joss Whedon on Angel, TV Guide, *7 December 2006*

A darker than dark, introspective hunk of man meat, square-jawed and far too handsome for his own bloodsucking good – it's become a cliché all of its own. Enter Angel, the vampire endowed/cursed with a soul.

Angel began his television life (or undeath) on *Buffy the Vampire Slayer* as the romantic obsession of Joss Whedon's eponymous heroine, regularly casting his brooding shadow over the first three seasons of the show. The pseudo-history of *Angel* stretches back to mid-eighteenth-century Ireland, and it's that old, old story again: boy meets girl, boy falls in love with girl, girl rips boy's throat out at the height of passion. The particulars this time around are: twenty-six-year-old Liam, rapscallion son of a merchant, is seduced and given the deadly love bite by the heart-stoppingly beautiful Darla. Technically, that means Angel predates his literary counterpart Dracula by almost 150 years, and, for that matter, nearly every other literary neck-biter. He is of the murky era of folklore and oral fable.

It is unlikely that Whedon set Angel's origin – or rather that of Angelus, the immortal demonic/vampiric aspect of the character – in this era to exempt him from the considerable constrictions of vampire tradition. But it nevertheless has that effect. Most of the common vampire conventions are still faithfully observed – the nocturnal perambulations, the lack of a reflection, fear of sharp pointy wooden

Spinning off from Buffy, Angel *was conceived as being far darker than its parent series.*

things, flame, sunlight, decapitation – but Whedon adds a few of his own, and discards others. Tellingly, the rules are never absolute within his mythology. They are stiff but not unbreakable.

Like many of the characters introduced in *Buffy the Vampire Slayer* (including Spike and Wesley), Angel was not intended to be a long-term inhabitant of the Buffyverse. He was introduced as the tortured vampire with a soul, the romantic lead opposite Buffy, the 'chosen one' whose cosmic mandate is the extermination of his fellow vampires. It's not quite Shakespeare but, with its star-crossed lovers, it almost certainly echoes one of the seven basic plots the Bard was so fond of playing with. This simple but compelling device was initially sufficient because the Buffy/ Angel relationship was adolescent and, while this was logical – Buffy being in high school and Angel being her first love – it did prove a limitation to the character's dramatic development. For quite some time, the title character remained that dark, brooding, enigmatic cliché.

Curiously, the show depicted Angel's ensoulment in 1898 well before revealing the details of Angelus's creation in 1753. According to Christian doctrine ensoulment begins with the creation of a life – the life here is Angel, the tortured, angsty 'good vamp' born out of the vile darkside of the creature known as Angelus. Angelus is cursed by gypsies, in reprisal for his brutal attack upon them, with the reinstatement of his soul, and thus Angel is born. Again. His human conscience restored, Angel comprehends the scope of the atrocities committed by Angelus and thereafter suffers from crushing remorse and self-loathing, hence the brooding part. The curse established a dual nature that became the basis for the growth of the character, eventually enabling Angel to move to his own series after three seasons in Buffy's fictional hometown of Sunnydale. While Buffy completed high school, Angel was almost entirely restricted to her suburban setting. In stark contrast, the spin-off series offered him a dazzling and very real Los Angeles. This relocation indicates not merely the growth of the character (moving to the big city being a common signifier of maturity), but of a paradigmatic reinvention of Angel and, by extension, the vampire genre. In other words, despite being immortal, Whedon's vampires continue to evolve.

As the arc of the doomed Angel/Buffy romance played out, Angel transformed from heroic teen heartthrob with a mysterious past into a complex and compelling adult character in his own right. Early in *Buffy the Vampire Slayer*, he appeared opportunely to aid her in her battles or to be rescued by her, and to fuel her hormones when the need for a little sexual tension was thrown into the mix. Over the course of the series it was revealed that Angel was on a quest for self-definition and purpose, having been mired in self-pity for the better part of the last century. Inspired by Buffy, he is motivated by some vague goal of redemption through good works (a contentious idea, but one of many Christian theological concepts to inform a reading of *Angel*). Given his heinous history, it is a redemption he can never achieve, and this notion of the unachievable goal, the impossible dream, in turn provided the thematic basis for the series. From it emerged one of most bizarre yet endearing of television protagonists, that of the anti-hero superhero vampire.

Angel the vampire possesses strength, speed, highly acute senses and immortality, qualities befitting any superhero. But Angel the human, back before he was Angelus the vampire, was a hedonistic brat called Liam. Seen in flashbacks, Liam is an objectionable figure with criminal tendencies, devoid of dignity or skills and a disgrace to his family. In a 'crossover' episode with *Buffy the Vampire Slayer*, Angel is granted full humanity but, in relinquishing his duality, sacrifices his supernatural strength. He discovers that he is now worthless in a punch-up, suggesting the plight of the anti-hero, the ordinary fellow trapped in extraordinary circumstances, desperate but impotent. Angel opts to return to his cursed condition, despite its ambivalence and danger. He chooses an existence of contrition, replacing the goal of redemption with the process of atonement. His superhero attributes are restored but his hollow core remains. It is this pathos and self-awareness that distinguishes Angel within the vampire tradition. He is much closer to the pulp-comic heroes Batman or the Shadow than to Anne Rice's Louis or Lestat. Her vampires may speak eloquently about their emotional tribulations ('Psychotherapy with the Vampire'), but Angel is

Unusually for a spin-off, Angel's popularity was such that its ratings sometimes surpassed Buffy's.

aware of both his delusions and his potential. He has the power and the will to act as a free agent, to determine his own destiny, and it is this self-actualisation which separates him from the pack. Viewers can identify with Angel as a figure of empathy, not some impossibly projected fantasy.

In contrast to many other vampire mythologies, the Buffyverse posits that vampires and innumerable other species of demon (not all of which are malevolent) have inhabited the cosmos since time immemorial, albeit mostly confined to other space-time dimensions. While *Buffy the Vampire Slayer* had characters (both human and non-human) of uncertain allegiance, there was always a clear demarcation between the forces of good and evil for the righteous. The selflessly penitent Angel – whose personality is fused with the unspeakably wicked Angelus – modulates from being Buffy's champion to that confused and morally ambiguous *noir* icon, the disillusioned private eye. He's Sam Spade with bite, so to speak. This internal transformation is externalised by the sprawling mess of modern LA, with its grand skyscrapers and desolate slums, celebrities and forgotten homeless, glamour and squalor. Sunnydale's models of justice and righteousness are outmoded in the big, bad City of Angels.

Upon his arrival in LA, Angel is quickly befriended by the Doyle – a half-demon, half-human character who has prophetic visions – and Cordelia Chase, the superficial high-school queen bee who has ventured to LA to pursue an acting career. This trio cements the *noir* theme by establishing Angel Investigations, whose mission is to 'help the hopeless'. It's hardly surprising then that, over the course of the series, each of the main characters descends into a hopeless (or even nihilistic) state of their own. 'Hopelessness' also suggests many of the existential themes which dominate the subtext of the series, as the characters repeatedly ask themselves if anything they can do actually matters; if there are boundaries to free will; if one can live with evil and remain uncorrupted.

In the first season the characters lived separately and worked from Angel's apartment, for season two they settled in the abandoned Hyperion Hotel, which functioned as office, fortress and residence. It established a metaphorical home for the extended family of 'Team Angel', which now included Wesley, the bumbling, priggish Watcher, another *Buffy* refugee. Season Two saw the addition of the streetwise Charles Gunn, the socially inept but brilliant physicist Fred, and the flamboyant yet kindly demon Lorne, to complete the core cast of the series.

In Season One, *Angel* imitated *Buffy the Vampire Slayer* in its anthology format with a self-contained mystery and monster each episode, gradually enhanced by longer story arcs and character growth. But from the initial episode, it was obvious that *Angel* was conceived to explore much darker themes than its parent series. Los Angeles is portrayed as an oppressive cityscape, a terrain of alienation, brutality and desperate loneliness. Several scenes from the first episode were reputedly cut and an entire episode intended to air as the second ever episode was scrapped, both at the insistence of the network which considered the material too dark. Employing *film noir* techniques, including a laconic voiceover from Angel, Whedon quickly established another genre hybrid. Sunnydale had been set above the 'Hellmouth', a portal from which demons occasionally poked their heads, but was otherwise depicted as an idyllic suburban town. Producers Whedon and David Greenwalt's fictionalised LA was a manmade incubator of monsters: demonic, human and, most especially, corporate. The moral solidity of quaint Sunnydale was replaced with a decentralised, amoral cityscape. It is this authentically resonating amorality – rather than zesty and facile immorality – which defines the series in Seasons Two though Five. Duplicity and mendacity are the coin of the realm, and sheer power is all that matters.

The characters transplanted from Sunnydale very quickly recognise that they are not in Kansas anymore, and each is confronted with dread existential quandaries as they 'grow up' in LA. There is no stability, no centre, nor any moral absolutes.

As Lorne says, addressing the mixed crowd of demons and humans at his kitschy karaoke club, 'In this city you better learn to get along 'cause LA's got it all: the glamour and the grit, the big breaks and the heartache, the sweet young lovers and the nasty, ugly, hairy fiends that suck out your brain through your face. It's all part of the big wacky variety show we call Los Angeles. You never know what's coming next. And let's admit it folks, isn't that why we love her?'

In LA even the 'powers that be' are inscrutable, unreliable and corrupt. Sacred prophesies might be bunk. One moment Angel is saving an innocent from certain death at the hands of a demon, the next he is served with a series of building code violations by dastardly transdimensional law firm Wolfram & Hart. The mundane reality of paying the rent becomes as much a part of Angel's mission as saving the world. Superhero one minute, anti-hero the next.

The maturation process for Angel's supporting characters entailed a disabuse of naïveté, a period of moral uncertainty, usually a descent into nihilism, then tribulation (assuming they were still alive at this stage) and final resignation as the world comes crashing down on their particular corner of the Buffyverse. To quote Angel, 'If nothing we do matters, then all that matters is what we do.' The path to self-awareness for each character is unique and, as the series progressed, these large character arcs came to dominate the later seasons.

The anthology format of Season One gave way to a much grander storyline in which the 'Big Bad' served both to immediately unite team Angel and to fracture the group over the long haul. With each character at different stages in their evolution, this created baroque and highly internalised narratives more akin to Icelandic sagas than American primetime television.

Throughout the series, the collective 'family' served to stabilise and guide each of the individual characters though their own development. Early on, Doyle was sent, as he stated, 'to connect' Angel to the world; later it was the larger group, particularly the females Fred and Cordelia, who served to hold things together. It's an unconventional family, to be sure. Each member is in some way an outcast or has been displaced: Wesley, the Englishman who has fallen from his post as a Watcher; Gunn, a black male marginalised and barely tolerated in his own city; Fred, the migrant from Texas, who was abducted and spent years as a slave in another dimension before her rescue; Lorne, an exile from his home realm, where music is unknown; Cordelia, newly arrived from Sunnydale, starting over after her life of privilege evaporated; and Angel – the ultimate loner, an outcast among both men and demons. Yet this disparate group, like a pack of runaways, coalesced into a family, incorporating another genre into the series – the good old-fashioned family melodrama, only this time it wasn't *Dallas* or *Falcon Crest*. The family ranch was replaced by a dilapidated hotel, the Hyperion, a place for those in transit. Just as there are no fixed moral landmarks is LA, so there is there is no fixed notion of home. The hotel is the signifier of transition, but it becomes their home by choice – a recurring choice made each day. After all the hardship and heartbreak, the many betrayals and a few beheadings, Angel's final words at the end of the series announce the choice that he's made: 'Let's go to work.'

There is a vast amount of reference material available on the extended Buffyverse. Both *Buffy the Vampire Slayer* and *Angel* have extended their canonical lives through comic books overseen by Whedon, respectively corresponding to *Buffy the Vampire Slayer* Season Eight and *Angel* Season Six. In addition there are comics and novels which cover early eras in the lives of the characters, even the lives of previous Slayers. Beyond these authorised properties there is a huge quantity of fan fiction of every style and dozens, if not hundreds, of tribute websites. You take your life into your hands by Googling the words 'Buffy' and 'Angel' – some fans have interesting ideas (it's safe to call them peccadillos) that they like to play out in the form of slash fiction.

Finally, there is a large and growing body of academic work in the area of '*Buffy* studies'. There have now been at least four major academic conferences held on the subject and, even though both *Buffy the Vampire Slayer* and *Angel* have been off the air for some time, the field continues to grow. Much of this work is first-rate and not, as might be expected, the scribbling of lazy undergraduates. There have been several books published in the field, and the website slayageonline.com manages a considerable archive of scholarly research on all things *Buffy* and *Angel*.

Nevertheless, these were just television shows, and if the academics can be broadly faulted it's for assuming that a multi-season TV series is a cohesive and consistent text. Any TV show is subject to the influence of several 'authorial' agents, most of whom are concerned with aspects apart from the consistency or quality of the product. The addition of the character Spike to *Angel* Season Five was requested by the network, solely because he was popular on *Buffy*. They were also behind the characters' departure from the Hyperion Hotel – although they did not specify how the producers and writers were to achieve this.

As noted previously, at the inception of the series the entire tone of the show was revised after only one episode. Scenes were regularly cut. Plots were altered. *Angel* also had to adapt to the departure of *Buffy the Vampire Slayer* to a rival network. Stories intertwined between the two shows had to be scrapped. None of these were creative decisions, but were imposed by external forces. Further, while *Angel* was the creation of Joss Whedon and David Greenwalt, who were the show's guiding forces, television is inevitably a collaborative process incorporating the input of hundreds of creative individuals. Scholars and critics are on thin ice when they assume, for example, that Lorne's green skin tone was chosen as an allusion to Kermit the Frog. (It may well have been that the art department decided green worked best with the established set colours.) Nevertheless, the very existence of so much scholarly work – not to mention the fawning fan texts – demonstrates that *Angel* was indeed something special.

When it happened, the cancellation of *Angel* was not expected either by the creators of the series or its audience. The Warner Brothers network requested changes

Angel *employed many* film noir *tropes as a stylish means of framing its core theme of redemption.*

for Season Five, including the addition of Spike – necessitating the resurrection of the other vampire with a soul after his glorious demise in the finale of *Buffy*. And so it was assumed that, with its solid ratings, the series would continue. Warner, however, wanted *improved* ratings, and thus announced the cancellation midway through Season Five's production cycle – thus allowing the producers to consider an appropriate closing for the series. As was true of its entire run, the final *Angel* episode did not conform to conventions.

The show's fans behaved even more unconventionally, mounting a campaign to save the series probably rivalled only by the efforts of 'trekkies' in the late sixties. The Saving *Angel* Campaign started as soon as the cancellation was announced. Borrowing tactics from the 'Browncoats', who attempted in 2002 to save another Whedon series, *Firefly*, the *Angel* supporters purchased ads in trade papers *Variety* and *The Hollywood Reporter*. They toured Los Angeles in a vehicular billboard named the 'Angelmobile', emblazoned with the campaign slogan, 'Looking for a few million good viewers? We'll follow *Angel* to Hell . . . or another Network.' The group raised over $40,000 through fan contributions for a live rally in LA and concurrent online rally. But, for the moment, it appears that their efforts have failed. However, it must be noted that five years after *Firefly* disappeared, it reappeared on the big screen as the feature film *Serenity*. Whedon largely credited the 'Browncoats' for their passion and support, although one suspects that exceptionally strong DVD sales of *Firefly* – which did not even complete its first season – might also have nudged unsentimental studio executives toward financing the feature. Given the many unresolved questions at the conclusion of the series' finale, and the obvious big one (did he slay the dragon after all?), it may well be that Angel will return from Hell one more time. He is, after all, immortal.

SMALLVILLE (2001 - PRESENT)

For anyone who thinks that myth is all about the Greeks bearing gifts (principally to the Romans, who adopted their mythology wholesale), myth in storytelling didn't end with the birth of modern civilisation. Telephones, computers and television didn't kill the monomyth. The genres of science fiction and fantasy have given us some beautifully rendered modern mythology, from J.R.R. Tolkien's *Lord of the Rings* to George Lucas's *Star Wars*.

Back in 1936, a pair of young men came up with a concept that would redefine the heroic ideal for generations. Jerome Siegel and Joseph Shuster (aged nineteen and twenty at the time) created the first, and still the quintessential, superhero: Superman. Humble in his ordinary persona as Clark Kent, this 'super man' was gifted with extraordinary powers. Even back at the outset of his heroing days, he was incredibly strong, faster than a speeding bullet and able to leap buildings in a single bound. Time and countless retellings have added to his abilities, raising them up to demigod proportions, along with hints about his boyhood in Kansas and his one weakness, kryptonite.

Smallville, the latest television incarnation of the Superman myth, has the benefit of over half a century of source information to draw upon, plus the hip writing of post-*Buffy* TV. *Smallville* is about Superman, and yet it isn't – because it takes place before Clark Kent starts wearing his underwear on top of his tights and dons the iconic red cape.

This new telling kicks off with a kryptonite meteor shower that brings with it the toddler Kal-El. Jonathan and Martha Kent – an attractive and still young farming couple – discover him, adopt him, and name him Clark. With the exception of the Kents being young, this should all sound familiar so far – it's tried and tested *Superman*, only in this version of the story the star child crashes to Earth in 1989.

Smallville is about Clark's teen and early adult years growing up in Smallville, Kansas. Thankfully, creators Miles Millar and Alfred Gough opted not to make it a Superboy story with young Clark flying around in a pre-shrunk superhero suit. But even *sans* suit, Superman is exactly what a mythological heroic figure should be. Millar and Gough recognised it, and worked it right into the pilot episode.

Then there's Superman's archenemy, the billionaire Lex Luthor. In most versions of the narrative, Clark doesn't encounter Lex until he is the maskless superhero with the big red 'S' on his barrel chest. But how much fun would a Superman show be without Lex? The answer lay in an old *Superboy* comic, in which the boy of steel and Lex were friends – as they soon become in the pilot episode.

It's a necessarily heroic introduction: Clark is standing on a bridge, ruminating on his life, when Lex, speeding in his turbo-charged sports car, swerves to avoid an obstacle in the road and goes careening off the bridge – ploughing straight into Clark on the way. Unhurt, Clark rescues Lex from the submerged car and resuscitates him on shore. Thus begins Lex's desire to make friends with the young man who saved his life, and, simultaneously, his obsession with just how Clark survived the collision. In pure Luthor fashion, he not only offers his friendship to Clark but shows his appreciation with a ridiculous slew of rich-boy gifts, including a truck that Jonathan Kent makes Clark return and, more tellingly, a party to help young Clark impress the woman of his super-dreams, Lana Lang.

It all goes swimmingly for a while; Clark and Lex become fast friends, they trust each other (to a point – Clark keeps *shtum* about his super secret), but as time wears on, several factors combine to cause their estrangement and Lex's slow spiral down to the dark side. In the simplest terms of the mythic structure, Lex is an ally who becomes an enemy.

In the first episode of *Smallville*, Clark is caught by Lana's jealous boyfriend, Whitney, and some of the blonde teen's football buddies. Every year the Smallville football seniors choose some freshman to haze. This year it's Clark Kent. They string him up on a cross in a cornfield, and paint a big red letter 'S' on his chest. It's all very symbolic. But they're only able to subdue Clark because they have a necklace belonging to Lana that sports a Kryptonite jewel.

It's Lex who spots his friend hanging there, shirtless and weak. As he helps Clark down, the necklace falls off and the superboy's strength is restored.

Visually this is very much a resurrection – the character coming down from the cross revivified. The mythological resonance is every bit as powerful as Clark's prodigious strength. It is not going out too far on a limb to suggest that *Smallville* draws an analogy between Clark Kent and Jesus Christ. In Christianity, Jesus was born as a divine blessing to the world, to teach us to love and forgive; Clark was sent to Earth from a dying planet to help guide and protect humanity. The parallel with Christ's crucifixion is clear, but other comparisons might not be so obvious. For we aren't just talking Christianity here, but mythological sun gods as well, particularly Osiris (while Ra is the name immediately associated with the Egyptian sun gods, Osiris also bore the title).

Superman mythology, reinforced in later episodes of *Smallville*, tells us that Clark draws his powers from the sun. And the resurrection analogy does not end at Jesus, as Osiris was chopped into pieces by Set, then reassembled and brought back to life by Isis.

And Lex? Does he serve as Judas to Clark's Jesus? Set to his Osiris? It takes years in terms of the story for Lex to go from morally ambiguous to morally corrupt, but like Judas he moves from an ally to an enemy. Even Osiris and Set were brothers and close friends, until Set betrayed him by chopping him up, putting him in a coffin and sending him down the Nile. (That kind of thing tends to put a crimp in any sibling relationship.)

Now bear in mind that *The Gospel of Judas* paints the man as still Jesus's friend; the Judas Kiss is orchestrated by Christ himself, making Judas the facilitator of the resurrection – probably the single most important aspect of Christianity.

The Gospel of Judas is one of the Gnostic gospels, a collection of writings about the teachings of Jesus, written around the second century AD. These gospels are not accepted by most mainstream Christians as part of the standard Biblical canon (and you thought *Doctor Who* and *Star Trek* fans were the only ones obsessed with what is or isn't canon). Rather, they are part of what is called the New Testament apocrypha, and the notion contained therein of Judas making the ultimate sacrifice and still being Jesus's friend isn't exactly part of what the Christian faith believes to be true.

Lex, like the Judas of the Gnostic text, is – in his own mind at least – not the villain. In fact, as the seasons progress he increasingly feels that Clark is. Clark betrayed him. Clark kept secrets. Even as Lex's megalomania builds and he assembles his own army of 'supers', he reasons that he is trying to protect the world, not destroy it.

Screenwriters Alfred Gough and Miles Millar had previously worked on big-screen heroics in *Spiderman 2* and *Shanghai Knights*, among other things. Their work on *Smallville*, however, is fascinating. Though it may seem a contradiction, the mythological theme gives it a solid sense of reality. Part of this comes from having the show take place in the present day; another aspect is the connection to archetypal characters; yet another lies in how it weaves in a sense of the ancient Kryptonian connection to Earth.

The most notable example of this is the Kiwatche Indian caves discovered in *Smallville*'s sophomore season. Ancient wall paintings depict Clark's arrival on Earth, and even Lex's two-faced nature. To the Kiwatche, Clark was known as Naman, and Lex, Segeth. Segeth's similarity to the Egyptian deity Set seems deliberate, emphasising the Lex/Set/Judas connection.

Epic themes aside, *Smallville* works at a more intimate level

Ever wondered what Clark Kent's high school days were like? Smallville *has the answers.*

because it explores the everyday concerns of coming of age. It is a *Bildungsroman* for the small screen: Clark's journey is our journey (minus the tights, the flying, and possibly getting the girl).

And like all good myths, loss is woven throughout Clark's story. Even before Kal-El makes it to Earth he is an orphan, and then some – his entire planet has been destroyed. He is, in fact, the archetypal American immigrant, an alien adopted and raised in the middle of the United States. (He could easily have come from Sweden, or Ireland during the potato famine.) Then, of course, he loses his humanity when Jonathan Kent tells him about the spaceship. Two of his girlfriends die – or make that three, though when Lana Lang is killed in a car crash Clark does the turn-back-time trick and saves her. But this still leads to our hero's greatest loss: the price of Lana's life is that of Jonathan Kent's.

Secrets and deception have been a staple of stories and myths for millennia. Because of this, a confidant of Clark like Pete Ross finds himself in danger; Lana

Smallville's pilot episode pulled in a massive 8.4 million viewers – a Warner Brothers record.

and Clark break up after they finally kindle a relationship; and Lois Lane is less than impressed with our hero. She even takes to calling him 'Smallville' – not just a reference to the town name, but her perception of his place in the world. And Lex's obsession with Clark's secrets is particularly significant.

It is a hero's friends and enemies that define him. Over the decades, the stories of Superman have developed a myriad cast of supporting characters – some brilliant, some downright silly. One of the strengths of *Smallville* is that it takes even the most ridiculous personages and makes them not only smart but relevant, light and dark reflections of Kal-El himself.

Case in point: the character of Krypto. Yep, Superboy's dog. A mutt with identical powers to the man of steel. Like *Doctor Who*'s K9, this notion appeals strongly to younger readers but tends to have the older ones rolling their eyes, disbelief no longer suspended. But Gough and Millar succeeded in giving a nod to Krypto in a rather ingenious manner. Clark finds a dog with heightened intelligence and super strength, due to experiments at Luthorcorp. Later, the dog loses its powers, but the Kent family adopts it. Clark suggests naming it Krypto, as in the *Superboy* comic. Instead, they decide on the name Shelby.

Since *Smallville* takes place before Clark becomes Superman, we already know how many things will turn out. Clark will fall in love with Lois Lane; work for the *Daily Planet*; he and Lex Luthor will be archenemies. The knowledge that Clark will become Superman also allows for some amusing foreshadowing and symbolism. Clark tends to wear blue shirts and red jackets, reminiscent of the suit and cape later worn in his secret identity. When he temporarily damages his sight he wears glasses, giving him that future bespectacled reporter look. The 'S' painted on his chest during the homecoming hazing echoes the symbol of the House of El, that familiar red 'S' that Superman wears on his chest. Indeed, that very symbol shows up in the form of a protective amulet that Clark obtains in the Phantom Zone.

Clark Kent and his secret identify of Superman may be but a myth, but mythology is powerful.

LOST (2004-2010)

The conceit is as old as *Robinson Crusoe* and it works just as well today as it did for Defoe. On 22 September 2004, Oceanic Air Flight 815, from Sydney, Australia to LAX, disappeared en route.

There were no survivors.

Except that you know there were.

Forty-eight passengers survived the plane tearing apart in mid-air and crashing into a tropical island. These people, from all over the world and all walks of life, banded together to fashion makeshift shelters, tend their wounded, and wait for rescue that wasn't forthcoming.

This isn't *Castaway*, or *Stranded*. There's no Oliver Reed romping on the beach with a lithe Amanda Donohoe. The survivors quickly realise that something is very strange about the island. Strange creatures stalk the night. Peculiar sounds rise from the jungle and split the silence. And all the while eerie visions haunt them.

This is the start of *Lost*. Originally conceived as a cross between *Lord of the Flies*, *Castaway* and *Survivor*, the show was created by J.J. Abrams and Damon Lindelof and quickly won a large (and rabidly enthusiastic) following, which has grown into a massive television cult over the five seasons that have aired thus far.

But why has *Lost* won such impressive loyalty? Obviously it can't be the originality of the concept; despite the fact that the mysteries of the Bermuda Triangle and fantasies of lost worlds have a perennial appeal, they have been done to death in just about every form of entertainment.

So what then? Is it the casting? Certainly, the executive producers showed surprising flexibility and insight when casting and tailoring characters to the actors and actresses they selected. Originally Jack, the doctor who takes charge after the crash, was supposed to die during the pilot, but they liked Matthew Fox's interpretation of the character too much to kill him. Hurley, created for Jorge Garcia after he auditioned for the part of Sawyer, was only supposed to be a small role but fans and the producers took the character to their hearts and he became a central figure. Charlie, the drug-addicted rock star, was supposed to be an older man but was altered to fit Dominic Monaghan (who had also auditioned for Sawyer). Josh Holloway, who auditioned for Sawyer as well, brought an angry edge to the role and the producers changed the former city slicker into a brash Southerner to match that.

Could it be the format? *Lost* relies heavily upon flashbacks – and, in later seasons, the rather unique device of flash-forwards. Each episode focuses on one character and uses flashbacks to provide insights into their history and personality. These tie back into the events occurring in the show's current timeline, explaining to the viewer why the character is acting as he or she is, and, more importantly, how events are having such an impact upon them. The flashbacks also provide clues to the deeper mysteries that link the various characters.

'The flashback element is one of my favorite things about the show,' J.J. Abrams told ABC News' Jake Tapper, 'And in theory you think, "Well, it's a flashback so it's not affecting the present-day story, therefore is it relevant?" I'm a huge fan of *The Twilight Zone*, and I love tuning into a show and not knowing exactly what you're going to get every week – it's sort of having a little surprise. It's a current network sort of no-no that you don't have an anthology, you have to have characters you're following every single week. But *Lost* allows us to kind of sneak in an anthology element into a series, which is: you don't know exactly who you are going to be following every week, and you have no idea where they are going to take you. The flashbacks are sort of a minipuzzle within each episode – what that means or why that little plane is so important to her.'

Nothing is simple, not the cast, not the format, not the set-up, not the writing. What makes *Lost* so compelling is the mystery at the show's heart. Why did Oceanic Flight 815 crash? Where is this fantasy island (*sans* Tatu)? And what is happening to the survivors? These three seemingly straightforward questions are all woven together, and, as the show progresses the viewers are teased with more and more tidbits of detail. But, rather like the real-time experiment of *24*, only as it progresses do the viewers gradually learn anything, and only at the same pace as the characters. They are never privy to secrets about how the island works, or who is running the show. They start out just as lost as the 48 survivors, just as confused and, thanks to the anyone-can-die aspect of the first few episodes, almost as scared.

As writer and executive producer Carlton Cuse explained to Jake Tapper of ABC News, 'The book *Incident at Owl Creek* we put in as a shout to people who are theorising that this whole show was taking place in someone's mind in the last moments of their life.'

So what is the answer?

The audience are there with the characters as they encounter polar bears in a tropical climate and a strange smoky-looking creature (like a will-o'-the-wisp gone supernova) that kills and then disappears. They are there when the survivors find a mad Frenchwoman living in the jungle, and when they discover a sixteen-year-old distress signal beaming out to no one.

The producers and writers effectively draw the viewer into the show by putting them on the same level as the main characters, making any information just as hard-won as it is for the survivors of the doomed flight. The flashbacks work to heighten

The Lost *survivors prepare for their ordeals at the series' inception.*

audience identification with the survivors, allowing the viewer to know them better and sympathise with them more, ultimately giving them a reason to care what happens on that mysterious island.

Of course, most televisual mysteries cannot sustain themselves for three seasons or more. But *Lost* is not built around a simple mystery. It is an incredibly complex web of deceit, with each revelation seeming to lead to more questions.

The sheer extent of Lost's *ensemble cast ensured that the series was one of the most expensive ever made.*

It is clear early on that many of the survivors have met one another, or at least had an influence on each other's lives, leading one to suspect that all of them are linked together somehow. But meeting isn't the same as knowing; none of them *knew* each other before getting on that fated plane. They might have shared a bus, queued at the same bagel stand, or almost run each other over – all of these little coincidental moments when their paths have crossed long before they ever got on the plane. Part of the appeal is undoubtedly watching these parallel lines of fate playing out. So is it coincidence that they would all be on the same flight together, or stranded on the same lost island? Divine providence? For if not, how could anyone besides the Omnipotent All-Seeing One have arranged it? Was the crash an accident? If so, how did it happen? If not, who engineered it? Are there other people on the island? If so, who are they? What are they doing there? Does their presence have anything to do with the crash, or with the survivors' interlinked lives?

At every turn, *Lost* throws up some new way in which the characters are connected. They have many common elements in their lives: companies, locations, acquaintances, even things as mundane as television shows and candy bars. But the most prevalent of these elements is a particular string of numbers: 4, 8, 15, 16,

23 and 42. These numbers appear over and over again in relation to the survivors; they are in the flight number, the flight's original departure time and gate, the survivors' seat rows, and many other places. Something about them seems to have been woven into the characters' lives. The mystery of what the numbers mean and why they recur so often is one of the show's central questions. Are they life's lottery *sans* power ball? Some complex code that would befuddle Fibonacci?

The most obvious question of the show, of course, is where are the characters? Their plane crashed onto an island, but where exactly is it? In this day and age of über-technology and gadgetry, is it feasible that they simply vanished off the radar? The pilot wound up off-course and was turning back when the plane crashed, which means they could be anywhere in the Pacific. The island appears tropical and, though the characters are attacked by a polar bear at one

A massively popular success, Lost *achieved an amazing average of around sixteen million viewers per episode across its initial ABC run.*

point, this seems more a part of the island's strange properties than a clue as to its location. The survivors spend a good deal of their time trying to figure out where they are and how to return home, though none of their plans or ideas appear to have much success. Akin to the force-fields of 1950s SF, there is something about the island that does not allow them to leave.

There are, in fact, many mysteries about the island itself. Injuries seem to heal there, even normally fatal ones. People and objects appear that should not be there. Sights and sounds, probably hallucinations but possibly revelatory visions, plague many of the survivors. Certain medical conditions seem to prevail. The island has peculiar properties, clearly. John Locke believes it is alive, and that it has brought all of them there for a reason. Locke is the island's self-proclaimed prophet, its voice and its servant. Is he deluded? Possibly. Prophets of all stripes often are. But certainly there is something going on that defies rational explanation. The name

'John Locke' was derived from the famous social contract philosopher who dealt with the relationship between nature and civilisation in his writings. One of his core propositions was that humans are born with a *tabula rasa* (the title of the third episode of the first season) an ethos which echoes their status as they arrive on the island, be they crook, doctor, junkie, the slate is wiped clean for them to start again. There are more similarities between fact and fiction, including the point during a flashback where *Lost*'s Locke donates his kidney to save his father. Though not identical historically, it is a matter of public record that John Locke saved the life of his mentor, Lord Anthony Ashley Cooper, by convincing him to have surgery to remove a cystic liver. There's no such thing as coincidence, meaningful or otherwise.

One interesting feature of the show is its support network. During the first season hints were dropped about a mysterious agency known as the Hanso Foundation, a supposedly charitable research company that may have far more sinister motives. The Hanso Foundation – specifically its Dharma Initiative – have something to do with the island and its other inhabitants (conveniently and imaginatively referred to as 'the Others'), though the specifics are unclear.

Curious viewers began searching for the Hanso Foundation online after its first on-air mention – and were excited to discover an official Hanso website, mirroring the interactivity of Britain's resurgent *Doctor Who* with its Bad Wolf campaign (the BBC hired writer Joseph Lidster to create and run a number of pseudo-websites for the Bad Wolf Corporation, scattering clues like a treasure hunt across the internet. Each one somehow related to one of the upcoming episodes and gave subtle hints about the 'big bad wolf' that was to come in the first season's finale). The site is equally mysterious, and raises further questions about the organisation, its shadowy founder and its vague goals. This meta-mystery only serves to entice the audience further, and keeps them involved in the story between the airing of each episode.

Likewise, fans can log onto Oceanic Air's official website, which was created by ABC specifically for *Lost*. There it is possible to check on the status of Flight 815 and discover yet more little clues, including an image of Boone's passport and Kate's mugshot. All of the elements are carefully orchestrated by the show's production team, and hint at answers without revealing anything directly. Various movies have created linked websites, including fictitious company sites, but *Lost* is one of the first television series to have such an extensively fabricated online presence.

This presence escalated when ABC unveiled the *Lost* Experience, part treasure hunt and part jigsaw puzzle, where fans could search websites, voicemails, television and newspaper ads, and even a novel for various clues. These led them to snippets of a video blog by one Rachel Blake, also known as Persephone. Blake had, she claimed, been researching the Hanso Foundation and had discovered the truth behind the Dharma Initiative, which also explained both the island's odd properties and the significance of the numbers. This was marketing genius. By involving viewers in such an interactive story, ABC were able to keep them interested even during the break between seasons and the inevitable falloff as new fodder hit the

Leader of Lost's *band of survivors, Doctor Jack Shephard (Matthew Fox).*

small screen. Online forums were filled with discussions of the game and its various clues, followed by rampant speculation about the meaning of said clues and the video footage that corresponded to them. The show's producers have confirmed that the game and its information is canon. And, as with the other elements, the site is not necessary for enjoyment of the television series – wandering through its pages gives added insight to events on the show, and points the way to answering some of the questions that pervade it. But viewers can still puzzle their way through the show without ever going online.

All of this points to the thing that makes *Lost* truly important and groundbreaking television: its vision. *Lost* was conceived from the start as not merely a show but a multimedia entertainment experience, and it is paving the way for even more outrageous promotions to satisfy the new generation of viewers. How far we have come from 'Danger, Will Robinson!' and jerky robot puppetry.

Lost has more than enough questions to keep forums buzzing for years, as people from all around the world watch the episodes and ponder the various details glimpsed or heard in every scene. The trick, as with any mystery, is revealing enough to keep the audience interested but not so much that there is nothing left to discover.

Lost was designed to have so many layers and elements that new details could be revealed and large questions answered without ever revealing the whole picture. And so far it has succeeded in walking that very fine line between not telling enough and telling too much.

The websites and novels and other media have only served to add to this complexity, but they also reveal the sheer expanse of the *Lost* vision. The story is capable of bridging the gap between television and internet, print and radio, precisely because it is so layered and so detailed. Anyone who wanders across the Hanso Foundation website can explore it and wonder about this strange company even without realising its connection to a TV series, because the site itself is so elaborate that it creates an experience of its own for browsers.

This is the twenty-first-century equivalent to a Shakespearean play, which had elements designed to appeal to each of its audience types: low comedy (including the infamous dancing bears) for the easily pleased, clever wordplay for the more sophisticated, and satire for the intellectuals.

Lost can be enjoyed as simply a supernaturally-tinged TV drama about the island-bound survivors of a plane crash. Or it can be seen as a show about a vast conspiracy with the power to span space and possibly time, manipulating people all over the world to bring about a very particular sequence of events, for reasons unknown.

The appeal of the show is, quite literally, a mystery.

HEROES (2006 - PRESENT)

The show *Heroes* debuted on NBC in the fall of 2006, and it fast became a smash-hit. It appealed not only to fans of superheroes and comic books, but to any viewers who could appreciate vividly realised characters, high-stakes plots, and sharp writing.

It wasn't the first superhero show we've seen, and not even the highest-profile one in recent history. That honour would probably go to *Smallville*. Still, it caught on better and faster than any of them ever had before and has quickly become a televisual phenomenon.

For those coming in late, *Heroes* concerns itself with the actions and activities of a select group of people who appear to be the coming of the next wave of humanity. These special folk are supposedly to homo sapiens as our ancestors were to the Neanderthals: people just so much better that the older kind had no choice but to eventually be shoved into extinction.

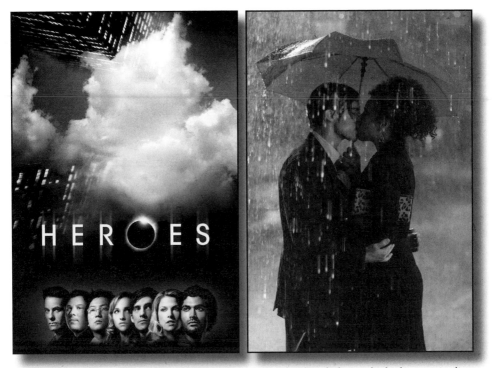

Heroes was initially greeted by widespread popular and critical acclaim before multiple alternate timelines undermined its plot credibility.

The heroes (and the villains, of course) come from all walks of life and can appear in any society. They include an LA cop, a New York politician, a Texas cheerleader, a Tokyo salaryman, a Vegas webcam girl, and many more. They become involved with each other in ways that imply that fate is pushing their buttons, shoving them together not despite their genetic advances, but because of them.

As the first season rolls on, we discover that the heroes hold the key to saving New York City from nuclear destruction, if they can only find it within themselves to grasp it. To complicate things, the story involves an artist who can see the future, a man who can travel through time and space, and multiple timelines.

Can the heroes escape fate? Or are all their efforts to do so in vain?

As you might imagine, these are questions that weigh heavy on the minds of most Americans today. In a world beset with problems far beyond the ability of any one of us to change, it's hard to feel like one person *can* make a difference. It seems that fate has already chosen its course, that history is already decided, that there's nothing we can do but hold on tight and try not to get thrown off the ride.

The central message of *Heroes* is that people – special people, at least – do matter.

Claire Bennet (Hayden Panettiere) and Peter Petrelli (Milo Ventimiglia) during their Season One showdown with Sylar.

More than that, we have no way of knowing who those people might be. Any one of us could be a hero at any time.

Unlike superheroes of an earlier age, the powers in *Heroes* arise not from radiation or wealth or strange visitors from other planets. No, these powers are the direct result of a weird combination of genetic code and the hot-housing effects of the modern world forging them into man-plus, homo superior, the next evolutionary leap. This means, of course, that powers tend to run in families.

As we're finding out in the second season, people with powers seem to become attracted to each other. When they have kids, chances are those offspring will have powers too. The forces of evolution push these people together to reinforce their superior lines and cause superpowered dynasties to begin.

Even so, not all of the major characters in *Heroes* have powers. Noah Bennet (the Man in the Horn-Rimmed Glasses, or HRG, as he's known) works with powered people, tracking them down for the shadowy organisation known as the Company. He tags them with a radioactive marker and then releases them back into the wild, none the wiser for the experience.

There's also Mohinder Suresh, the Indian scientist whose father began the groundbreaking research into the heroes, defining not only how they work but also puzzling out a formula for who they might be. While not a superpowered person himself, his blood holds the cure for a new virus that seems to affect such people. He is related to powers but has none of his own.

In a world in which superpowered people exist, it's the normal ones who have to make the hardest choices, and who come out as the most heroic and the most flawed. They can't rely on impossible abilities, after all, just their own skills and their often-conflicted sense of judgment.

That's not to say that the people with powers have an easy time of it. They just have other options available to them.

Key players from Heroes' debut season (clockwise from top left):
Mohinder Suresh (Sendhil Ramamurthy), Isaac Mendez (Santiago Cabrera),
Sylar (Zachary Quinto), and Niki Sanders (Ali Larter).

247

Two of Heroes' *ensemble of heroic leads: Peter Petrelli and the hugely popular Hiro Nakamura (Masi Oka).*

However, since they have the ability to stop disasters from happening, they also feel the responsibility to do so. In this sense, they're like soldiers in an army. They may not have a solid grasp of the larger picture, but they use their skills to do whatever they can to help those who don't have the ability to fight for themselves.

Ironically, it turns out that the superpowered people are unwittingly the source of many of the problems they're trying to solve. More than once they struggle with the question of whether the world would be better off without them. Should they kill themselves or ask others to do it for them? Or should they accept the fact that people like them exist and that the most they can hope for is to do the best they can to use their powers for good rather than ill?

The central heroes must also struggle with the question of perhaps letting fate take its course. Should they let the disaster happen so that they can take advantage of its ramifications, possibly for the greater good? No matter how many people might die? (There's a strong resonance here with the strike on the Twin Towers, the notion that somehow 5,000 died to forge a stronger, more united America, tempered in the heat of tragedy to stand firm in a war against terror. If the planes hadn't crashed, if the tragic waste of life had never occurred, would borders have been tightened? Would

Homeland Insecurity have been formed? Biometric passports and limitations on transport, increased spending on defence, arms budgets, and Gung Ho Americanism? Not a prayer – so the science fiction writer's impulse here, obviously, is to go beyond what we've already seen and extrapolate it into a worst case scenario, first a holocaust of nuclear proportions in Season One, and then a glimpse at a totalitarian America fronted by one of our heroes in Season Two.) Or should they stick to their values and try to save the world, however unpragmatic that might be?

Heroes is unusual among superhero TV shows in that it is not based on an existing comic book. However, the producers take great pains to use common comic-book tropes and even to involve prominent comic-book creators in the production of the show.

For instance, the paintings of the future that Isaac Mendez creates in the show are actually produced by acclaimed comic-book artist Tim Sale. Sale is best known for his work with writer Jeph Loeb on books like *Batman: The Long Halloween*.

Not coincidentally, Loeb is a co-executive producer on the show and one of the regular writers. He and series creator Tim Kring have known each other for years, having co-written the film *Teen Wolf Too* long ago. That movie, of course, also featured a hero with strange, secret abilities.

Before the show even hit the air, the producers brought an extra-long pilot and aired it at Comic-Con International in San Diego in the summer of 2006. Their booth featured cheerleaders in *Heroes* uniforms passing out literature and showing clips to all potential fans.

The team behind *Heroes* use the internet to promote the show better than possibly any other show to date. They publish a regular comic on the show's website, which is soon to be collected into a hard-copy graphic novel, complete with covers by superstar artists Jim Lee and Alex Ross.

Heroes writers regularly blog about the show, either on their own sites or on promotional ones like ComicBookResources.com. While they are careful not to reveal spoilers about what's coming up, they offer nearly unprecedented access into how the show is created and what the creators are trying to do with it.

The show has also spawned a tie-in novel and a mobile phone game. As hot as it is, fans can expect many more *Heroes* items to come, including next-gen computer games.

So far, all of the products tie tightly into the series. They respect the original stories and add to them, even revealing details that have not yet been displayed in the show. The producers keep tight control over the content, but unlike other shows in the past, they seem eager to broaden their story into other media rather than trying to keep all the good parts to themselves.

This gives fans the sense that they can trust the *Heroes* brand. They know that if they read a *Heroes* novel or play a *Heroes* game, they can be sure that someone who knows what he's doing took the time to vet the product. These new bits then fall into the *Heroes* canon or continuity, which encourages fans to track them all down so they can learn as much as possible about the show and the characters in it.

Unlike many previous superhero shows, *Heroes* takes itself as seriously as any drama. It certainly has its funny moments, but these arise from the situations in which the characters find themselves. The show never mocks its own premises.

Heroes has many precedents in comic books themselves. In tone, it's closest to the *X-Men* comics, particularly the legendary 'Days of Future Past' story arc. However, its modern sensibilities fall closer to *The Ultimates*, a recent reinvention of *The Avengers* in a new Marvel Comics universe in serials like *Gods and Monsters and Grand Theft America*. Here a classic hero like Captain America has been reimagined as a considerably more violent and pragmatic character. Nick Fury is more rage-fuelled, we've got an abusive relationship between Hank and Janet Pym, and a womanising drunk with a homosexual butler. Clean cut is long gone. Curiously Fury and Janet Pym have also undergone a racial shift in this reimagining so that they might appeal to a broader spectrum of readers. *The Ultimates* also consciously addressed the issue of the war on terror and grooming normal folk into super soldiers to fight the good fight.

Possibly the most interesting wrinkle to the show is the character Sylar. He starts out wanting to be special, to be someone important, and the fact that he's not frustrates him to no end. Then he discovers he can steal the powers of other special people, but only by murdering them.

While the earth-shattering disasters the heroes face are clearly the larger threat to the world, it's Sylar who is the most dangerous to them individually. If the heroes are the celebrities of the superpowered world, the secret stars that live among us, then Sylar is the madman who stalks them.

Sylar has no powers of his own, no fame. He has no talents. He can only steal those of others by killing them, much in the way an assassin's fame comes only from being associated with the important people they kill. He is the ultimate leech, hollow inside but for the energies he steals.

This adds another element of suspense to the show. Whenever Sylar shows up, anyone could die. With such a large ensemble cast, any character is disposable. And with time-travelling powers like those shown by at least a couple of the heroes, it's even possible they could come back.

It reflects another element from modern society, the feeling that any of us could be killed at any time. Random events are one thing. We know that we don't have much control over lightning strikes or car accidents. But Sylar's attacks aren't random.

Sylar represents the risk of being talented. If you stand above the crowd, you're bound to be noticed, and that makes you a target. While most people won't try to kill you, they might hope to steal your thunder, to take your glory for themselves.

Some of Sylar's victims keep their talents secret, telling no one and using them for little or nothing. In fact, his first victim doesn't even want his powers at all, which drives the jealous Sylar to his murderous fury. The point here, of course, is that if you have talents you should use them, no matter what the risks might be. You can't

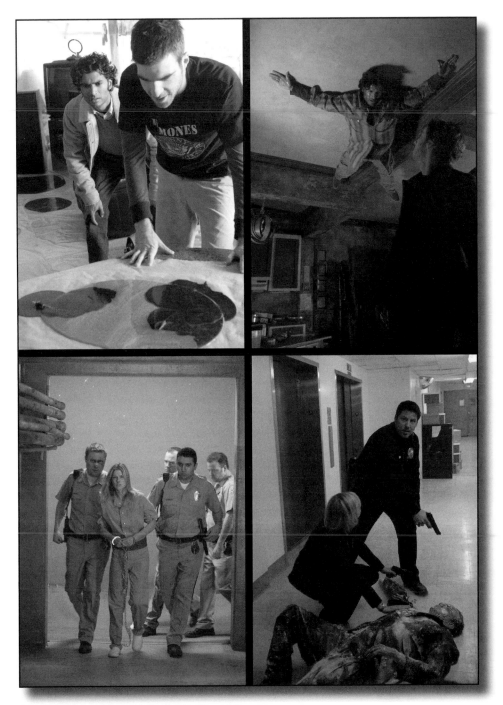

Strongly influenced by comic books,
Heroes *featured regular action-packed set-pieces.*

keep them secret forever, and sooner or later someone will take advantage of them (and you) if you don't.

Heroes follows squarely in the footsteps of *Lost* in terms of its narrative structure and style. The show is a serial thriller in which each episode builds upon the last. It's possible to jump into the show in the middle of a season, but it's hard and not nearly as rewarding as following the whole thing from day one.

While shows like these clearly have some soap-opera elements, the plot moves along at a brisk pace. Big things happen. If you only see one episode out of five, you're missing out on tons of juicy stuff. You need to follow every bit, or you may find yourself wondering what the heck is going on.

Given the modern means of getting our hands on TV shows, though, catching up isn't all that hard, even barring illegal methods. You can watch a selection of older episodes for free at NBC's website. You can pick up the Season One DVDs. You can plumb the depths of the internet for show guides and episode encapsulations and reviews.

As screenwriter John Rogers likes to say: 'We are all writing for the box set now.'

Before the internet, before the advent of the DVD box set that allowed you to watch entire seasons of a show in one sitting, writers and producers had to assume that people would miss some of the shows. Episodic television had to remain relatively static because of that. The writers could take the toys off the shelf at the start of each episode and play with them however they liked. Still, at the end of the show they had to put the toys back on the shelf in roughly (if not exactly) the same condition in which they found them.

Star Trek is a classic example of such storytelling, as are the vast majority of media related tie-in novels. The characters in any given episode are roughly the same. They might change a bit from season to season, but mostly they are the same people with the same relationships, never growing or evolving from episode to episode. *Heroes* is the exact opposite of that. The episodes link together. They stand upon each other and build something greater than just a series of barely related short stories featuring the same protagonists every week. They form an epic tale with teeth, a story in which they characters can learn and grow. Something more akin to real life.

Ten years ago, shows like this would wither on the vine, just from natural rates of viewer attrition. While they might have a strong base of viewers to start with, they could count on some of them dropping away as the show went on, for a variety of reasons. Back then, it was almost impossible for new viewers to catch up, no matter how much they might want to. The audience inevitably faded away until it got to the point where the show was no longer sustainable.

Now, with the internet, BitTorrent clients, TiVo, Freeview, streaming shows from network homepages and those beautifully packaged (and cheaper by the year) box sets making missed episodes easily available, hit shows can build on their buzz and draw in more and more viewers every year. Didn't catch any of Season One?

Watched by the enigmatic Haitian (Jimmy Jean-Louis), Noah Bennet (Jack Coleman) 'dies' in the arms of his adopted daughter Claire. In true comic-book style, he'd be back.

Pick up the box set a couple weeks before Season Two starts, and you're good to go. This is unequivocably a case of technology mutating our viewing habits and television shows being stronger for it.

Tim Kring and his crew clearly had this in mind from the show's inception, and it allowed them to engage in the kind of bold storytelling unseen in previous generations. In this sense, *Heroes* is the model for a new kind of show, a return to the kind of meaningful, epic stories previously found only in longer works of literature.

Despite making some serious character development mistakes in the opening gambits of Series Two, giving us more 'origins' storylines instead of driving on with the cast of characters they'd already established, and thanks to the Writer's Guild of America Strike putting pay to the proposed miniseries *Heroes: Origins*, we've been denied what promised to be a fascinating journey into the backstories of our heroes. One can't help but think that the quality of writing and the epic (and possibly ultimate) extrapolation of the monomyth means that *Heroes* is going to resonate with television viewers for years to come.

Which can only be good for fantastic television as a whole.

8 WORLDS OF THEIR OWN

A Round Robin Interview with Joe Ahearne, Adrian Hodges, Kenneth Johnson, Stephen Volk, Keith DeCandido, Andrew Cartmel, Joseph Lidster, Paul Cornell and Kevin J. Anderson

A ROUND ROBIN INTERVIEW

We've spent the last few hundred pages in the company of their creations, so what better way to close *Fantastic TV* than to allow some of the creators and writers to share what they love and loathe about genre television?

I have been lucky enough to sit down with a number of the very best and most influential proponents of science fiction television of the last few years, including:

Joe Ahearne, whose credits include *This Life* (writer and director), *Ultraviolet* (writer and director), *Strange* (director), *Doctor Who* (director), and *Apparitions* (writer and director).

Paul Cornell, whose credits include *Primeval* (writer), *Doctor Who* (writer), and *Robin Hood* (writer).

Kenneth Johnson, whose credits include *The Incredible Hulk* (creator), *V* (creator), *Alien Nation* (creator), *The Bionic Woman* (creator), and *The Six Million Dollar Man* (writer).

Andrew Cartmel, who served as John Nathan Turner's script editor for the final three seasons of the classic *Doctor Who* series and is a novelist in his own right.

Kevin J. Anderson, a science fiction novelist with over 100 books to his credit including countless tie-ins to popular shows and films such as *Star Wars, The X-Files, Dune, Fantastic Voyage, The League of Extraordinary Gentlemen* and *Sky Captain and the World of Tomorrow*.

Keith DeCandido, a genre novelist with over 50 books to his credit including tie-ins to *Supernatural, Star Trek, Doctor Who, Spider-Man, Buffy the Vampire Slayer, Andromeda,* and *Farscape.*

Stephen Volk, whose claim to fame in 1994 was convincing the British public he was responsible for killing a BBC presenter on live television in *Ghostwatch* (writer), and more recently traditional supernatural thrillers including *Afterlife* (writer) and *Telepathy* (forthcoming, writer).

'You write science fiction? So that means you won't be producing anything worthwhile or of merit,' was the accusation levelled at Rod Serling when he announced *The Twilight Zone* – how would you as a writer of SF respond to this today?

AHEARNE: The accusation wouldn't be stated in the same way today but the prejudice is still there. You only have to compare the number of classic period adaptations or contemporary series that are done compared to science fiction. The assumption remains that the audience is not large enough to warrant the expense (not that science fiction always has to be expensive). There are any number of cop/doc/lawyer shows but no remotely comparable range of sci-fi (on British TV). When a period drama flops that doesn't mean the broadcasters stop making them but the position of science fiction is more precarious. That said, the situation is much more hopeful than ten years ago. Things are moving in the right direction. When *Ultraviolet* was pitched ten years ago we were told by one commissioner that the audience simply wouldn't believe there was a conspiracy of vampires out there – i.e. the suspension of disbelief was not expected or required. However with the success of *Doctor Who*, *Torchwood* and many more science fiction projects in development we have to be careful not to squeal too loudly about being victims. The climate has changed and will hopefully change further. I'm currently working on a show about an exorcist which is for a mainstream channel and star which I would never have envisaged ten years ago. But we will have to fight to get adult science fiction/fantasy/horror perceived as more than an occasional risk.

ANDERSON: Today, that's an easy question. Thanks to the undeniably brilliant work in so many episodes of *The Twilight Zone*, or *The Outer Limits*, or *Star Trek*, audiences began to see the potential of science fiction. George Lucas faced the same thing when he wanted a non-cheesy budget to make *Star Wars*, and he proved to everybody that there was big money in science fiction. Today, thanks to the consistent efforts of those early SF television shows, a whole generation grew up remembering how much fun and how thought-provoking SF could be. And we picked up the candle and carried it forward – I can remember running home from school every day to watch *Star Trek* reruns on TV; I can remember sitting in the theatre watching *Star Wars* in its first run and being blown out of my chair with amazement. Now I've written for *Star Wars*, and I've written for *Star Trek*, and many others. Some fans applied that excitement to writing SF-based videogames, or have written new television shows, all of which are now considered *mainstream*. We're no longer the weird 'sci-fi buffs' – we've won the battle.

CARTMEL: I think SF is still perceived as a ghetto, although the huge success of *Doctor Who* may have gone some way towards altering perceptions like that, at least in TV commissioning circles. It's interesting, though, how literary masterpieces (Orwell, Huxley, Atwood, Cormac McCarthy's *The Road*) are somehow seen to be exempt from the ghetto label of science fiction, despite very clearly being SF.

CORNELL: I think this attitude is fading over time. The number of mainstream writers getting into genre, even the ones quick to disavow that that's what they're doing, and the number of genre writers entering the mainstream, indicate that the barriers are coming down. Of course, for a genre to thrive it actually needs those barriers. *Doctor Who* is now the biggest TV drama in Britain. It's also one of the most prestigious popular shows you can work on. It's also SF. So doing it all at once is entirely possible. Russell doing that changed everything.

DECANDIDO: I'm sorry, I can't hear you over the sound of my cheque being cashed. Seriously, when I get this accusation levelled against me, I consider the source. Someone who says such a stupid thing isn't someone whose opinion I'm going to take in the least bit seriously.

VOLK: The unspoken accusation that science fiction or horror is, let's face it darlings, 'low art' is the subtext of every single meeting I've ever had at the BBC in the last twenty years! It drives me completely crazy! Frankly I've had enough of it! (When I was writing a vampire story for David M. Thompson I must've reeled off about fifteen movies as reference – *Rosemary's Baby*, *Near Dark*, *The Hitcher* – and, surprise surprise, he hadn't seen *any* of them!) The problem is that most of the commissioners and producers are English Literature graduates and their genre of choice is either literary bollocks or Jane Austen. They simply don't like the genre the rest of us love, and even if they are forced by some dictat from above to 'find science fiction!' – they don't know it because they don't read it and don't instinctively like it or get it. Hence they cry: 'Time travel!' or 'Dinosaurs!' as if they are the first people to think of it – rather than knowing there have been hundreds of stories about time travel and dinosaurs for the last 200 years. Also they're inherently snobbish about it because it is populist. Today, still, they put it in the box called 'family entertainment' as convenient segregation to avoid their middle-brow embarrassment – but *I* want to see on TV the kind of stories that excited and challenged me when I was young: Moorcock, Harlan Ellison, J.G. Ballard. BBC Two made an astonishing anthology of SF stories that had a huge impression on me in the seventies, *Out of the Unknown* – stories like Asimov's 'Liar' and the one about the future doctor's black bag: they had important ideas and themes and were inventive without being silly. With the present crop of SF, I don't think anyone is too worried about being 'silly' – well, they bloody should be!

JOHNSON: I wonder not only how Rod Serling felt about that but how Aldous Huxley and George Orwell felt about the same thing. I think the beauty of working in science fiction that I have always felt is that one can work in allegory and in metaphor and can get into some very, very deep and important subjects but do it at arm's length, which gives us a new and better lens through which to view the human condition.

What excites you about television as a medium for telling your stories?

AHEARNE: I think in pictures more than words so it has to be film or TV. The most exciting thing is to photograph a character thinking rather than just speaking. And when you can tell the audience the story by juxtaposing images rather than exposition. Very difficult to do on TV because of time pressures and the prejudice that TV is fundamentally different from cinema. It isn't. Or needn't be. Movies play very well on TV and don't always cost the Earth.

Which shows, old and new, would you say have had the most influence on you as a writer – why/how? What, for you was the high/low point of genre TV?

VOLK: Low point has to be *Blake's 7*. I just thought it was trash from the first frames. Maybe I was too old then. But after the wonder and awe that came with *Star Trek* (a ship with 500 crew members – the *idea* of that blew my mind!) it really was very badly made, and very badly acted. I think it was the kiss of death for SF TV, actually. It said, 'We can't make this anymore.' It was Robin Hood, only with less charm than the Richard Greene series – which I loved. I had a Robin Hood suit as a kid I think. Or was it the Lone Ranger? Zorro, certainly – I remember the chalk-tipped rapier! (My brother, eight years younger, had a Captain Scarlet outfit: and actually looked like him!)
I really got sucked into my whole fascination with TV by the ABC/ITC adventure shows of the late sixties, early seventies. I got hit by the Emma Peel era of *The Avengers*. And then – *in colour*! Wow! Not so much the sex appeal as the surrealism of the stories: killer clowns, cybernauts, shrinking spies. Just fantastic. My mates and I were obsessed by them. Then *The Champions, Department S, Randall and Hopkirk, Jason King*. We were making our own Super-8 films at the time, slapstick and horror shorts, but we wrote to Monty Berman and he gave us a tour of Elstree where they were filming *Jason King*. It was just so generous of him, and he showed up an episode that had just been cut, in the screening room. What a gent! We felt we were in heaven, us, three TV-obsessed lads from a grammar school in Pontypridd!
At various stages I wanted to be Dennis Wheatley, Richard Matheson, Robert Bloch – but I also wanted to be Brian Clemens, or Dennis Spooner, the script supervisor and creator of these marvellous, imaginative TV series: I didn't think there could be any job in the world better than that. And maybe there isn't!

CORNELL: The original version of *The Outer Limits* I think is the high point of genre TV. It certainly had the most influence on me. It's genuinely nightmarish. It doesn't feel it has to sum everything up neatly, its poetic writing, stark, shadowy photography and genuinely deep mind beasts really get into one's brain and stir things up. You can feel trapped in it. The second season is nowhere near as good, mind you. *Sapphire and Steel* also didn't feel the need to explain itself, showing that a mainstream audience in a primetime slot will accept, indeed, may even prefer, emotional and character-based 'explanations' for what just happened rather than ones based in rational systems. And I think I probably nicked all my heroic motifs from *Robin of Sherwood*. Richard Carpenter knows his mythology and history. I haven't mentioned *Doctor Who*: it's not a TV show, it's a lifestyle choice. And ever since I was a kid I was always more interested in the fandom than in the show.

CARTMEL: My favourites were and remain the original *Outer Limits* (chiefly the episodes Harlan Ellison wrote – 'Soldier' and 'Demon with a Glass Hand') and the original *Twilight Zone* (which was full of good writing: Richard Matheson, Charles Beaumont, Rod Serling, et al) and what I think of as Nigel Kneale's 'black and white' *Quatermass* stories (i.e. everything before the Euston Films *Quatermass*, which was interesting but didn't have the same impact). In more recent decades the real stand-out in fantasy television has been Joss Whedon's *Buffy the Vampire Slayer*. I'd say that these all had a profound effect on me. They are my high points. The low points, thankfully, haven't stuck in my mind and in any case, whatever dumb, cheap show I nominated, there would be a dumber, cheaper one out there somewhere that I don't know about.

But, interestingly, in some ways *The X-Files* embodies both the highs and lows of genre television. At its best, I loved *The X-Files* and thought it was a terrific show (though, tellingly, I'd never dream of listing it with the others above). But it also contains some of what I thought was the worst television science fiction in its meretricious story arc about alien abduction. I think John Brosnan put it best when he described this as 'all that alien conspiracy crap'. Such crap was the Achilles heel of what should have been a great and classic show.

AHEARNE: *Doctor Who*, Gerry Anderson, Irwin Allen. All the ones which had visual ambition and weren't entirely close-ups of people talking. An element of larger-than-life situations – not just two people arguing in a kitchen about their relationship (not that there's anything wrong with that, but there is quite a lot of it). Late seventies was probably the high point of genre TV and the low point maybe the late eighties/early nineties after the cancellation of *Doctor Who*. In contemporary TV, Jimmy McGovern has always been an inspiration since *Cracker*.

ANDERSON: Classic *Star Trek* really shaped me when I was in high school.

I was so enamoured with the show that I outlined maybe 70-80 original *Trek* episodes because I wanted to see more adventures with my favourite crew. Just doing that taught me a lot about plotting, and I even received a response from Paramount when I queried them (as a Junior in high school) on whether I could publish my stories. They said no, alas, and so I wrote my own original fiction . . . published that, then got asked to write *Star Wars* novels, and eventually worked on some *Star Trek* books and comics. Nice, neat full-circle there.

For me, the high point in old genre TV was probably 'City on the Edge of Forever' from *Star Trek*. Low point . . . I'd have to say the carrot-man episode on *Lost in Space*.

DECANDIDO: Probably *Doctor Who* and *Star Trek*, simply because they've been important parts of my genre life since I was a wee tot, and have remained part of my life all along.

JOHNSON: As I think back on what shows that had the most influence on me, particularly growing up, none of them were science fiction really. I was a big fan of a show called *The Defenders*, which was a very literate show about a father and son lawyer team with E.G. Marshall and Robert Reed. I was also a big fan of *Have Gun – Will Travel*, which was a very well-done character show, and also, of course, *Maverick*, the original *Maverick* with James Garner, which had a terrific sense of humour about it. I think those three in particular had a big impact on me as a young person.

Why do you think we respond so well as viewers to supernatural, scary, or just plain fantastic stories? How does this fit into your own work?

ANDERSON: What's the point of a story if it can't take you to strange and amazing places? When I was in an advanced creative writing class in college, I was living in a small Wisconsin town, working as a waiter in a restaurant, and I wrote stories about alien invasions and starship battles. My creative writing teacher, a gruff old writer of self-labelled 'literature' grew very impatient with my wild tales and said, 'Why don't you write about a young man who lives in a small farming town, who puts himself through college by working as a waiter in a restaurant?' My jaw practically hit the table. 'I live that every single day of my life,' I said. 'Why on Earth would I want to waste my imagination on that?' As a reader, or a viewer, we want to live adventures we can't really live, see places we can't really see. In my original work, I try to push the envelope and develop worlds and conflicts that stretch the abilities of my imagination.

VOLK: I think cop shows and detective stories appeal to one side of the brain – the logical side where you want to solve the puzzle – and ghost stories and weird tales appeal to something else, the bit that doesn't want things totally explained because we know the world is like that: scary and unknowable.

The poet Lorca said that the mystery is always superior to the solution to the mystery, and that's where my interest lies. I can't plot a 'who-dun-it' like *Foyle's War* to save my life. I'm interested in shoving a great big terrifying catalyst into people's lives, usually something they can't comprehend or explain, and see what happens. What shakes their foundations. I can't see the point of a story, like on the Stephen Fry ITV series *Kingdom*, where it says in *Radio Times* something like, 'The WI are worried their guest speaker might not turn up.' What? Who gives a shit?

At one stage I tried to resist writing horror and science fiction. I succumbed briefly to the notion, absorbed from others, that it isn't really a respectable pursuit. Stupid. But then I realised it is the way my mind works: I can't think any other way. If someone says, do a story about a refrigerator, I'll think of a refrigerator on a town dump with a child trapped inside it. So I'd better go with the flow and just try and get good at it.

I think supernatural stories are as old as the hills: almost in our DNA. We tell scary tales to prepare ourselves psychologically for the scary things out there. I think stories generally are preparatory routines, experiments in cause and effect. If a greedy person does this, this will happen, or might happen. Or if the idiot goes down the cellar on their own without a flashlight – this surely will occur. Or maybe not. And whatever subtlety or symbolism you put into your stories, I think it is still that.

Which is why superstition and stories are closely related. Stories play out cause and effect to try out patterns to prepare us for life and understanding other human beings and ourselves. Superstition is when cause and effect goes awry: the stars cause our future, a rabbit foot will help me win the race, etc. That's why superstition will always be there – because we will never be prepared to accept the cold reality and brutality of real cause and effect.

Also I find it interesting – and maybe this is what draws me to it – that Freud thought the 'uncanny' genre was unique in that it is the only genre in which our experience of the fictional is greater than our experience in life (e.g. no love story makes us feel quite to the level as when we are really in love).

CORNELL: I think, like dreams, these stories are ways to say things that are difficult to say directly. 'Father's Day' talked in realistic terms about the relationship between a child and an absent father. That relationship is real, but the only way you can dramatise it, as opposed to representing it in prose, is through fantasy.

CARTMEL: I suppose people need fantasy as an escape from humdrum reality. I have a much clearer grasp, though, of why people like scary stuff. To be scared, while ultimately knowing you're safe (in your chair, watching television) is a tremendous pleasure. The adrenaline buzz is related to, though less intense than, a rollercoaster ride.

AHEARNE: People sometimes like stories that appeal on a visceral level and don't need much explanation. They like to enter a new world and be surprised and delighted by something purely imaginative. It's sometimes been forgotten in the UK with the overwhelming emphasis on social realism. Drama here tends to operate on the basis of recognition and identification rather than asking the audience to witness something out of their experience. Ten years ago it was almost impossible to get a science fiction project off the ground, now it's just difficult. Movies go through the same cyclical process where a genre is pronounced dead until someone revives it – movie science fiction was dead until *Star Wars*. In British TV, mainstream science fiction was, if not dead, definitely moribund until the revival and success of *Doctor Who*.

DECANDIDO: Because folklore is full of stories like that. Look at the myths of most cultures – they're all SF and fantasy stories! Hera turning one of Zeus's lovers into a cow, powerful beings breathing life into the world, Beowulf and Enkidu fighting a big scary monster, and so on. These are the stories that have formed our species.

JOHNSON: I think the reason that human beings respond to supernatural and scary or just plain fantastic stories goes all the way back to the early days of cavemen who would sit around the fires telling each other legends they created about the stars that were in the sky or the elements. I think that human beings have always had a desire to be inspired by the imaginative, and having their own imaginations stretched in such a way that it made them think about things or see their dreams put into a context of story. I have always tried to approach storytelling from that point of view but also it was really important to me to keep it as realistic as I could. I believe that an audience will only give you so many 'buys'. They will only buy so much in the context of any one story so it is very important not to stretch them beyond the edge of credulity in whatever particular story you are telling.

Why do you think there is such an enduring appeal to all things supernatural when it comes to storytelling – from the campfires to the big screen? What about it fascinates you?

AHEARNE: People like to step outside the rulebook and be challenged by something they know probably isn't real. People like to be scared in an enjoyable way. Not just by terrorism stories or domestic thrillers. Most TV is about reassurance and reinforcement of social cohesion and can be quite politically correct. Good horror and supernatural stuff is about unsettling and undermining social norms. There is no negotiation in horror and that is uncomfortable for a lot of people.

DECANDIDO: Look at Kripke's show on the CW, the reason why it continues to do well against powerhouses like *CSI* and *Grey's Anatomy* is, I think, twofold. One is that the show is much better than it needs to be. They could easily have just done 'pretty boys drive through town and shoot demons in the head', but they've gone to the trouble of actually developing a metastory and mythology, and giving the brothers an impressive depth of character.

The other is that the show touches on urban legends and tropes that everyone's familiar with and does interesting takes on them.
VOLK: I'm very proud of *Ghostwatch*. It was a bit of an event in TV history, which is great. It's disarming when a young man comes up and tells you that he saw it aged ten and he's never quite recovered from the experience!

Of course you never know the impact of your own work at the time, but over the years it's garnered quite a reputation, which delights me. When the BFI released the DVD they called it 'legendary', so you certainly can't complain about that!

The thing I always want to put right is this notion that it was a 'Halloween hoax'. It wasn't. It was a drama commissioned by BBC Screen One and it was written and produced by the drama department as a drama. Of course once we hit on the idea of pretending it was 'live', that demanded that we made certain choices and did it in a certain way, for instance with real presenters like Michael Parkinson and Sarah Greene – but that was to be true to the material and the intent. Which was (a) to create a good modern ghost story for TV, and (b) to smuggle in a bit of satire about the nature of reality TV and the way television was going, generally. Hopefully, we managed to do both. Certainly it's been pretty well imitated in the interminable *Most Haunted* – which has made the fatal error of really pretending to be true!

What only a few perceptive critics (like Kim Newman) realised about *Ghostwatch* was that it was also pretty much a homage to Nigel Kneale and his stunning BBC single drama *The Stone Tape* in particular. I took the 'man in rubber mask' joke from that: an excellent way to soften up the audience. And the whole 'science-to-answer-the-paranormal' is essentially classic Kneale. On seeing his ITV series *Beasts* again recently I was astonished how some of the sequences – the poltergeist in the supermarket, the cry of 'clear the studio!' in 'Dummy', reminded me so much of *Ghostwatch*. I guess if you dredge your unconscious you never know what might come up.

Are there any motifs you consciously seek to explore? Should genre TV be looking to examine taboos or merely to entertain?

DECANDIDO: Nothing specific. I don't think there should be any storytelling limits on any story being told. Usually if someone complains that they just look to something for entertainment, it means that a nerve was struck, and any story that can do that has done its job.

CARTMEL: Motifs – no, absolutely not. On the other hand I do occasionally write a deliberate polemic.

Taboos – I think a better question would be whether genre TV should be seeking to tackle real issues (back to the polemic again). And I believe it should. Certainly Serling's *Twilight Zone* showed that fantasy material could usefully shed light on real world topics. As for taboos, I suppose touching a nerve is always effective. But unless you have something genuine to say (back to the polemic yet again) you're going to end up with empty sensationalism. A supernatural version of *Red Shoe Diaries*.

VOLK: I hate the word 'entertainment' – I really do. It's like an implicit directive to leave your brain at the door. TV, like any (ha!) art form has to *challenge*, and mostly it doesn't. Your guy advertising PC World or the new Vauxhall Vegan doesn't particularly want to challenge, of course: he just wants a guarantee of millions of viewers. But I like to believe that eventually audiences, in drama anyway, don't want blandness and will grow tired of the same old reheated pap.

Danger is, the shows that break taboos aren't entertaining: *Secret Life*, about the paedophile, and *Boy A* were worthy, almost documentary explorations: I would question whether either was really a drama – drama meaning something made-up, folks.

It's hard to know what motifs and themes preoccupy my work. I try not to think about that. Sometimes I write about childhood, sometimes I write about fathers and sons, sometimes about brothers. I'm interested in outsider characters, monsters, murderers – broken personalities rather than the *Wire in the Blood* abuse of women gorefest. It's all about what makes people tick, even in fantasy, or I'd say, *especially* in fantasy.

I often come back to exploring, as in my ITV series *Afterlife*, the clash between rational and irrational: I think very much that there are two sides to human beings – certainly two sides to me – and though on a nice bright day like today I'm the supreme atheist/disbeliever/rationalist, second only to Richard Dawkins, in the cold of moonlight on a country road I am scared shitless of things unknown and things that go bump in the attic. Being paranoid and anxiety prone. Being a control freak. Being a writer.

CORNELL: It should be looking to do what I talked about above, to tell the truth, like every other kind of fiction does. I always seem to come back to fathers, and to sacrifice.

ANDERSON: Genre TV has the unique ability to perform thought experiments, show extremes and make viewers confront their own prejudices, or ignorance, or revulsions. *However*, if you're using science fiction as a cudgel to hammer home your point and preach at your audience, then you'd be better off staying home. The number one rule should be to tell a good, compelling story, and the big lesson should be subtly hidden in the fabric of the tale, like a stealth bomber strike rather than a frontal assault.

AHEARNE: The only motif I come back to is credibility. The more thought that goes into making it 'for real', the more the audience can buy into it. I'm not a great fan of camp. Humour should be within the story, not aimed at it from outside. Genre TV should be allowed to both entertain and examine taboos like any other drama. Some people are anxious about using what they in their heart-of-hearts consider a non-serious genre to explore serious issues. *Ultraviolet* took a lot of people by surprise by not going for the easy laughs with vampires but treating them for real.

JOHNSON: I don't know that there are particular motifs that I have sought to explore but there certainly are themes. Thematic material is very important to me, particularly regarding intolerance, discrimination, prejudice, it is a theme I have returned to again and again, particularly in *Alien Nation*, which was not about aliens and that sort of thing. What it was really about was what it was like to be the world's newest minority. Likewise there was a strong theme running through *V*, the theme of power and how some people are in power and how some people abuse it, others suck up to them because they want to be close to that power and others will say wait, this is being abused and we have to fight back against it. I think that is the great beauty of what we can do in science fiction and speculative fiction in general, it is to approach the world and storytelling from the standpoint of really getting deep into taboos and deep into thematic material in addition to 'just entertaining'.

Certain shows, like *Doctor Who* and *The Twilight Zone*, seem to have become a part of the public consciousness – what, to you, explains their appeal?

JOHNSON: I think that that same thing is the reason why shows like *The Twilight Zone* have become a part of the public consciousness – because they do have thematic material. Rod Serling was always interested in examining the human condition and using his anthological series to do that. I have hopefully tried to do much of the same thing in my work.

CORNELL: All SF is about what's happening now. *Doctor Who*, at its best, is about what's happening now, down the road, or in your house, in a single British consciousness that everyone thought had vanished, but hasn't. It's fantasy fiction that's a shared experience for British households, doing exactly what pantomime does.

CARTMEL: *The Twilight Zone* was the flipside of buttoned-down, cold war, conformist Eisenhower-era America. It was the dark collective id being allowed free rein in a time of great restraint, when a conventional façade was being strictly maintained despite the H-bomb hanging over everybody's head. It was jazz in the fallout shelter.

Doctor Who I think is successful for very different reasons, in very different times. I think the essence of *Who* is that it can go anywhere and do anything in story terms. Which should be a recipe for chaotic disaster. Too much freedom, in storytelling, can be a very bad thing. With no constraints you can easily end up with a shapeless mess. But *Who* has this beautiful, basic, very simple but very strong structure. That is, you have the Doctor to lead you into these endlessly rich and strange situations, along with the companion(s) to provide audience empathy and a standard of normality. The Doctor, like the Tardis, is the doorway to these other dimensions of fantasy storytelling.

AHEARNE: *Doctor Who* has a very pleasing format – go anywhere and anywhen – and a satisfying central relationship between the alien and his human companion. Also a freshness which is built into the concept because there's no precinct – little time is spent in the Tardis – every story is a completely new situation.

VOLK: I think it might have to do with *comfort*, on TV anyway. I think it's easier to be 'challenging' in a feature film where you pay your $5 and sit in a seat and know what you are in for, or are promised something *horrifying*: in TV it beams into your home and, on an individual programme basis, you didn't ask for it – so that makes the contract different. On a fundamental level, TV is there to reassure, to make safe, not to rattle.

I think *The Twilight Zone* didn't really rattle – it wasn't terribly subversive or mega-shocking but it did have scary, memorable moments that people would talk about the next day. It wasn't an aberrant phenomenon though, I think there were other scary shows like *Boris Karloff's Thriller*. But I think Serling's genius (and the other writers like Matheson and Beaumont) was that the shows were thematically rich, politically rich, which is why they really endure.

The secret of *Doctor Who*? Ha! It is up to greater minds than mine to work that one out! And if I could, I'd be in Hollywood! You could say it's the appeal of the alien amongst us – like Spock in *Star Trek*, but in the original series he was more 'weird grandad' and 'space pixie' rather than alien. He's the mad professor. I think part of it is he is a great anarchic figure who sits outside the norms of society – it is funny he has clown-like incarnations, the scarf, the bright clothes, the mercurial wit – because there is a bit of the Lord of Misrule about him: a bit of Punch, with the sonic screwdriver instead of a big stick. (The Master – especially in John Simm's portrayal – even more so.) And there is a bit of the Punch and Judy Man's call and response about Russell T. Davies's interaction with his Whovian audience.

I don't know. How can such a character endure if it doesn't tap into some sort of ancient archetype? That's my guess.

ANDERSON: In *The Twilight Zone*, because it was an anthology show, week after week the audience watched everyday people 'just like me' thrown into extraordinary circumstances. It was like throwing gasoline on the sense-of-wonder fire, and made us consider the possibility that something strange was out there.

Doctor Who is a different circumstance, I think. A constant barrage of quirky characters (including sexy babes), fun adventures, covering the full gamut of science fiction (and even fantasy to a certain extent); even mainstream audiences could find something to like if they watched a couple of episodes.

DECANDIDO: I think because both shows have/had a format that allows for almost infinite storytelling possibilities. *The Twilight Zone* was an anthology series, and *Doctor Who* may as well be. The former had the advantage of Rod Serling's genius to guide it (which is why other anthologies have been less successful), and the latter has a single hero (and companions) to follow along with, but who can also go anywhere.

How would you say modern technology has changed the approach to storytelling? I remember *Doctor Who* and *Lost in Space*, for instance, fondly for their cardboard walls and bubblewrap monsters . . . is the story still king?

AHEARNE: I don't think modern technology makes much difference to the bulk of the audience. It's only anoraks and programme-makers who agonise about the special effects. People in 30 years will be laughing at our CGI just as much as we laugh at cardboard sets. I also believe storytelling norms will change. Just as some today feel superior to the character-lite, plot-heavy stories of the seventies, people of the future may be contemptuous of the storytelling quirks we can't see in our own work but are just as much a mark of the era we live in.

ANDERSON: Sadly, I would say the opposite. In the early days, when TV shows could afford only cardboard sets and silly rubber makeup, they *had* to rely on great stories because the special effects could not carry the show. Now, effects are so spectacular and jaw-dropping that a weak story can be covered up by eye-popping visuals, enough to entertain the viewer just long enough to distract him from realising that the story doesn't make sense. My favourites were the old *Outer Limits* episodes, which had incredible stories and incredibly silly rubber-faced monsters.

DECANDIDO: I don't think it's changed the approach to storytelling at all, it just reduces the number of distractions. I don't think there's a single story that Russell T. Davies and his gang of writers has done on twenty-first century *Who* that couldn't have been done with William Hartnell or Patrick Troughton in the 1960s. The cat nurses would probably have been much less convincing, and we likely would not have had flying Daleks, but otherwise . . .

VOLK: The shaky wall syndrome certainly did for the Doctor. It was just too embarrassing to the Powers That Be: but they didn't give them the dosh to do it well any more. As usual the BBC was about fifteen years behind the times. (I bet they're currently trying to dream up a 'British *Buffy the Vampire Slayer*'!)

Yes. The important thing is *story, story, story*. Good story and good writing will get you good actors. (Not necessarily good *acting*, but that's another story!)

But SF doesn't *have* to be expensive. It's all about the ideas. We had some wacky ideas in *Afterlife* and it literally cost not a penny more than a standard ITV hour – in fact I was trying to prove a point that it *wasn't*. Imagination doesn't have to be costly. This is my contention – and I've been saying it until I'm blue in the face – you can make SF on TV like you make *Dalziel and Pascoe*, or *The Bill*. You can do a science fiction or horror story with two people in a room for 30 minutes. Stunning! One person in a house. Terrifying! What matters is commitment to the genre, long-term, from commissioning editors. To get them to commission 24 episodes of a horror anthology, not five. Enough to syndicate it, right off, instead of this terminal hesitation they've got about committing to anything.

CORNELL: Of course it is. TV still can't compete with movies, and tight budgets always mean innovation and getting the audience to fill in the gaps. *Lost* does that in a wonderfully precise way, a bit of a masterpiece of genre writing, that show. If you watch most straight-to-DVD animated fantasy movies with an action bent to them, you'll get bored quite quickly, because they can afford, through their nature, big action sequences, but generally without the characters and audience connection that would make that action interesting. In effect, they shouldn't do the big action even though they can.

CARTMEL: The notable thing about CGI is that it is only as good as the creative artists who are operating the computers. The software and the hardware are a common denominator. What distinguishes the great stuff from the terrible stuff is the ability of the people doing the effects.

JOHNSON: I think that modern technology has only changed the approach to storytelling in that it has freed us up in some ways to do things that we couldn't do before. Until the sort of liquid technology was developed for the movie *The Abyss*, for example, Jim Cameron has said that he would not have been able to do the second *Terminator* movie the way that he envisioned it. Certainly when I look back at the visual effects and such in *V* they are a far cry from what happens in motion pictures and television today, although at the time they were state of the art, but still back then there were many times when I cringed because I couldn't make them look as seamless and natural and real as I wanted them to look and I didn't have the freedom of the camera, but ultimately the story is always the king. We always say, 'If it ain't on the page, it ain't on the stage,' and that's ultimately true. I am a big believer that stories have to be character-driven and emotionally driven. As soon as we begin to rely upon visual effects then we are going to be in trouble. The tail will be wagging the dog and the story or the movie will suffer because of that.

Are studios and TV executives more receptive to fantastic TV now than they were? What kind of debt do we owe to the pioneers of TV? We do, after all, have our own dedicated science fiction and horror channels on TV now. . .

AHEARNE: They're more receptive after *Doctor Who* but I suspect they're still much more at home with period and social realism.

CORNELL: Hugely. In the fifteen years between old *Who* and new, you couldn't get a fantasy show off the ground in Britain, now there are loads of them. It's all down to Russell.

JOHNSON: I don't know that studios are any more receptive to fantastic TV now than they were. If anything I would probably think it is less so. Everything seems to be much more reality-driven and I think that the pioneers of early TV would be delighted to have the kind of tools that we have now but overall I think that we all learn and stand on the shoulders of giants. That's what Isaac Newton said, if he has seen further it is only because he is standing on the shoulders of giants. I also have to credit the wonderful republic serials that were made in the late thirties and forties and into the early fifties because they inspired a whole generation of filmmakers including myself and Steven Spielberg and George Lucas.

CARTMEL: The TV networks in the UK are somewhat less sceptical about fantasy material at the moment, and that is all down to the success of *Who*. *Primeval* (which I like) is a manifestation of this. But I imagine all it would take is a few high-profile flops for the major networks to go cold on this kind of show. The dedicated science fiction and horror channels are basically niche programming which perhaps say more about the fragmentation of television in the twenty-first century than about the rising popularity of genre material.

VOLK: I've never been approached by those dedicated channels and I've never had a meeting at one, so I don't know.

Commissioning editors will listen now to a 'fantasy' pitch or look for fantasy projects, but in my heart of hearts I don't think they are excited to do them. They would prefer to import American shows like *Lost* and *Heroes* rather than go to the trouble of making our own, because they don't understand, they don't know how, and (again) – they don't get it.

My bugbear about *Sea of Souls* was that every episode became a detective story. They weren't constructed as supernatural mysteries so much as something that had to be solved: I think that's a mistake because, as I say, the appeal of 'detective show' and 'uncanny' are diametrically opposed. I am absolutely sure that the reason that happened was that the BBC understands how to script edit a police show, but not a supernatural show.

So there are all these hurdles of prejudice, still.

It is probably easier to get a 'family fun' science fiction semi-comedy going, but would they do an adaptation of *The Kraken Wakes*? No – because I tried to. Would they do Ballard's *High Rise*? Almost certainly not. Too dark. Too serious. And, most fatally of all, it's *about* something.

That's the burning question for the next five years, to me. Can SF TV get out of the 'family entertainment' ghetto and can we get really exciting, really thoughtful, really adult SF on our screens?

Those great old TV shows have literally got me where I am today – not being grand, but at least writing TV for a living. ITV's *Mystery and Imagination* still gives me the creeps just to think about it. Ditto the BBC M.R. James and Charles Dickens *Ghost Stories for Christmas*. Everyone remembers these programmes and they were just superb, and superlatively made. A week doesn't go by without me thinking back on them, tonally, or in detail. They're my equivalent of a library, in my head. I'm really indebted to them all. That's when I first saw the credit 'Written by'. I thought, hang on. They're what touched and excited me and made me want to be a writer and write this crazy, some would say pointless, terrifying stuff in the first place – long before I got into books.

DECANDIDO: I think it's part of two things – one is the technology you mentioned in the previous question. It's easy to dismiss *Lost in Space*, or even *Star Trek*, because of the papier-mâché rocks and the guys in suits. It's a lot harder to dismiss, say, what Peter Jackson did in *The Lord of the Rings*. Also, just in general, there's been, over the past twenty years or so, a sea change in attitudes toward popular culture and genre fiction. It's not just in TV and film, but in literature as well.

ANDERSON: Absolutely – I don't think a label of 'SF' is a detriment at all. *Battlestar Galactica* is widely celebrated as one of the best shows on television, even from mainstream critics. In fact, our satellite recorder picks up so many new genre shows that I honestly don't have enough hours in the evening to watch them all, even if that's all I watch. Us geeks who watched *Star Trek, Lost in Space, Voyage to the Bottom of the Sea, Doctor Who, Land of the Giants, The Twilight Zone, Space: 1999, UFO*, and all the others – well, we grew up and now we're not only the main audience but we're also the creators.

Where do you see the future of the fantastic? Is the novel as a format losing a lot of very talented writers to the small screen? After all couldn't it be argued that the most original SF or accessible horror is coming out of TV rather than short stories and novels?

VOLK: It pisses me off somewhat because there are great genre writers out there. Fantastic people. I know a lot of wonderful British horror and SF novelists and reading their work over the last few years I would dearly love them to write for TV. To write *fantasy* for TV, that is. Some have been tempted to 'Do *The Bill* for the money,' which is tempting, naturally, but I said: 'No, no, no, write something that *you'd* want to see! Don't do what *they* want to do! That is fatal!' But I think writers like Tim Lebbon, Mark Morris, Sarah Pinborough, Conrad Williams, are all at the very top of their game. They would write *amazing* TV given the chance – and it would reward them a lot more lucratively than most deals for books, I have to say. Not that they should exclusively change horses mid-stream, but do both. Why not? I think they'd get an enormous kick from it. It would stretch them, and get some smart, genre-savvy stuff on the box, from new voices.

I hope also that writers going straight into TV have a genuine love of the genre, and are not trying to write it because it is a 'fad'. You can't do it, you'll be found out, just like if I tried to write a Mills & Boon. But I hope writers from whatever discipline will respond to the challenge if there are some open ears out there, and create some great new off-beat and in-your-face shows, and taking some risks, for heaven's sake – rather than the self-censorship that goes, 'Oh, they probably won't commission this idea I'm passionate about, so I'll just do an *Inspector Lynley*.' Crap to that.

CORNELL: I don't think that's true, it's horses for courses. The novel offers a complete mental experience that no TV show or movie is going to replace.

CARTMEL: I think the novel is king and always will be, because if the writer has sufficient power of expression they can get directly into the minds of the reader, without having to deal with layers of TV executives, creatives and technicians, all of whom may be great or terrible but in any case dilute the purity of the author's vision.

It would be nice to stretch a point and include Troy Kennedy Martin's *Edge of Darkness* as a science fiction show (it is after all a shadowy conspiracy thriller about stolen uranium and space weaponry) or even a horror/fantasy show (Kennedy Martin's original script ended with the hero turning into a tree!). However you decide to stretch the point, Troy Kennedy Martin is a great screenwriter and *Edge of Darkness* is a magnificent, classic piece of television which deserves attention.

I would also like to make mention of a British TV show that deserves more recognition. *Ultraviolet* was a good series, if not a great one, and if it had been given a decent chance it might have progressed towards greatness. Created by talented writer-director Joe Ahearne (later to work on *Doctor Who*), it was an ingenious updating of the vampire myth with a special police unit in London delegated to fight the fiends. There was cool terminology (a vampire was called a Code Five – think Roman numerals) and cool technology (guns with charcoal bullets and video sights – to distinguish between humans, who register on video, and the Code Fives who don't). This was a quality series, well-acted and well-made with a nice sense of foreboding. But someone at Channel 4 cancelled it, presumably turning up their nose when they realised it was about vampires. And presumably only a few weeks later, they paid through that same nose for the British syndication rights to Joss Whedon's *Buffy* spin-off *Angel*.

JOHNSON: I think that unfortunately we have become a society that is more anxious for having stories fed to us rather than taking the time to sit down and read them, which is a shame because there is a lot of wonderful, wonderful literature out there that particularly young people miss because they just haven't accustomed themselves to being readers. It is my favourite thing to do, read. I watch very little television. I always have. I tend to read a great deal. Particularly the classic writers, the eighteenth- and nineteenth-century works of both literature and theatre. And poetry as well. There is so much to learn from that as a writer that I always focused on that. I would really hope that young people especially would turn off a TV once in a while and pick up a novel or a book of short stories because they are wonderful. And what happens in your mind as you are reading more often is so much more fascinating than what you see on the screen. That was one of the great joys of writing *V: The Second Generation*, because I could get into the heads of the characters much more so than I could in a screenplay or in seeing it performed before me. It engages the reader so much more so, I think, and stimulates their imagination much as the imagination of people has been stimulated for centuries, for aeons, by sitting around listening to storytellers. So I would encourage people, especially young people, not to wait around until somebody serves it up to them on their MP3 player or their iPod or their cellphone, but rather dig in yourself and discover the great wealth of literature that is out there that will open your mind up to so many wonderful things. Go back and read H.G. Wells and Conan Doyle and some of the great writings of all of the early writers in the genre, as well as every other genre. It's so great. Go back and read *Moby Dick*! It's a fantastic read!

DECANDIDO: I don't agree in the least, in part because a lot of what's being done on screen is stuff the literature already moved past twenty years ago. Nothing on TV or in the theatres has come close to being as innovative as the 'new wave' stuff of the late 1960s or the cyberpunk of the 1980s (lots have had the veneer of cyberpunk, but that's really it). Also, while the compensation is better in Hollywood, you are also but one part of a big whole, and it's a part that the people who own the whole don't take all that seriously (the recent shameful negotiations during the writers' strike, for example), whereas when you write a book you are *God!*

ANDERSON: I see a blurring of boundaries as writers 'think outside the page' – but that's not a bad thing. A story is a story, even if the 'delivery device' changes. A lot of great writers used to create radio dramas, but they lost their jobs when people stopped listening to radio plays. Magazine short story writers are already a dying breed, and it's nearly impossible to make a living by writing an original novel per year. But writers can work for TV, for games, for websites, for comics, for movies, and plenty of other alternatives. It's an exciting world and science fiction writers – of all people! – should not complain about being forced to adapt to new circumstances.

I learned a great deal about how to be a good writer by studying and dissecting the best TV shows. I applied the skills I learned from writing *Star Wars* to my own series – creating likeable and legendary characters, adding humour, building spectacular scenes, telling epic plots. And my readership has crossed over in droves, too. Fans of my *Star Wars* or *The X-Files* or *Dune* novels have faithfully followed my *Saga of Seven Suns* series or other novels. AHEARNE: Haven't read novels since Asimov, so can't help you there. . .